The Belli Files

MELVIN M. BELLI

Reflections on

PRENTICE-HALL, INC.

THE BELLI FILES

the Wayward Law

ENGLEWOOD CLIFFS, NEW JERSEY

Prentice-Hall International, Inc., *London*
Prentice-Hall of Australia, Pty. Ltd., *Sydney*
Prentice-Hall Canada, Inc., *Toronto*
Prentice-Hall of India Private Ltd., *New Delhi*
Prentice-Hall of Japan, Inc., *Tokyo*
Prentice-Hall of Southeast Asia, Pte., Ltd., *Singapore*
Whitehall Books, Ltd., Wellington, *New Zealand*

A version of the chapter entitled "Law in the 'Good
Old Days'" originally appeared as an article in
The Common Law Lawyer, volume 6, no. 3, May/June 1981.

Library of Congress Cataloging in Publication Data

Belli, Melvin M., date.
The Belli Files.

Includes bibliographical references and index.
1. Trials—United States.
2. Law—United States. I. Title.
KF220.B44   1982   345.73'07   82-13326
ISBN 0-13-077974-1 347.3057

Printed in the United States of America

Dedicated to
PROFESSOR MAX RADIN
Boalt Hall Law School
University of California at Berkeley

IN 1932 GOVERNOR EARL WARREN, also of Boalt Hall and later a United States Supreme Court Chief Justice, tapped Professor Max Radin for a vacancy on the California Supreme Court.

While the nomination was pending and during the course of the candidate's usual formal investigation, two derelicts were arrested for vagrancy in Stockton, California, and, for good measure, tagged, as many of the "have nots" in those days were, as "communists." They immediately sent for and asked the gentle and learned professor to represent them (for free, of course).

The faculty, also interested in the honor to the law school of his appointment, argued with Professor Radin, pointing out that he didn't even know the men, owed them nothing, they could find other competent counsel, and most importantly, if he represented "these communists" he'd surely lose his pending appointment to the California Supreme Court.

But the professor took the case. And he lost his Supreme Court appointment—can't be mixed up in "that sort of thing," you know. Max said if he couldn't first be a fearless lawyer doing his legal duty without concern for the consequences, he shouldn't be a justice—or even a judge, for that matter.

Trial law is a lonely art. In the middle of cross examination or argument, a lawyer can't turn to his partner for help or resort to the big books. He must courageously and conscientiously present the word or act, even if it is unpopular and embarrassing at the time. Perhaps seconds or days or years later he'll be accolated for his bold and courageous stand. But he doesn't act counting on that.

Professor Max Radin taught me English common-law history and legal ethics, both of which you'll find quite a bit in this book. I've tried to practice his teachings and his life examples. I just wish more of the judges I've stood before these almost fifty years at the bar had been more like Max Radin—whom the establishment sure enough found wasn't qualified to be a judge.

Max, sartorially, was Mr. Chips. I suppose with my cowboy boots and scarlet-lined coats and "flamboyant" press doings around the world as the King of Torts I'm the opposite of Professor Radin in many respects.

However, he did teach me that "you've got to ring the church bells to get the people into the temple to hear the sermon!"

He who knoweth the law and knoweth
not the reason thereof, soon forgetteth his
superfluous learning.

—Lord Coke

Contents

A Word from the Author
Look Backward, Reader

THIS BOOK IS A distillation of some of the ancient and more recent customs, statutes, opinions, and decisions that flavor present-day law. It is a result of my own unquenchable curiosity to know how people thought and governed themselves in earlier days.

You will find much here to wonder about, chuckle over, and, I hope, ponder. These pages are meant to entertain, but I suspect they will also inform. Some of the cases described herein shaped my own legal career. They may also spark research and creative thought for you.

In fact, the most valuable course of study I can think of is ancient and old legal history, all the proceedings and procedures we've long ago discarded, even, unfortunately in some cases, forgotten. These ashes of the law can provide clues to where we've been, and to where we are going. Modern law schools that pride themselves on teaching modern law sometimes overlook the answers to everyday perplexities lying buried in shallow ground.

Our law developed gradually over many centuries and still undergoes constant change. The cornerstone of American and English law is *stare decisis*. This means that a judge should follow the rulings of other judges who have gone before him or her.

If you look closely at His Honor, you will see sitting on his right the eminent Sir William Blackstone and Daniel Webster, on the left chief justices John Marshall and Charles E. Hughes, and if these are not enough, in his chambers, awaiting his call, are my lords Coke and Mansfield, and every justice from the beginning of time up to that moment.

There are few troubles and problems from which the human race has not already suffered. When the client comes in and says, "Counselor, here's the summons; it happened this way," the counselor scurries for the big books to see what his brethren prescribed in yesteryears, and he generally finds what he's looking for.

When a case is found "on all fours" (factually identical), all the wisdom of Solomon, all the logic of Plato, and all the personality of a blonde plaintiff cannot make for a different result, unless current conditions make the result inapplicable to modern life. In the latter case, the result is overruled.

But let the question be novel and the experts, engineers, plumbers, photographers, and bookkeepers parade into court. Analogous cases are cited from South African law reports, Territory of Alaska records, Chinese extraterritorial courts, and the sayings of Mohammed, and the court timidly decides a new point, which by sheer declaration then becomes *stare decisis* for future judges.

Thus, the picture of our history reflected in law's mirror is the result of an interplay of two forces: *stare decisis* or the principle of looking backward for guidance in going forward, and the need for responsive, modern law applicable to new conditions that didn't exist when the venerable leading case may have been decided in the past. To deal competently with both of these forces, judges and lawyers need a thorough grounding in law's history and past decisions.

The history of the law is a fascinating study. The story follows a continuous thread, but the thread changes color and direction many times.

For example, after a hung (deadlocked) jury today, a defendant may be tried as many times as the district attorney desires until there are twelve minds on the jury with but a single thought: "guilty" or "not guilty."

Directly trace this modern rule back, let's say, to the 1795 North Carolina case of *State* v. *Job Garrigues*.[1] The thread is continuous, yet it has abruptly changed color, for in that case, amidst weighty remarks about "the law since the Revolution," the court decided that once a defendant is tried with a jury disagreement, "we will not again put his life in jeopardy—more especially as it is very improbable he shall be able to possess himself of the same advantages." This is the exact opposite of the modern rule.

Yet trace the thread back still further to the cases cited in the 1795 decision, and we find under the Stuarts in England cases being dismissed and retried and retried until the prosecution successfully marshalled sufficient evidence for a verdict of guilty. The thread has changed color again, and becomes the same as the modern rule.

Looking backward, therefore, is as essential as it is entertaining. The study is so vast, however, that we should take it in manageable bites. There should be a stopping place now and then.

I am reminded of the story told by my criminal law professor about someone who didn't know when to stop:

A drunk was brought into police court. The officer testified that he had found the defendant prowling a house in an exclusive residential district.

"Your Honor," testified the officer, "the defendant told me he lived there and as proof showed me his front-door key. He took me into the house and showed me the library and I was convinced he really did live there. But he insisted I follow him upstairs, and I did, and he showed me his room and his closet full of suits."

"Well, why did you arrest him, then?" inquired the judge.

"Well, Your Honor, I was convinced he lived there all right, but he wouldn't let me go. He wanted to convince me further, so he took me down the hallway and said, 'That's my wife's room. We'll go in.'

"Judge, I didn't want to, but he made me go in and it was then I arrested him. He opened the door and turned to me and said, 'You see that man in bed with my wife? That's me.'"

The law is full of surprises. I hope you enjoy these recollections, reflections, and refractions of many of the curious cases that have molded the law.

Melvin M. Belli, Sr.
San Francisco and Los Angeles,
April 1982

Notes

1. *State* v. *Garrigues*, 2 N.C. 241 (1795)

The Belli Files

1

See My Lawyer

S EE MY LAWYER" is an expression of majestic finality. It is as imperious as "I'm a union man." It is also a magical phrase, at once giving respite and respect. When meek Mr. Jones, the seventeenth assistant teller at the Holy Grail National Bank, is unexpectedly assaulted with the heart-rending news that his wife has left him, the mortgage on his home has been foreclosed, his six-foot Sony television screen has been repossessed, and the policeman's knocking at his door about those unpaid traffic tickets, he's still able to come off the canvas with one final punch: "See my lawyer!"

That punch is a telling one. It's as though someone had screamed "Plague!" There is a moment of dead silence and then argument and action against the beleaguered Mr. Jones cease. Even police (because of the Miranda Rule) must immediately cease asking Mr. Jones any questions.

Unlike the mystical words of wise old Merlin, this phrase is neither secret nor available to a select few alone. "See my lawyer" is every man's semantic sword. Ali Baba's "Open sesame" unlocked a poorhouse in comparison. At the uttering of these words, heavy troubles are lifted from aching and tired shoulders and transferred to the stronger ones of those more eager to bear them, those who cannot have troubles of their own, the lawyers.

Consider the matters the lawyer is called upon to decide. They include the liberty, the property, the happiness, the character, and the life of any citizen or alien. The lawyer touches the deepest and most precious concerns of men and women and children, born and unborn. Indeed, he is even cloaked with the priestlike quality of having his lips sealed to that which is told him by a client. His learning may snatch the innocent from the gallows; he draws the will that provides after the death of a client and he may, thereby, prepare for generations yet to be born. Only he among professionals is licensed to traffic with utmost finality in the affairs of humans for all time.

There's no law without lawyers. Judges don't bring cases to themselves; only lawyers can bring them. The Constitution of the United States rests in a glass case in the Congressional Library in Washington. It is not self-executing. Only lawyers can bring it to court to make it work and grow and survive.

IN ANCIENT "LAWSUITS," however, there were no lawyers. A party had the right to settle a dispute through a "trial by battle" wherein God was thought to reward the innocent and righteous with victory and a consequent "verdict." A disputant might have need of a stronger substitute to assist God in giving him a favorable verdict. A list of professional champions or pugilists consequently grew from which one could choose. These "gentlemen" of the earliest English "bar" became "lawyers," "witnesses," and "jury."

When trial by battle disappeared, parties at first appeared in court themselves. Court procedures rapidly became complicated and, since one was bound even by a slip of the tongue, the litigants began to bring friends to court for counsel. Soon the friends did the talking or pleading since the pleaders' words were not binding until adopted by the litigants. These pleaders were the earliest trial counsel. Since the relation of narrator and client was that of alleged friendship, the narrator could not charge a fee. They were given gifts, however, and to this day there is a hidden pocket on the shoulder of all barristers' robes for this gift.

The first attorney, however, was an entirely different person. He did not appear in court but represented and stood for his client in all business affairs and the acts of the attorney were binding upon the client.

An attorney (or solicitor) cannot go to court to this day in England; that privilege is reserved for barristers. The English barrister doesn't see or interview the client until court time. He is instructed by the solicitor's brief, usually a very learned and concise statement of the case and of the witnesses.

With the establishment of the profession in America, no distinction was made between the pleader or barrister and the attorney or solicitor, as still remains the English practice, although the common law of England was accepted as the law of all the states, except Louisiana where a modified French civil law prevails.

The term *lawyer* or *counselor* in America includes the roles of office lawyer, or advisor, and of trial lawyer.

THE LEGAL PROFESSION had a poor image in the early days of colonial America. The Puritans had suffered under priests and kings, the law being the weapon used, so during the greater part of the seventeenth century no legal profession was allowed in New England.

It was further felt that the existence of a legal profession in the New World would create a caste or ruling class, so the Body of Liberties, adopted in Massachusetts in 1641, provided that "every man that findeth himself unfit to plead his own cause in any court can employ any man, against whom the Court does not except, to help him, provided he give him no fee or reward for his pains."

It was felt that to stop a lawyer's fees would be the surest way to stop his tongue. In 1658 Virginia, the prey of unscrupulous lawyers recently fled from England, enacted that all persons, attorneys or others who should assist in pleading causes for a compensation were liable to a fine of 5,000 pounds of tobacco.

Today the cost of legal help is a major source of the layperson's dissatisfaction with the law and with lawyers. Lord Brougham's definition of a lawyer is "a legal gentleman who rescues your estate from your enemies, and keeps it for himself." In England, the loser pays *both* sides. In the United States, a suitor generally pays only his own lawyer, but he may win a case only to lose the award in the cost bill and the lawyer's fee. Noted an Eastern court, "A facetious writer says of a lawsuit, 'Nothing is certain but the expense.'"[1]

LAWYERS ARE OFTEN maligned by the layperson. The principal criticism of lawyers is that they represent guilty people. A vivid example of this general criticism is the celebrated Courvoiser case tried in England in 1840.

One of the leading members of the English bar, Mr. Charles Phillips, had been called for the defense. Lord Russel had been murdered in bed and Courvoiser, the valet, was named defendant. It was apparent that someone in the household had murdered the elderly lord. However, Phillips successfully scattered blame upon the other servant members of the house until the ever-fateful moment of all trials occurred: Someone recognized Courvoiser as the man who had sold silver stolen from Lord Russel's home. Courvoiser sent for Phillips and to him alone whispered the confession. Phillips demanded that he be allowed to withdraw from the case, but Courvoiser refused the request. (An English barrister, unlike his American cousin, cannot refuse a case and, once in a case, cannot withdraw.)

Phillips, sorely perplexed, sought a private audience with one of the trial judges. This judge not only advised that it was highly improper for Phillips to inform him, the judge, of the confession of guilt, but His Worship also insisted that Phillips continue on the case.

The trial went to the jury and Phillips, with the secret in his breast, made an eloquent plea in behalf of his client in which he said, "God only knows if the prisoner is guilty."

The jury, however, usurped the divine prerogative and voted the prisoner guilty. After the case, a full account was given of Phillips's conduct and he was severely censured by the press of England for his eloquent plea to the jury and for continuing on the case.

Had Phillips brought a similar case the next day, as a matter of English law, he would have had to proceed in the same manner and subject himself again to censure by those who made the law, and, having the power to change it, would not.

> Every man charged with an offense in a court of law stands or falls according to the evidence there produced. If that which is brought forward against him is weak and insufficient, or the charge itself is so inartificially framed that the law, if appealed to, must relax its hold upon its prisoner, it can be no violation of moral duty to point out these deficiencies to the court, although the effect must be that the criminal will escape.[2]

I very seldom really know when the person I am charged with defending is guilty. I don't ask my client about guilt because he doesn't know himself. It is for the jury to say. I ask my client if he did certain acts, and I cannot put him on the stand to deny the facts of what he has told me he did.

Do I not have a suspicion sometimes that my client is guilty? I may on occasion, but really that's none of my business. That is society's determination to make through a jury under the rules of the game with me giving all of the admissible and demonstrative evidence in the best imaginative manner I possess, but at no time offering as fact that which I know to be untrue.

Perhaps it is no answer to say that the lawyer is an officer of the court and that it is the lawyer's duty to see that the forms of the law are carried out irrespective of his individual knowledge. This makes law a game (see chapter 4). Furthermore every accessory to a crime could urge with equal vigor that he could not know a crime had been committed because a person had not been legally adjudged guilty when he helped him.

As in the Courvoiser case, the answer lies with the layman. When his son has run down a pedestrian with the family car, does the layman retain the most ethical but also ineffective member of the local bar who will put in an honest if somewhat uncertain defense? Ninety-nine percent of us will retain the criminal lawyer who is most likely to assure results. (To the credit of the law, and the discredit of the layman, law has made it increasingly difficult for the criminal lawyer to "assure results.")

Behind every crooked lawyer must be the dishonest layman. The story is told of a young lawyer trying his first case. The client had to leave the courtroom while the jury was out, but he instructed the young lawyer to wire the results of the verdict as soon as the jury came in.

The jury brought back a verdict of acquittal for the worried client and the young lawyer dashed out of the courtroom to the nearest telegraph office to wire naively to his client, "Justice prevailed."

Quickly came back the reply: "Appeal the case, we'll win the next time!"

In a democracy, the layman may change any rule of law, court, or legislature; he may even amend the national constitution itself. That he has done so in so few respects shows his satisfaction with the law as it is. All classes of lawyers still do his bidding, and he, to ease his conscience, criticizes the law for it.[3]

THE HATRED OF the legal Frankenstein the layperson himself has created is nothing new. Peter the Great is said to have asked, when being shown through Westminster, "Who are all those people running about in black robes?" Upon being told that they were lawyers, he remarked in disgust, "Why I have but four in my entire kingdom and I propose to hang two as soon as I return!"

Judges themselves, forgetting they were once and should continue to be lawyers as a matter of learning, unfortunately lend credence to some popular ideas of the law. Said an august federal judge, "By the time the questionable arts of the advocate, which are practiced to persuade and delude the judge as well as the jury, are eliminated from the profession, there will be little use for lawyers; the millenium will have come."[4]

In May 1978 when President Carter visited Los Angeles, he joined the outcry against lawyers and roundly denounced us as the "hierarchy of privilege" who "accommodate the interest of the public only when forced to."

President Carter condemned "unnecessary litigation" as if that were the fault of the lawyer and not the layman who brings the unnecessary litigation to the lawyer. He urged both legislation and action by the Bar to remove many cases from the courts, shorten the time of trials, cut the costs of legal service, and equalize the treatment of rich and poor.

Joining the cry was Chief Justice Burger of the United States Supreme Court who is sure that "juries don't serve the common man." He would try cases by arbitration or commission, as they do in New Zealand.

A little legal history showing what we've tried to do to accommodate the suggestions of both Mr. Burger and Mr. Carter would make them think perhaps a little more deeply before discarding our legal system. This system, which I see as the best in the world, is now in its golden age, with better laws being framed by the national and state legislatures and better, more *pro bono*–slanted lawyers coming out of the law schools every day.

As for the law's delays, I have to admit that this is an area that legal history shows has always been a deficit and threatens today to break down our otherwise splendid system. If we allowed the plaintiff 20 percent interest on the ultimate judgment from the day of the occurrence of the event for which he later goes to trial, the insurance companies, which are the majority of real defendants, wouldn't be so anxious to delay trials. In some cases, trials are delayed five years in the trial court and another five years in the appellate court—a total of ten years! An insurance company can make 20 percent and more a year on this money, which belongs to the judgment creditor, thereby in ten years making over two million dollars on a one million dollar judgment. Of course, they don't want to go to trial, but that's not the fault of the lawyer. Simple legislation or even court action could adjust this.

P EOPLE ALSO CRITICIZE the law because of the very shortcoming they and nature have imposed upon it.[5] The law is not an *exact* science. It cannot be, because it deals, not with such immutable laws as mathematics, but with words.

Words, not skyscrapers or guns or x-rays, are the lawyer's stock in trade. And, as one court said, "Words are evanescent; they are as fleeting as the perishing flowers of spring."[6]

For example, *dunce* was once the term applied to a learned man, but the meaning of the word has now so changed that it could be actionable slander to call a man a dunce.[7]

To complicate the problem of an imprecise language, (scientists wrote in German rather than English), the lawyer has, like the head of an Eastern lodge, a predilection for philological flourishes.

A Connecticut lawyer once addressed the jury this way:

> And now the shade of night had wrapped the earth in darkness. All nature lay clothed in solemn thought, when the defendant ruffians came rushing like a mighty torrent from the mountains down upon the abodes of peace, broke open the plaintiff's house, separated the weeping mother from the screeching infant, and carried off—my client's rifle, gentlemen of the jury—for which we claim fifteen dollars.

The layperson's expectations of a lawyer are high. He wants his lawyer to be not only logical and brilliant, but also a consummate actor. A lawyer is an exceedingly versatile individual.

An enthusiastic juror describing his ideal lawyer said:

> In my time I have heard [the lawyer] Sir Alexander Wedderburn in pretty nearly every part; I've heard him as an old man and a young woman; I have heard him when he has been a ship run down at sea; and when he has been an oil factory in a state of conflagration; once, when foreman of a jury, I saw him poison his intimate friend, and another time he was a crippled soldier about to be hit by the railroad. He ain't bad as a desolate widow with nine children of which the eldest is under eight years of age; but if ever I have to listen to him again, I would like to see him as a young lady of good connections who has been seduced by an officer of the King's guards.

In a Tennessee case, the court said:

> Perhaps no two counsel observe the same rules in presenting their cases to the jury.... Tears have always been considered

legitimate arguments before a jury. . . . It would appear to be one of the natural rights of counsel which no court or constitution could take away. . . . Indeed, if counsel has them at command, it may be seriously questioned whether it is not his professional duty to shed them whenever proper occasion arises.[8]

Years ago, a friend of the author and one of the ablest criminal lawyers in California, actually practiced the art of crying. Daily he set aside a certain time to retire to a private room to call forth the various types of tears. There were the tears of anger, or remorse, and of the broken-hearted mother.

Since every criminal is presumed to have a mother, the tears of this white-haired old woman, her head bowed, her gnarled hands clasped—were among the best this lawyer could vicariously shed and he shed enough for all motherhood since the beginning of time.

His every sob was calculated to wring the heart of the most callous juror and the ever-present audience of lawyers that never tired of hearing the same performance. Despite himself, even His Honor, who had witnessed the same Niagara a hundred times before, would find his eyes becoming a bit misty.

One was made to feel a mother's heart dropping to the floor to be shattered there as the round tears profusely welled and splashed. At each performance a different defendant sat quite embarrassed as the lawyer laid a kind hand upon the head of "this innocent, bewildered lad."

Yet the "lad" (anyone up to forty-eight) felt decidedly that he was getting his money's worth.

Only once was this lawyer almost at a loss for tears: He usually laid a handkerchief upon the counsel table at about tear time. This was a certain sign to the knowing that the dam was about to burst. One day a police officer slipped a large Bermuda onion under the handkerchief. As counsel reached for the handkerchief the onion rolled to the floor in front of the jury. A roar of laughter swept across the courtroom.

But our lachrymose pleader was equal to the occasion. Solemnly picking up the onion he exhibited it to the jury and announced in a voice shaking with emotion, "Gentlemen of the jury, can you believe the evidence of anyone who would thus trifle with a mother's sacred emotions?" (Their verdict showed they couldn't.)

THE LAYPERSON SEES the lawyer in many ways, as shown in the foregoing illustrations. In at least one instance, a defendant claimed his lawyer was crazy.

The defendant in a famous 1912 criminal trial had been found guilty of murder and was sentenced to be hanged. On his motion for a new trial he pleaded his insanity and—the insanity of his lawyer.

The latter accusation was not necessarily because counsel had lost the case, but on the grounds that the lawyer had been in the insane asylum before he had tried this case and returned immediately thereafter.

In substance, the defendant argued that the attorney had more or less tried his case as a coming-out party—to test his wits, as it were. Seeing they were not all they should be, and like the groundhog awaiting a more propitious time to emerge, he retired to his place of refuge.

The supreme court of a Southern state refused to grant a new trial, saying the lawyer "did a better than average job at the trial." (Therefore was the lawyer sane, or are all average lawyers crazy?)

The defendant was hanged and the lawyer went back where the defendant would rather have gone: to the asylum.

Whatever your opinion of lawyers, they are essential to our way of life. And should a legal difficulty arise, it is reassuring to be able to say, "See my lawyer."

Notes

1. *Carlton v. Rockport Ice Co.*, 2 A. 676, 678, 78 Me. 49 (1885).

   No more beautiful or purposeful a life could the lawyers have picked to guide them than that of their patron saint, Yves De Ker-martin, or, as he is now called, St. Ives.

   If you think your lawyer's fee too high, remind him of his patron saint and his teachings. Your lawyer might have forgotten all about him and need but your suggestion to mend the error of his ways.

   St. Ives was born in 1253 in Brittany and came of a noble family of the diocese of Treguier. As was the custom among noble sons, Ives studied both civil and canon law and theology at the University of Orléans and at several other schools of learning.

   He quickly established a reputation for legal knowledge and, once ordained, was made a church official, a judge of an ecclesiastical court. From the bench and as a pleader he exhibited those qualities that have endeared him to the hearts of lawyers and made him their patron saint.

   A friend of the poor, he disdained riches and turned his father's house into a hospital where bodily evils might be cured or, if not cured, at least eased. His success and fervor in pleading the cause of the "forgotten man" earned him the title of "the advocate of the poor."

   In an age of venality he was inaccessible to bribes. Discouraging litigation, he urged the rich to accept apologies from the poor instead of judgments.

   In the midst of an active life he practiced self-denial and austerity. His charity was boundless. One day while trying on a new coat he saw a beggar admiring it through the window. To the beggar he gave the new coat and kept the old, saying, "There is still plenty of wear in this."

He was canonized shortly after his death and for all lawyers he left the postulate for true legal service: "He scorned delights and lived laborious days."

2. The advocate "may honorably say to the accuser: 'Prove my client guilty if you can. You use the law as a sword, I will take it as a shield,' and as long as he keeps within the lines which the law has traced for the protection of the accused, he may—nay, he must—afford his client the benefit of its shelter.

   "If the law allows a loophole of escape, he is a traitor to his trust if he does not bring this before the attention of the judge. He would incur a fearful responsibility indeed if, knowing an objection which, if taken, would be fatal to an indictment, he were to suppress it, because he was satisfied of the fact of his client's guilt. It is no doubt difficult to observe the proper medium and herein, in a moral point of view, consists one of the chief trials of the profession."

3. Sir William Blackstone at one time in his life had decided to quit the profession in disgust. Peculiarly enough, his freedom from excessive learning was his greatest asset. His lectures at Oxford became popular because he explained the law in simple terms. But he was a prophet without honor in his own land. In his home country, *Blackstone's Commentaries on the Laws of England* was merely another book on the law; in the United States, before and after the Declaration of Independence, this work was the oracle of the law. In some places it was the only law book to be had. When a monument was erected to Blackstone in England, it was not the English bar that built it but the American and Canadian bar associations.

4. *Gulf, C. & S.F. Ry. Co.* v. *Curb, et al.*, 66 F. 519, 521,(1895).

5. "Jurors are the best known doctors of doubt," said a Georgia court. *Central Ry. Co.* v. *Ferguson & Nelson*, 63 Ga. 83, 85 (1879).

6. *Fonville* v. *McNease*, 31 Am. Dec. 556 (1838).

7. *Clarges* v. *Rowe*, 1 Freeman 280, 89 King's Bench 201 (1681).

8. *Ferguson* v. *Moore*, 39 S.W. 341, 343, 98 Tenn. 342 (1897).

9. "No attorney is bound to know all the law; God forbid that it should be imagined that an attorney, or a counsel, or even a judge, is bound to know all the law." *Montriou* v. *Jeffreys*, 2 Car. and P. 113, 116, 172 Eng. Rep. 51 (1825).

2
Law in the
"Good Old Days"

Y OUR LAWYER IS INCLINED, particularly before a jury when the smoke of battle is in his nostrils, to orate for those "good old days" and to demand for his client those "ancient rights of the Magna Carta—rights acknowledged from time immemorial!"

But he really doesn't mean that. His law teachers should have thoroughly schooled him in legal history so that he may appreciate for himself just how "modern" law is in every age. The "good old days" really weren't that good.

Today, an arrestee must be brought immediately before a magistrate, warned of his right to remain silent, informed of the charges against him, allowed to subpoena witnesses in his behalf, send for a lawyer, have his lawyer paid if he hasn't funds, consult in private with him, prepare his defense, and be admitted to bail pending the trial or even after being found guilty and pending appeal.

In the sixteenth century he had *none* of these rights. He was secretly arrested and secretly confined, could not be visited except upon special permission, and was kept ignorant of the cause of his arrest and the charge against him until he was suddenly popped up out of a secret passageway in the floor into the courtroom and the trial begun. A statement taken from the defendant upon arrest was read in court against him upon any charge the crown elected to bring against him.

The defendant had no right to call witnesses in his behalf and indeed it would have done him little good, for he could not have consulted with them beforehand to know their testimony. At the trial there were no rules of evidence and the defendant might even be accused by complainants whom he had not the right to see. There was no right of cross-examination and not until 1837 was the defendant even allowed a lawyer as of right.

How many days did the trial take? It was rather how many trials could a day take, for the judge instructed the jury (which consisted generally of his giving his opinion on the guilt of the prisoner in no uncertain terms),[1] and proceeded to the next case before the same jury, and so on until the jury complained that their memories had been taxed. The judge then grudgingly allowed them to retire to consider *all* the cases at one time.

Jury deliberations were expedited by two practical rules: From the time the first case was called to the announcement of the several verdicts, the jurors must remain standing and they could neither eat nor drink.

As late as 1880 the Vermont statutes provided "if a party obtaining a verdict in his favor shall . . . give to any of the jurors in the cause, knowing him to be such, any victuals or drink, . . . by way of treat, either before or after such verdict, . . . the verdict shall be set aside and a new trial granted".[2]

If the defendant cried "I want an appeal," the judge would have thought him mad for there was no such thing as a new trial and not until 1907 was an appeal given in a criminal case in England.

Furthermore, in a capital case an appeal might well have been moot as little time was lost in subjecting the defendant to quartering or disemboweling or to one of the other nicer forms of capital punishment then common. There was, of course, no constitutional admonition against "cruel and unusual" punishment.

A S THE PROSECUTING WITNESS in the old criminal case, you would indeed have been surprised to see the defendant march into court, throw a precisely stitched glove at your feet, and, instead of submitting his case to a jury, challenge you to battle.[3] Yet this would be sound law in the good old days.

The early judges, in attempting a method of trying issues of fact, and perplexed by man's false swearing, sought to pass the problem on to God in the "trial by battle," as mentioned in chapter 1. While the acts of tongue and fact might not be consistent, if the litigants were made to do battle, it was thought that God must protect the truthful in battle by vanquishing his foe.

So, the defendant, upon being accused, loudly proclaimed his innocence and threw a meticulously patterned glove at the feet of his accuser, announcing that he would defend the same with his life. Then, to make God's task the easier, the litigants, taking glove and Bible, and hand in hand, gave oaths against amulets and sorcery: "Hear this, ye justices, I have this day neither eat, drank, nor have upon me neither bones, sotness, or grass, nor any enchantment, sorcery, or witchcraft whereby the law of God may be abased, or the law of the devil exalt, so help me God and his saints."

The battle began at sunrise. If the defendant won or could stay his accuser's victory till the first star shone, he was acquitted. If he quit the fight he was adjudged guilty. If the battle were going against the accuser he could cry "craven" and withdraw. He was not hanged, but by uttering the most vile word of surrender he became "infamous" and forevermore disgraced.

If it were a civil case involving property, then the litigants hired substitutes from the lists of professionals to fight for them.[4] If the accuser were a woman, a priest, infant, cripple, or a peer, he or she might decline battle. Yet where an accused in this latter class desired battle, the odds were equalized and God thereby again assisted to pick the truthful: The accused was placed in a hole half his height in depth or had one hand tied behind his back.

In England in 1824, one Thornton, accused by Asher, followed the procedure of battle to the exact stitching of the glove—upon the advice of counsel. The startled judges were by then unfamiliar with this practice but, upon scurrying to the ancient books, deemed it still the law of England and reluctantly upheld Thornton's challenge to do battle.

Thereafter, Parliament hastily changed the law in England, but the word "craven," though shorn of its legal meaning, remains as a reminder of man's first trial, the mirror of his history in the good old days.

B UT WHAT ABOUT trial by jury? Surely here we may talk about the good old days. No, Fourth of July orators to the contrary, jury trial did not originate in America or England, and it was not guaranteed to everyone by the Magna Carta because at the time of the Magna Carta it was "unconstitutional"; it was not a matter of right but actually had to be bought, and, finally, the jury was never intended for the trial of cases because jurors gave evidence instead of hearing it.

Charlemagne's son, Louis, probably originated the jury in Europe when he decreed that in all cases involving royal right he would hear only the sworn testimony of a group of people from the district chosen by him. This "jury" was called the *inquisition* and gave evidence instead of hearing it because they were chosen for their familiarity with the facts in dispute. If a private litigant wanted to use the inquisition, he had to *pay* the king for the privilege.

This custom was brought to England around 1066 by the Norman conquerors and we find the king asking the inquisition to name the *neighbors* suspected of a felony, a function similar to that of the *grand* jury today. These juries provided the royal officers with a good number of suspects, but since suspicion is not proof, how were they to be tried?

No one had ever heard of the *petit* or *trial* jury and the only means of determining guilt or innocence was by "the ordeal," a form of torture in which God manifested the innocence of the accused by preventing physical harm to him. To the ordeal and its various refinements went those suspected (we might call them "indicted") by the inquisition.

Refusal of an ordeal was often an admission of guilt, and it is thought by the police even today that to refuse a lie detector test is proof of guilt, since the innocent have nothing to hide.[5] This same reasoning was likewise applied to those who refused the ancient tests of torture and they were quickly punished as undoubtedly guilty.

In the common "ordeal of the cursed morsel," the accused was given a lump of food with a foreign substance hidden therein. If he was able to swallow the morsel without gagging, he was acquitted; but if he gagged, God had shown his guilt. This ordeal and the "ordeal of rice" were possibly pseudoscientific tests of guilt, for fear leaves a dry mouth, and the innocent, firmly believing that God would see them through, feared not and had saliva to assist them to chew and swallow. For the guilty, the morsels stuck in their throats, or in the ordeal of chewing rice, blood appeared upon their dry gums.

Another means of trial was the "ordeal of the cross" used in criminal cases. Two sticks were chosen, upon one of which was carved the image of a cross. Both were wrapped in identical cloth and laid upon the church altar. The priest was then called in and if he picked up the parcel with the carved cross, God had acquitted the "defendant."

The administrator of the ordeal, usually the priest, prejudging the guilt or innocence of the "defendant," made the "trial" more or less severe, according to his opinion, thus assisting God to a true verdict.

W HILE A CONFESSION made today under torture is not admissible as evidence, at one time only confessions and evidence received after physical and mental torment were deemed reliable testimony.

Slaves of the ancient Greeks, fearing their master's reprisals, refused to testify against them in court. So the punishment for refusal to talk was made so terrifying that only the bravest and most loyal heart could endure it long. This torture opened hitherto dumb mouths to such good effect that it became the regular means by which the so-thought "truthful" testimony of a slave was obtained, and by peculiar reasoning any evidence from a slave became unreliable unless extracted under torture. Athenian gentlemen began to offer up their slaves as witnesses to be tortured and if the opponent did not so offer up his slaves, judgment went against him.

The modern rule is that confessions actuated by force or fear are inadmissible since the defendant, knowing the answer desired, may be inclined to give it, rather than the truth, for physical relief.[6]

Today, at no time during an entire criminal proceeding, from coroner's inquest through grand jury to trial before jury, must the defendant speak or testify unless he signifies his desire to do so.

The modern rule is so strictly followed in criminal trials that, should the defendant desire not to testify on his own behalf, the prosecution is forbidden even to *comment* upon this fact in front of the jury. Civil trials do not absolutely protect the defendant's silence. It used to be that if a defendant was *confronted* with a statement that an innocent person would deny, the defendant's *failure* to speak would be admissible—although he still need not speak at trial. It was the defendant's *conduct* in the face of an accusatory statement that counted.

A NOTHER METHOD OF TRIAL was invented later to attempt to solve the perplexing problem of how to know the cause of death when only Richard Roe and John Doe were present and later John Doe was found dead. At first, if Roe but took an oath to swear to his innocence he was acquitted, for the oath was a solemn, terrifying thing invoking God's wrath forevermore.

It soon became apparent, however, that the criminal was more concerned with the present noose than the heavenly reward. So in

Anglo-Saxon law, the accused was made to repeat the oath in four different churches. But if a plaintiff had the fees to take oath and call his opponent a liar in twelve, the plaintiff won the case by a wide margin—exactly eight.

A more intricate system was devised. As in early law one called his family about him to resist attack, he now sought them to resist suit. So besides taking the oath himself, his family and later his friends took oath with him. He called this *wager of law* and the oath makers were *compurgators*.

The remarkable thing, however, was that the compurgators were not witnesses, and neither saw nor knew the evidence; they merely swore that "the oath which William has sworn is clean, so help me God and his saints." The church collected another fee, giving sanctity to the custom and, during the eleventh and twelfth centuries this was an accepted method of trial in place of the trial by ordeal and torture. The number of compurgators that could be called was limited only by friendship and finances. One case is known where the whole town of four hundred appeared and swore that an oath was "clean."

I N 1215 THE CHURCH, administering and having full authority over the trial by ordeal, abolished it and, with the jails full, left no known way to try any of the defendants. A comparable dilemma today would be the closing of all the courts!

The perplexed king called in all his judges and told them that since they could not keep all the defendants in jail awaiting a trial that no longer existed, they could either free the defendants at random or devise some new method of trying them.

Although history leaves them unnamed, certain of these judges decided to ask the inquisition, which presented the suspicious persons, to decide further if they thought them guilty. This is one theory of the beginning of trial by jury. It was the same grand jury (inquisition) and composed of the actual witnesses of the alleged crime, and the judge would accept or reject their verdict as he saw fit.[7]

But then came the cry, and quite correctly, that trial by jury was "unconstitutional." The defendant could be forced to the ordeal but the majority of the judges determined that it was unreasonable to make him submit to the innovation of trial by jury. So the defendant was asked the astonishing question, "Will you *consent* to be tried by your country?" If he objected, nothing further could be done. The defendant might be sent back to jail, or freed, or the judge might summarily lynch him from mere force of habit.

Then came an amazing distortion of an ancient phrase in a hideously cruel manner: Since a *convicted* felon forfeited all his lands and property to the crown, if the defendant, awaiting a trial in which he knew there would be a conviction, could die before pleading, he might make one last noble gesture to his heirs and at least leave them his estate. To do this he could choose to return to a "prison forte et dure," a "prison strong and durable." But by some diabolical twist the word *peine*, or pain, became substituted for the word *prison* and the expression then took on the dread significance that the defendant who would not plead or consent to be tried by jury was to be returned to a pain strong and hard rather than a prison strong and durable.

This "pain strong and hard" consisted of placing the prisoner upon the floor of his cell, putting a weight on his middle and increasing the weight until either a plea or consent to jury trial (and foregone conviction)—or life—was squeezed from the body.

Today for a defendant who stands mute and refuses to plead, the judge is required by law to enter a plea of "not guilty" and accord him a jury trial. But the ancient "squeeze play" was not abandoned in England until 1772.

GOING ON JURY DUTY in the past could be as hazardous as being the defendant himself. Since only those who knew the facts of the case were eligible for the jury duty, and since the judge might also assume he knew the facts, if the verdict of a jury displeased him, he could conclude that the verdict might have been "attainted." The defendant was immediately forgotten and the judge proceeded to summon a jury of twenty-four men to try the original jury of twelve. In some cases even a third jury was called to try the jury that was called to try the jury that tried the defendant—something on the order of "The House That Jack Built."

If the jury was found guilty, and this often meant nothing more than bad judgment, the law stated that they "shall be committed to the King's Prison, their goods shall be confiscated, their possessions seized into the King's hands, their habitations shall be pulled down, their woodlands felled, the meadows plowed up and they themselves forever thenceforward be declared infamous."

There was sufficient reason in the good old days to avoid jury duty if possible. In the trial of one case in 1600, one stubborn juror held out for an acquittal, though all his colleagues were for "guilty." The result of this judgment was that the defendant went free and the judge sent the recalcitrant juror to jail for attaint.

Today juries still render strange verdicts, but the court has no power to punish them, in the absence of actual malfeasance, if he disagrees with their verdict. He may administer a severe tongue-lashing, but even for this there is absolutely no authority in the law. He may grant a new trial to the defendant but, in most jurisdictions, not to the prosecution.

Gradually the two types of jury evolved, the grand jury (inquisition) to indict, or present suspicious characters, and an entirely separate petit jury of twelve men to try those presented. Thus, from a European monarch's instrument of oppression, and as a substitute to trial by torture, grew this most coveted guarantee of liberty and freedom in England and America—the "right" to trial by jury.

WHILE THE LAW may have been slow to start in the good old days, once started, it was tenacious, and though man may have shuffled off his mortal coil to the satisfaction of the coroner, the law by no means even then put an end to the litigation. A person might still be brought to trial and punished, called as a witness, or might be kept legally alive for many purposes.

As late as 1609, Robert Logan of Scotland, then in his grave three years, was exhumed and tried for treason against King James. Being found guilty, as punishment his memory was declared extinct and abolished, his land and all possessions forfeited to the king.

While the church canonized her departed saints, she also tried the dead for heresy and accused their memory.

Though the health authorities may prevent it today, many were the cases in a not too ancient past where burial was held up until the dead man's debts were paid.[8]

Physical punishment directed against the corpse was not un-common. It was customary at a relatively late date to take a dead wretch from the gibbet and "burn his bowels before his eyes." The corpse was drawn and quartered and boiled in oil.

In "bier law," dead men did tell tales, for the deceased could be "summoned" as a witness, and the accused made to suffer the ordeal of touching his wounds. If the accused refused, or if upon touch the body stirred or blood ran forth, this was more con-clusive evidence of guilt than the verdict of any jury. Properly arranged and manipulated by a not too tolerant court, the corpse might seem to move or bleed; witness Siegfried's bleeding when his murderer came into his presence.[9]

Marc Anthony erred when he spoke of Caesar's wounds as "poor, poor dumb mouths."

U NLIKE THE LAWYER, the labor organizer is too wise to evoke the good old days for, while no more revolutionary are its changes in this field, perhaps law is more obvious in its advance-ment here.

By the Statute of Laborers in 1350, any worker who refused to work for the customary wage was thrown into jail. A penny a day or five pence the acre was the usual wage for hay mowing. In the time of good Queen Bess it was enacted that all men between the ages of twelve and sixty, who were not in the arts or sciences, or gentlemen born, were compelled to work for anyone requesting them to—or go to jail. Women between twelve and forty who were unmarried and born out of the "genteel" class were likewise compelled to work or be committed as a ward until they did.

The local sheriff often fixed the wages, and hours were from five in the morning until eight at night. A laborer was required to have a permit to leave the town in which he was born and laborers who fled to another town were burned in the palm of their hand with the letter *F.* Even the dress and living conditions of the laborers were regulated by law.

In 1800 the Combination Acts in England made it a crime to contract between employer and employee to raise wages. Any worker who refused to work with other employees or who attempted to raise the customary wage was liable for a jail sentence.

The Philadelphia Cordwainer's Case, an 1806 Pennsylvania decision, held that workers combining for the purpose of improving their own conditions by raising their wages and lowering their hours of work were guilty of criminal conspiracy.

But a scant 100 years ago, England indulgently gave her laborers the right to combine to effectuate shorter hours—without being criminal conspirators. Some years ago I sat in the United States Supreme Court and heard that tribunal announce that the Wagner Act prohibited the employer from interfering with the union.

Labor law, too, has marched on from the good old days.

IF YOUR LAWYER is a woman, she too is unlikely to recall the good old days. In those days the law forbade women from practicing law.

Law is not a profession for women, said the Supreme Court of Wisconsin in 1875,[10] denying Miss Lavinia Goodell and all women the right to practice law. The court explained:

> The peculiar qualities of womanhood, its gentle graces, its quick sensibility, its tender susceptibility, its purity, its delicacy, its

emotional impulses, its subordination of hard reason to sympathetic feeling, are surely not qualifications for forensic strife. . . .

It would be revolting to all female sense of the innocence and sanctity of their sex, shocking to man's reverence for womanhood and faith in woman, on which hinge all the better affections and humanity of life, that woman would be permitted to mix professionally in all the nastiness of the world which finds its way into courts of justice; all the unclean issues, all the collateral questions of sodomy, incest, rape, seduction, fornication, adultery, pregnancy, bastardy, legitimacy, prostitution, lascivious co-habitation, abortion, infanticide, obscene publications, libel and slander of sex, impotence, divorce: all the nameless catalogue of indecencies, *la chronique scandaleuse* of all the vices and all the infirmities of all society, with which the profession has to deal, and which go towards filling judicial reports which must be read for accurate knowledge of the law.

This is bad enough for men. . . . No modest woman could read without pain and self-abasement, no woman could so overcome the instincts of sex as publicly to discuss the case which we had occasion to cite, the *King* v. *Wiseman*.[11] [The King case was a prosecution for the crime of sodomy.]

As with the rights of laborers, women's rights have advanced too far for women to feel nostalgic about law in the past.

I N ONE INSTANCE perhaps the good old days were good. In days gone by, when men fought the year round in civil and foreign wars, the church made certain days holy or sanctuary, on which days it was against God's law to fight—blood feuds were to be suspended. These were days of God's peace, and the offense of fighting on these days meant trial and fine by ecclesiastical courts.

The king and his lesser lords also had their days of peace and consequent fines in their courts. Since the lords were sometimes more powerful than the king, and since he had difficulty in communicating with remote parts of the kingdom, the king often sold for a flat sum a part of his peace to a favored lord who then held court and kept the fines for breaches of the king's peace. The sheriff had his peace, the lord of a *soken* his, and even the household had its peace.

In criminal offenses, it was the injured or his family alone who was wronged and who could demand the fine or compensation. As the crown grew more powerful, the king began to decree that certain acts outraged *him* as well as the injured man or his family. These became *pleas of the Crown* and the idea of days of peace was extended to these acts, which became offensive the year round. Thus "treason, ambush, attack on a man's house, or neglect of military duty" became breaches of the king's peace. The culprit was tried in the king's courts and although, at first, the fine was divided between the injured man and the king, later the king took the whole fine and considered himself the party injured.

The action came to be called, and still is: *Rex (King)* or *Regina (Queen)* v. *Smith*, or *U.S.* v. *Smith*, or *The People of the State of* ———— v. *Smith*, instead of *Jones* (the injured) v. *Smith* (the defendant). (The family of the deceased or the injured man has redress today in the civil courts where it is still *Jones* v. *Smith* and the state has no part.)[12]

Even now the indictment must state that the offense is against the "peace and dignity of the state." To omit these ancient words, which show that it is the king's (or the state's) peace that has been breached, until fairly recently rendered an indictment invalid.

The law of *sanctuary* was a romantic respite from the rigors of what we have seen to be the harsh, rather than tolerant, law of the good old days.

The idea of "king's" or "sanctuary" days came from the church's institution of holy days—originally the only days of peace were such holy days. The extension of the idea also brought about sanctuary of place as well as of time. It may have been man's universal love of a game, or it may have been the quality of mercy, but the institution was everywhere.

In the Old Testament, according to the Book of Numbers, six cities were appointed by Moses to be cities of refuge where no officer of the law might pursue the criminal farther. In Deuteronomy and the Book of Joshua reference is made to "the slayer that flee hither that he may live."[13]

With the Greeks, could the criminal but reach the oratory of

Theseus he was safe. In Rome, the temples were sanctuaries and consequently became dens of thieves, robbers, and murderers. (Santa Claus or St. Nicholas, by the way, became the patron saint of thieves!)

In England it was truly "Come unto me, all ye that labour and are heavy laden, and I will give you rest," for the churches provided sanctuary. It was a race to the church between the exhausted felon and the posse.

The side door was always the sanctuary door with a large knocker for the nocturnal felon. A seat of stone was erected beside the altar. It was the "chair of peace." After the exhausted felon had reached the chair to cry a grateful "sanctuary," custodians, stationed in the room above the door, tolled the church bell to announce that another had found surcease.

Pursuers had to rein up at the church door under penalty of the wrath of God. Seldom was sanctuary violated. There was one famous instance in 1191, however, when the Archbishop of York was seized at the altar and dragged, vestments, robes, and all, through dirty streets to the castle.[14]

While in sanctuary the felon was still playing the game and had to obey the rules carefully.[15] The church didn't waste an opportunity to save a lost soul during the felon's involuntary sojourn. He and others were mustered daily for long prayers. These he could not avoid for to set foot off church property was to fall into the hands of the lurking coroner and his men, who used every device and lure to empty God's house of its reluctant penitents.

For forty days and forty nights, the felon had to be fed and sheltered by the church. After that he could not be put out, but he could be starved into surrender or to "abjure the realm."

To abjure, he again had to follow the rules carefully: He made an oath to leave England forever or until pardoned; his goods and lands were confiscated by the monarch and he had the letter *A* burned on his thumb.

Then, bareheaded, covered only by a sack cloth, and carrying a large wooden cross, the felon marched forth from the church and had to take the most direct route to the nearest seacoast. There he might tarry but one ebb and flow of the tide unless it were impossible to come by a ship. In the latter case he must wade into the water up to his knees each day until a boat put out. To vary but minutely from these ceremonial rules meant instant capture and hanging.

Today all this romantic game is gone and the only sanctuary is in a land that has no extradition treaty. Even in prison, where the prisoner is "civilly dead," he may still be served with process.

Today the side door of the church is still called the sanctuary door, though the knocker is stilled, and, though without legal effect, one may still sit in the "chair of peace."

WITH THE WORLDWIDE PERSECUTION of the Jew, and England and the United States offering sanctuary in recent times, it should be interesting to consider the past legal status of the Jew, since Jewish lawyers too may long for the law of the good old days.

At one time, any Jew setting foot within the British Isles became as much the personal property of the crown as the goods cast upon the English shores by the sea.[16]

After the Norman Conquest, Jews came to England in great numbers. They were merchants and in one business they thrived: The church did not allow her members to charge interest, so this became the Jews' particular province at a time when the rate was about forty-three and a third percent per annum.

Since the Jews belonged bodily to the king, it was to the King's benefit to protect them; they were his honey bees and were even given special privileges. Thus it came to pass that in all cases between a Christian and a Jew, the Christian plaintiff had to produce two witnesses, a Christian and a Jew. If a Jew was sued by a Christian who failed to produce due evidence, the Jew could clear himself merely by his oath on the Pentateuch; the Christian, in like case, had to produce eleven witnesses to swear "his oath was clean."

In their own quarter, Jews were left to try their own cases by their own courts, except when a Christian was criminally involved.

All this good fellowship must have caused the Jew forebodings and his worries were not unwarranted, for by the practice of *tallaging*, Jews were taxed an amount equal to half that taken from the whole country.[17]

As is often the case, the work required to overcome oppression breeds prosperity and jealousy. Edward I, in 1290, confiscated their property and banished Jews from the kingdom, thus keeping the one golden egg, but killing the geese.

THEN THERE WAS that delightfully cozy institution, the prison, Dickens's "gaol."

One may not be jailed solely for a debt today. Yet in 1700, a debtor arrested for debt in England entered such a labyrinth of financial perplexities that only by desperately clutching the hand of death was he led therefrom.

If he somehow raked together the amount of his debt, a greedy warden took that as evidence of hidden wealth and demanded of the piteous wretch a delivery fee. For the man once in jail, it was ludicrous to expect a speedy verdict of "not guilty." In jail he stayed until an exorbitant fee was paid. No court in the land would sooner free him.

Only in fiction is the filth of the debtors' prison of old England imaginable today. There were swindlers, debtors, and malefactors of all sorts, in all stages of sickness. Segregation was unknown. If he wanted food, clothes, bedding, warmth, or sanitation, the prisoner furnished them himself, robbed his neighbor, or went without.

Prison gangs terrorized the prison. One warden once testified, as to the cause of his ignorance of a prisoner's death, that his prison was so fearsome a place that he was afraid to step within the walls. The judges believed him.

The filth was so great that it often took the form of "jail fever." "A whole courtroom, sitting at the trial of a prisoner, was once destroyed by its contagion." Of course, when a dead prisoner was found it was convenient to whisper "jail fever."

But if a man had money—ah, then it was different. Bribe upon bribe, fee upon fee, furnished separate accommodations to his taste; the season's luxuries graced his table, his friends came to his sumptuous banquets in jail or he even went to theirs—outside the walls.

One warden in London went so far as to refuse to admit his prisoners to the prison. He quartered them in his private inn and "fee collector." There the guest, introduced to the "strong room," eight by eleven feet, built over an open sewer, the walls steaming moisture, with no fire, no bedding, and no food, was soon convinced that the more desirable rooms were worth the outrageous tariffs demanded.

Yet, immaculate blooms grow from jungle rot. From the filth and graft of Fleet Prison grew a man's noble ideal. General Oglethorpe, in 1732, disgusted with English jails, started a new prison system by founding Georgia as a penal colony. Thus, the United States, and Australia as well, grew partly as a result of experiments in prison reform.

Today, a prisoner does not forfeit all rights, health, and dignity when entering prison walls. Although conditions are far from ideal, in most prisons man's inhumanity to man has lessened enormously in 200 years.

Our constitutional guarantee against "cruel and unusual punishment" requires that jailors provide a reasonably safe place of confinement. The very idea of the "prisoner's rights" movement of today—assuring mail, attorney, library, and legal privileges—would have been laughable 200 years ago. In fact, the routine beatings, gang rapes, and homosexual assaults that the prisoner of old endured are now in some states actual legal defenses to prisoner escape.[18]

As we've seen, there was little goodness in the good old days of law. Comparing the various incidents of justice recounted herein with modern law, one is forcibly reminded of its progressive and modern character.

Notes

1. The argument presented to the California electorate when it was called to pass upon a constitutional amendment allowing a California trial judge to "comment upon the evidence—as in his opinion is necessary," was that it would follow the English practice. It did not specify at what time. The author tried the first case involving this law. Earl Warren, D.A., later U.S. Supreme Court justice, prosecuted.
   People v. Gosden, 6 Cal. 2d 14, 56 P.2d 211 (1936).

2. *Baker v. Jacobs*, 64 Vt. 197, 23 A. 588 (1891).

3. An 1857 South Carolina statute still permitted this until very recently.

4. The Emperor Otho in 983 very heroically put an end to perjury in his court by making all potential litigants wage their battles.

5. Most courts, except under mutual stipulation by both the defense and the prosecution or plaintiff, bar polygraph evidence. But as the reliability and acceptance of polygraph tests grow, courts are again beginning to change their views to accommodate modern technology, another example of the fluidity of law.

   It is still often reversible error for a witness to bolster his believability by referring to the fact that he passed a lie detector test. *Commonwealth v. Johnson*, 272 A.2d 467, 441 Pa. 237 (1971).

   But a few state and federal courts have become the vanguard of the future by admitting polygraph results. *People v. Cutter*, Calif. Sup. Ct. 12 Cr.L. 2133; *U.S. v. Ridling*, 350 F. Supp. 90 (1972); *State v. Dorsey*, 87 N.M. 323, 532 P.2d 912 (1975).

   The day when polygraph and, inevitably, voiceprint tests

become routine evidence, just like fingerprints and photographs, may not be far off.

6. Since also the confessor may more vividly, but perhaps less truthfully, paint the confession expected of him under promises of immunity or reward, confessions taken under such circumstances are also inadmissible, and so far has the modern rule digressed from the ancient, that where the defendant, before making the confession, was told by the officer, "It is always better for you to tell the truth," the court refused to hear the confession presuming the same to be under "promise of reward."

7. Judges may still reject the jury's verdict in equity matters such as a jury in a divorce case—it is "advisory" only.

8. Rembrandt was more fortunate, although when he was buried he was a bankrupt. In 1935 his memory was "brought to court" and the justices were moved to strike from the rolls the record of his bankruptcy.

    An ingenious undertaker of old San Francisco employed a most effective method of collecting his delinquent bills. He would drive up to the door of the widow, ring the bell, hand the bill to the widow and, without saying a word, glance over his shoulder at the large empty dirt wagon in which he had driven up.

    The widow, following his gaze, would see in the wagon three burly Irish grave diggers armed with pick and shovel, spitting on their hands, their sleeves rolled up ready for action. So eloquent was the pantomime that it was not necessary to threaten in words that if the bill was not paid forthwith, the remains of the late Mr. O'Leary would be summarily dug from the place of his last abode!

9. In France, by carrying the hand of the murdered man before the court, the dead thereby demanded vengeance against the living.

10. *In the Matter to Admit Miss Lavinia Goodell to the Bar*, 39 Wis. 232 (1875).

11. *King v. Wiseman*, 91 Fortescu 94, 92 Eng. Rpts. 774.

12. In some countries, the crime and the civil action can be tried together. Thus, at the same time, the court case can determine whether defendant shot victim and how much victim's life was worth to his bereaved family.

13. Oddly enough, until recently there was a sanctuary for known criminals in one of our large Midwest cities, known to every law enforcement officer. So long as they robbed elsewhere only, the criminals were unmolested. This tacit agreement was solemnly kept by police and robber—in Kansas City.

14. The "Murder in the Cathedral" of Saint Thomas á Becket was another celebrated violation of the shelter the church provided.

15. No felon could be turned away unless the church already had twenty sanctuaries, and this the claimant of the privilege could not know until inside the church, when it was possibly too late to seek another.

16. Even before 1066, Edward had decreed, "Be it known that all Jews wheresoever he may be within the realm are of right under the tutelage and protection of the King. Jews and all their effects are the King's property, and if anyone withhold money from them, let the King recover it as his." Like the fatherless children of the law, they had no place in society.

17. At the coronation of Richard, an unfortunate experience both for Jews and the crown happened. The Jews coming to pay their respects were jostled and set upon and all their homes, with moneys, bonds, and securities, were burned. When Richard returned from the Crusades, he ordered registries of all bonds made in duplicate so thereafter he would know the Jews' wealth when "initiation" day came.

18. In 1974 the first California court to allow sexual assault by prisoners as a defense of escape considered the problem thus: "While we must confess a certain naiveté as to just what kind of exotic erotica is involved in the gang rape of the victim [a woman] by a group of lesbians and a total ignorance of just who is forced to do what to whom, we deem it a reasonable

assumption that it entails as much physical and psychological insult to and degradation of a fellow human being as does forcible sodomy." *People* v. *Lovercampt*, 43 C.A.3d 823, 118 C.R. 110 (1974).

Ms. Lovercampt fared better in California than Mr. Green in Missouri: five-fold sodomy couldn't justify his escape. *State* v. *Green*, 470 S.W.2d 565 (Mo. 1971).

3

Is the Law a Ass?

WHEN THE MYSTIFIED LAYPERSON is asked to sign seemingly endless piles of papers, when he is paraded into and out of court for formal appearances that may consist solely of an unintelligible muttering of counsel to court, and when he is finally about to unburden himself to a jury and is allowed to say only that which in his mind is meaningless and unimportant, without hesitation the layperson says: "The law is a ass."

But to the initiated the law is not a ass.

Like medicine, religion, politics, and architecture, the law carries into its modern dogmas much of the ancient ritual because it possesses the dignity of age.

Perhaps you have performed the arduous task of searching the title to a piece of property you were about to buy. If you have, you appreciate the modus operandi of the law.

You examine the records in the recorder's office to see from whom your prospective seller bought the property, then the grantor to that grantor, and so on back until you arrive at the very beginning, which may be the notation "Conveyed by the United States." (How the United States got title to the land from the Indians is not considered.)

So it is with the law. When a problem is presented for decision, the lawyer first looks for an analogous case, preferably in his own state. Finding it, he will see cited therein the authority for a certain rule and going to *that* authority another authority still further back will be cited and so on until eventually is cited an English case, for American law is based upon the English common law. The English case will cite even more ancient authorities until the lawyer comes upon an original decision first announcing the rule of law he found in the modern book at the beginning of his search.

The original decision may have been made in 1700 or 1500 or even earlier. It may have been the first written expression of an ancient custom or common law, or it may have been the deliberate effort of a judge to decide, with all the logic then at his command, a novel point of law, called a case of first impression.

The thread may be continuous, but it may also abruptly change color, as when a court announces it will no longer, because of changed times or social conditions, follow the old rule. The court then overrules (reverses) itself—or another court.

It may seem that the law is slow to respond to changing social conditions. Despite popular opinion to the contrary, however, within the last two decades the law has done a great deal of housecleaning. The cases following, remnants of an earlier age and unfairly seen in the modern mirror, no doubt corroborate the sentiment that the law can at times seem a farce.

THE FIRST CHARGE of crime against a defendant is by an *indictment* voted by the grand jury or, as an alternative, the less formal *information* or *complaint* filed by the district attorney.[1] California recently held that a grand jury alone could no longer present one for trial without a preliminary rite of examination or cross examination by the magistrate. The grand jury is on its way out or its functions have been stripped!

In 1908 one Campbell was found guilty upon the following indictment: "assault on Willie Clark in the County of Green, and State of Missouri." On appeal the conviction was reversed because the indictment did not read "*The* State of Missouri."[2] The question of guilt was not raised on appeal, merely the omission of the word *the*. The same error and reversal occurred again several years later.

An indictment against one Carter for desertion read that he "unlawfully and willingly" deserted his wife. After his conviction, and upon appeal to the Texas Court of Criminal Appeals, the typographical error was discovered for the first time. The indictment should, of course, have read "unlawfully and *willfully*." Although it is difficult to see wherein the defendant was prejudiced or wherein he could be willful and not willing, the case was reversed upon this error, the court saying, "If the defects mentioned are the result of carelessness in preparing the transcript it is inexcusable, and, if they actually reflect the record, the defects are even more inexcusable."[3]

In another Texas case one Grantham was convicted of burglary. He had confessed, but the case was reversed upon appeal because the indictment charged he burglarized a house occupied by six Japanese people. Although it was proved he burglarized the house, it was offered in evidence and proved that but five Japanese people lived in this house, a fatal variance.[4]

Many were the reversals of convictions because the indictment, after charging the offense, did not end with the formal phrase "against the peace and dignity of the state." The Alabama Supreme Court held that unless that language appeared, the indictment did not state an offense and though the evidence pointed unquestionably toward the defendant's guilt, the omission of these formal words justified a reversal.

In one case, the assault set forth in the indictment was alleged to be upon one Edward Oscar Williams. The evidence, though it showed he was the same man, proved he was actually called Oscar Williams. The conviction was reversed upon appeal.

In a 1911 Illinois case, one Hunt was charged with the theft of a pocketbook and fifty-five dollars in lawful money of the United States, "a more particular description of said personal property and money being to the grand jurors unknown." Hunt was speedily convicted of the theft but the conviction was reversed in "one important element of the proof"—there was a failure to prove that the description of the exact money stolen, whether in bills or coins, was really *unknown* to the grand jurors.[5]

In the North Carolina case of *State* v. *Morgan*, the indictment alleged that defendant discharged a gun against the head of Berry Bunch causing a wound that "produced instant death." There was no question of defendant's guilt, but on appeal the conviction was reversed because the indictment failed to charge that a mortal wound was given of which deceased died. Said the court:

> The prisoner had been charged with a heinous crime and found guilty by a jury of his county and it is with some degree of reluctance that we have come to a conclusion which opposes an obstacle to the counsel of justice. This case shows the impropriety of draughtsmen departing from established precedents and attempting to simplify legal pleadings.
>
> The day of the stroke and the day of the death must be stated in every indictment for murder that the court may see that the death ensued within a year and a day after the stroke. One not a lawyer would suppose that they were sufficiently stated in this indictment for the reason that it stated the wound produced instant death, but "instantly" is not inconsistent with a death 20 days later. Unless the indictment further states that the wound was "mortal," it is not a sufficient indictment.[6]

In an old English case of assault it was alleged that a broadsword split a man's head so that "half lay upon one shoulder, half on the other." The court said the pleading was not sufficient because it was not further specifically alleged that the man died from the wound.

These are actual flesh-and-blood cases. They brought tears, laughter, rage, joy depending upon which side one was on. Of course, there were cries of "lawlessness" and "law technicalities" then even as now. But it is significant that these technicalities, the growing pains of the law, are so few today.

Counsel for the defendant in a Georgia criminal case searched the record long and hard for an error that would justify a reversal of his client's conviction. Thinking he had found one, he appealed to the Georgia Supreme Court.

He wrote in his brief: "The error was that the District Attorney had introduced into evidence a map drawn in red ink; the red color so inflamed the minds of the jury that they found his client guilty." Although the Georgia court disagreed with him, they didn't take away his right to appeal again for future clients.

A JUROR IS REQUIRED to render a verdict in one word or two as his conscience, or lack of it, directs him. Like the hand that "writes and having writ moves on," no tears nor pleas can move the judge's will to bring the verdict back to cancel half a word of it—or to spell it properly.

Twelve jurors deliberated long and bitterly upon the guilt of a prisoner in an early Texas case. Finally the presumption of innocence was laboriously overcome and twelve minds thought "guilty." But what they actually wrote for the verdict was *guity*.

The foreman just wasn't a speller. A disgusted appellate court reversed the conviction, saying, "We cannot hold that guity is the same as 'guilty.'" [7]

Oddly enough, the same appellate court in the same year decided that a verdict handed up from another unlettered Texas jury, which read "guily" instead of "guilty," was really in fact "guilty," and affirmed the conviction. Defendants' luck for that year in Texas had run out. [8]

Louisiana was not so particular with the spelling of her jurors. When a jury brought back a verdict of "mansluder" for "man-slaughter," the high court of that state said, "The court does not require jurors to be philologists." [9]

Again in Texas the Supreme Court had to reverse a conviction because penitentiary was spelled "penty." [10] But, seemingly, only one mistake of a kind is allowed in that state, for the same court later held, in affirming a conviction, that "penitenture" suffi-ciently described a "penitentiary." [11]

OUR LAW IS NOT a philosophical system. It is a growth, having its origin in the customs and usages of half-barbarous tribes. [12]

This being so, let it not be condemned for its past sins, of which, as in any other field, there are many. What it has done to "clean house," to rid itself within the last decades of the technicalities that resulted in thousands of reversals like these is more important.

Half the reversals of convictions lay in faulty wording of the long, overly-technical law indictment requirements.

California, following the lead of other states and followed soon by yet others, abolished this form of indictment in 1927 and permitted a short indictment or information that "A killed B," thus by one statute abolishing the source of 30 percent of technical reversals. No longer can a defendant reverse a conviction because the word *the* is left out of the indictment.

Aimed directly at technicalities, California amended its constitution to provide that no judgment should be set aside on technical grounds unless the error complained of resulted in a miscarriage of justice.[13]

One change in the criminal law was directed at both technicalities and the jury system. It authorized the trial judge to "comment upon the evidence" for the obvious purpose of guiding a bewildered jury through the legal labyrinth of a difficult case where a miscarriage of justice either in conviction or acquittal might arise.

This was a constitutional amendment[14] and the argument to the voters was that California judges would be allowed to "comment on the evidence," or a witness's testimony, as had the English judges. (But it didn't say as the English judges did at what period of history.)

Earl Warren, then eyeing California's attorney generalship and later to become governor and then Chief Justice of the United States Supreme Court, was the district attorney in Alameda County, Oakland.

Louis Gosden was charged by indictment of poisoning his wife. I was just out of law school six months but had already tried two widely publicized homicide cases and was representing Louie. The evidence was tough on Louie but the new law was tougher.

Earl Warren tried a doggedly pursued case for the prosecution. He was widely respected by all judges and jurors, and for the first time at the end of the trial, the "commenting on the evidence" statute was used by the late Judge Ogden after consultation with

District Attorney Warren, to which consultation I had not been invited.

The judge noted that Louis Gosden had defended his actions in buying strychnine by claiming that he had purchased it "to kill some rats." Then the judge said, "This does not square with some of the other evidence or with an innocent frame of mind to me—of course you may decide any way you want to, but this is my judgment."

Worse than that, when instructing the jury on punishment the judge went on to say "Ladies and gentlemen of the jury—in California we have life imprisonment and capital punishment. In order to reduce a penalty from capital punishment to life imprisonment you must find 'extenuating circumstances.' To my mind there are none."[15]

This was the first time an American jury had heard such directions from a judge both on guilt and punishment. They followed the suggestion of the trial judge and brought back a guilty verdict with a capital punishment penalty.

I remember telephoning Earl Warren when he was governor, after my appeal to the United States Supreme Court for Louis had been turned down. I told him that I had just come upon some new, important evidence.

It was two evenings before Louis was to be executed and the former district attorney said, "Ah, Mel, there may be new evidence, but I'm pretty sure he's guilty and I'm not going to save him."

Years later, after Earl Warren had gone to the United States Supreme Court as Chief Justice, I came across a homicide case from San Diego, *People v. Friend*.[16] It was a California Supreme Court case and said that "Jurors have unbounded discretion and judgment in reducing a penalty from execution to life imprisonment; they may not like the color of the district attorney's hair or they may like the color of the defendant's eyes, but their discretion is unbounded and arbitrary and cannot be bridled by suggestion from the trial judge that there must be *reasonable or any other kind of extenuating circumstances.*" (Emphasis added.)

I never did get a reply from Chief Justice Warren to my letter enclosing the opinion in the *Friend* case. We did remain friends until his death. I was a great admirer of his work on the United

States Supreme Court, although I didn't approve of his conduct in the *Gosden* case.

Louis was executed. He was one of the early ones to go by the gas chamber instead of by hanging, California having changed its mode of execution. He insisted I come to the execution, as did George O'Meara, the San Quentin chaplain. Louis further insisted that I stand right next to the glass, just inches from him, as he sat in the lethal chair under which the cyanide pellets were to be dropped and he would communicate his last thoughts by lip language.

He did. At first Louie said "There's nothing to it." Then his body started to jerk and stutter and as a look of agony came across his face, his lips formed the words "It's terrible!"

CHANGES IN THE LAW continue, but the "Blindfolded Lady" is very, very old and the process of face-lifting must, of necessity, be slow and gentle. Other rheumatic pains and wrinkles of age remain and successive legislatures will ease an ache here, smooth a wrinkle there.

In one specific instance, civil law up to the twentieth century was the same as that of 1200 A.D., and all the more remarkable because this law was in common use, daily defeating the ends of justice in many states.

In the year 1200, if A were injured by or had a personal action against B, and if A died before suit could be brought, this right of action died with him; his heirs could not sue in his name.

Furthermore, if B died before A brought suit, A's claim was extinguished and he could not sue B's estate no matter how righteous his claim, no matter how wealthy the estate. These laws have been reversed and changed in modern times.

Shortly after 1200, law began to allow creditors of a deceased person to sue his estate, but only in contract actions (for broken promises to pay rent and the like). But for some quite arbitrary and historical reason, in personal actions, such as personal injury suits, the law of 1200 prevailed. Suits did not survive the death of either the injured or the injurer.

In a leading California case, the plaintiff's husband had been willfully killed by the defendant. The defendant was wealthy, but before the widow could bring suit, the defendant died. His death prevented the widow from collecting a justifiable debt. The defendant's fortune went to his heirs free of any claims by the widow. The mere coincidence of his death purged his estate under the ancient rule. (California law has since been changed on this point.)

In another case, a passenger was injured in a bus by the negligence of the driver. Because of the death of the bus driver, the bus owner (actually the insurance company) escaped a just claim by the severely injured passenger.

"Lord Campbell's Act" in 1849 allowed heirs to recover for the wrongful death of their relatives, and England, lover of precedent that it is, changed the anomaly and provided for survival of many more personal actions in 1934. New York changed its law in 1935, and most states followed suit.

A great many states, however, plugged along year in and year out under the ancient and arbitrary rule of common law, and only because in 1200 A.D. that had been the law. Suits of injury to reputation (libel, slander, malicious prosecution, and other types of mental anguish) are still often barred after the plaintiff's death.

Errol Flynn's children, knowing I was his good friend and lawyer, asked me to sue the author and publisher of a book about him libelously reporting he was a Nazi spy and a homosexual. I knew both these assertions to be untrue, but I could sue in no U.S. jurisdiction because there is no U.S. law protecting a deceased person from defamation. I finally brought suit in California claiming the defamation went over directly to Errol's children and defamed them directly. Our case is pending in the Superior Court of San Francisco.

Will the law of 1200 defeat a recovery by Flynn's children? Law sometimes has all the suspense of waiting for next week's episode of a soap opera. With the law, however, we must wait much longer for the next episode. It will come eventually on my appeal to the Supreme Court of California from an adverse decision below.

Notes

1. Both merely accuse defendant of crime and cannot be taken as evidence; only upon these specific charges does he go to trial. Evidence admitted must bear upon these charges.

    At one time man did not have the right to know with particularity the offense for which he was being tried. He fought for a *precise* indictment and got it. But the very precision of the indictment, until recently corrected, *became* the abuse rather than the abuse it sought to correct.

2. *State v. Campbell*, 210 Mo. 202, 109 S. W. 706 (1908).

3. *Carter v. State*, 115 Tex. Cr. Rep. 614, 27 S. W. 2d 821 (1930).

4. *Grantham v. State*, 59 Tex. Cr. Rep. 556, 129 S. W. 839 (1910).

5. *People v. Hunt*, 251 Ill. 446, 96 N. E. 220 (1911).

6. *State v. Morgan*, 85 N. C. 581 (1881).

7. *Taylor v. State*, 5 Tex. App. 569 (1879). See also *Wilson v. State*, 12 Tex. App. 481 (1882); *Harwell v. State*, 22 Tex. App. 251, 2 S. W. 606 (1886).

8. *Curry v. State*, 7 Tex. App. 91 (1879).

9. *State v. Smith*, 33 La. Ann. 1414, 40 L. Rep. 965 (1881).

10. *Keeller v. State*, 4 Tex. App. 527 (1878).

11. *Stepp v. State*, 31 Tex. Cr. Rep. 349, 20 S. W. 753 (1892).

12. *Foster v. Retail Clerk's Intl. Protective Assn., et al.*, 865, 39 Misc. Rep. 48, 78 N. Y. Supp. 860 (1902).

13. *California Constitution*, Art.6, Sect. 13 (1966).

14. *California Constitution*, Art.6, Sect. 19 (1934): see now Art.6, Sect. 10 (1966).

15. 6 Cal. 2d 14, 56 P. 2d 211 (1936). *People v. Gosden.*

16. 47 Cal. 2d 749, 767–68, 306 P. 2d 463 (1957). *People v. Friend.*

4

Beating the Rap

TRYING TO "BEAT THE RAP," as the underworld and some criminal lawyers put it, makes of law a game. In this game the "house" that must be beaten is "the people." Unfortunately, too, making a game of the law lends a certain romanticism to the players, for no matter how crookedly they play, they are seen as clever if they win.[1]

Here again are the technicalities that lead to the miscarriages of justice that the layperson rails against. Such technicalities are for the most part outmoded laws taken advantage of by the clever. As with income tax laws, these loopholes are being noticed and plugged by each succeeding legislative session and panel of judges.

ONE OF THE EARLIEST ways of beating the rap, strangely enough, was called "benefit of clergy" and was accomplished with the aid of The Church. Under the early law, the clergy, thought punishable solely by God, were tried in ecclesiastical courts where they were not subject to capital punishment. The lay felon was tried in the monarch's courts where capital punishment was the cure for a great number of crimes.

In those days, at least half the population had some connection with holy orders; when hailed before the crown's court for some legal infraction, the clergyman would be transferred immediately to the more tolerant church court by pleading his benefit of clergy.

How did one plead his clergy? Only a clergyman was supposed to have sufficient education to be able to read in those days. By passing a reading test any defendant could save his life and beat the rap. He was conclusively presumed to be a clergyman.

The clerk of the court would cry to the accused "legit" (read) and if the accused read from the Bible he passed—to the ecclesiastical court. By a fortunate coincidence (for the layman), the test was given on the same easily memorized passage each time and these verses came to be known as the "neck psalms"; the copy of the psalter kept in each court to administer the oath came to be known as "the clergy."

Soon it appeared that those hailed into the king's court and obviously not in orders had memorized the verses ("Whoever on this book with scorn would look, may he at Sessions crave and want his Book"), and were piously chanting them while their unreading eyes peered into the book.

That some innocent laymen thus escaped came to be the only merit of the privilege, since in just hands it stood as a mitigation of a rather severe and savage early criminal law. (One then could be hung for stealing a loaf of bread.)[2]

A distinguished layman who beat the rap by pleading his clergy was Ben Jonson. Jonson was indicted for murder but because he could read, he escaped to the church court and suffered no more than being branded on his thumb, and losing his lands and chattels.

Ben Jonson's criminal record comes down from 1598. The original indictment by the grand jurors of Middlesex county charging Jonson with murder today reposes in the Guildhall of Middlesex, London.

Gabriel Spencer, an actor of Henslowe's Globe Theater, was appearing in Jonson's *Every Man in His Humour* when Jonson, even exceeding the temperamental prerogative of men of letters, put a stop to the actor's employment by "running him through."

Says the indictment in part:

> The jurors for the lady of the Queen present that Benjamin Jonson late of London, yeoman—with a certain sword of iron and steel called a Rapiour worth 3s gave Gabriel Spencer then and there with the sword aforesaid in and upon the right side of the same Gabriel a mortal wound six inches in depth and one inch in breadth, of which certain mortal wound the same Gabriel Spencer then and there instantly died at Shorediche aforesaid county of Middlesex in the fields aforesaid.

Today the indictment would be much simpler, merely stating that "Jonson murdered Spencer," naming the time and place. But then today, Jonson might have been hanged.

These "lay clergymen" were given but one "free" crime. For the next crime they were hanged. The thumb branding ensured that it would be impossible for them to plead "benefit of clergy" a second time without being recognized.

IN 1692 WILLIAM BRADFORD was being tried before two Quaker judges for printing an "obnoxious pamphlet." There was good reason to believe that the defendant had printed the pamphlet, yet none had seen him do so and he would not admit the authorship.

The prosecution with great exultation finally discovered the metal form from which the alleged pamphlet had been printed and testimony was introduced that this form was found in the home of defendant.

Bradford rightly contended, when the form was offered for proof, that he could not be convicted until it was shown that the print on the form corresponded to that on the paper. The prosecuting attorney willingly obliged, then believing the case easily won, and passed the metal form to the jury for their inspection.

As the foreman passed the form to the next juror the quoins came loose and the mass of type fell into his lap, an indecipherable pile of pi. The evidence thus disappeared with the prosecution's chances for a conviction. The defendant won his seemingly hopeless case, which leaves the moral that no case is hopeless (until the verdict is returned—and then there's always appeal).

IN 1750 KING GEORGE II OFFERED a reward of forty pounds for the conviction of any highway robber. Stephen McDaniel and company were particularly interested in this offer, because they were highway robbers.

They had no intention of giving themselves up, but forty pounds was a lot of money, often more than they realized on the job. So they set about to rob the crown of the forty pounds offered for their own capture. Their bold scheme led to one of the first double crosses reported in the law books.

The plot opens with McDaniel, Thomas Blee, James Eagan, and John Berry in deep conversation at their hangout, The Bell. Blee was selected for the job and he returned shortly with two known thugs, Kelly and Ellis.

Blee had told these two that he had a plan to steal valuable linen in the parish of Saint Paul at Deptford. As they walked by The Bell, McDaniel nodded his head, and as the law report says, "approved of Kelly and Ellis as fit and proper persons to rob James Salmon."

Rob James Salmon? Yes, but Kelly and Ellis didn't know this. Only the original robbers and John Salmon himself knew. Blee, Kelly, and Ellis departed for Deptford, but on the way Salmon conveniently appeared alone on the road and, presenting an invitation to robbery, Kelly and Ellis robbed him at Blee's suggestion. They found little of value on his person. After the robbery, Blee disappeared and McDaniel informed the king's officers of the robbery and informed them that Kelly and Ellis were the robbers.

The latter two were convicted of highway robbery and sentenced to be hanged. The forty pounds reward was paid over to McDaniel, who divided with Berry, Eagan, Blee, and Salmon.

But what of Kelly and Ellis? They didn't know of the plot. They intended to rob Salmon and did rob him. Weren't they guilty of robbery? The court held there could be no robbery of Salmon as he had willingly parted with his goods. Kelly and Ellis were reprieved and discharged.

Robbery was kept among robbers, the crown kept its forty pounds, one of the first cases of blackmail reached the law books, and though seven highway robbers stood in the shadows of the gallows, a perplexed crown discharged them all.

Four years later, these enterprising robbers were still at it. In 1754 one Joshua Kidden was tried in England for the robbery on the king's highway of Mary Jones, a widow. At the trial Mary made positive identification of Kidden and her testimony was corroborated by John Berry. Even though the prisoner swore he had never seen Mary Jones before the trial, and that he was a respectable citizen, he was speedily convicted. Since execution was the penalty for all robbery in those days, Kidden was hanged.

After the execution, Mary Jones and John Berry collected a reward of forty pounds for aiding in the conviction of a highway robber. This reward was divided between them and Stephen McDaniel and Thomas Cooper. Why did Mary and John share their reward with the latter two? Because the story told by Kidden at the trial was true. He had not robbed Mary Jones and had not seen her before the day of the trial. His protestations of innocence from the gallows were sincere. No more innocent man was ever hanged.

McDaniel, Cooper, Berry, and Jones conspired to accuse Kidden of a fictitious robbery that they might collect the reward. The fact that Kidden must be hanged in order for them to collect their reward did not disturb them. Forty pounds was a lot of money, the reasoned, and after all, they didn't owe Kidden anything. They had merely picked him at random as their victim.

But murder will out, even when committed by the state. Thomas Blee, a member of this reward-collecting gang, was later arrested in connection with yet *another* fake holdup. He told the whole story, and the four recipients of the reward were indicted for the willful murder of Kidden, convicted, and themselves sentenced to death.

The judgment was not carried out, however, upon doubt that an indictment for murder could lie in a crime of this nature. The prisoners were ultimately discharged from custody, this being the *second* time McDaniel and Berry had "beaten a rap" for an offense of this kind.

If this conspiracy were committed today, an indictment would undoubtedly lie for murder.

ONE TRULY AMAZING STORY is the case of *Queen v. Hartnett*.[3] Because a judge forgot to order them buried within the walls of the prison after they were to be hanged, two Irish murderers once "beat the rap" and were set entirely free!

Almost 100 years ago in Ireland, James Hartnett and Thomas Casey willfully murdered one Patrick Lawlor. Nothing could be said in their defense and they were both sentenced to be hanged within the week.

Yet caprice was their lawyer; for them was saved the most technical of technical legal defenses. The judge discovered this and wrote the following letter to the Twelve Judges of Ireland: "I did not direct that their bodies should be buried within the precincts of the gaol. When ruling the book a day later I noticed and so directed. The prisoners were not in court on this latter occasion."

Six out of the Twelve Judges held the sentence illegal since there was a mandatory act of Parliament that executed prisoners be buried within the confines of the prison. Though the prisoners were still in prison awaiting execution, though they had killed Patrick, though they might be called back and resentenced, though they could still be buried within the prison walls, the highest judicial minds in all Ireland decided the trial judge could not *amend* the sentence.

The only thing left to do was to discharge the prisoners. That was consequently done and the case stands as a rare instance in which the location of a man's grave saved his life.

NO FILIBUSTERING SENATOR in Congress ever watched the clock with more anxious eye than did the lawyer for Robert Spier as he made his closing argument to a North Carolina jury in 1827.

Spier had been indicted for murder and notice had been given his counsel that trial would be held on Wednesday. Came Wednesday and the solicitor of the state, not being prepared, asked that the case go over to the following day. The next day he repeated his request and Spier's lawyer graciously agreed.

On Friday, the jury was sworn and the case rapidly proceeded to trial. By Saturday evening all evidence was in and the counsel for the state and the defendant were preparing to argue to the jury. When it came time for Spier's lawyer to argue, he argued loudly and long and it was noticed that he frequently glanced at the clock. At twelve thirty the judge was also seen to look suddenly at the clock and in a startled voice he announced, "My term of court ended at midnight Saturday." Without further comment he adjourned court and a bewildered jury dispersed to their homes.

Spier returned to jail and the next week appeared before the Supreme Court of North Carolina. His filibustering lawyer argued that since the first jury had lost jurisdiction within the term of court and had disbanded, the jury could no longer render a verdict. What was more, he further argued that for another jury to be empaneled would put Spier in "double jeopardy," a fate forbidden by the Fifth Amendment. Therefore, no way being left to try him, he was entitled to his freedom.

Said the Supreme Court: "In this case the guilt or innocence of prisoner is not the subject of inquiry. Although the prisoner if guilty may unfortunately escape punishment in consequence of the decision this day made in his favor, yet it should be remembered, that the same decision may be a bulwark of safety to those, who, more innocent, may become the subjects of persecution and whose conviction, if not procured on one trial may be secured on a second or third whether they were guilty or not."

Because this had happened before (in 1795) in the same state, as reported in an ancient law book weighed down with dust and the majesty of the law, the legislature later changed the statute.

Such a change could not apply to Spier as it would have been *ex post facto*, or operating on a defendant retroactively, and forbidden. So Spier went entirely free.[4]

Suppose His Honor were to step to the bench and declare: "Ladies and gentlemen, for the coming year law will take a holiday. There will be no punishment for murder this year; court adjourned."

A fantastic supposition? Perhaps so, yet in Iowa in 1855 the Old Lady of the Law grew so tired she took a whole year's holiday and declared a moratorium on all crimes, including murder.

Here's how it happened.

One Jones murdered one McArdle in Iowa in 1840. Had Jones been tried in that year he could have been punished by the law of 1840. But for some unaccountable reason Jones was not brought to trial until 1855, when he was convicted of murder and sentenced to prison for life. It was then that Jones's lawyer, scurrying through the big books, found the murder moratorium.

In 1843 a new Iowa criminal code was enacted, which repealed the 1840 law, yet provided that anyone who had committed a crime before the passage of the 1843 law, and was not punished before it went into effect, could still be tried under the old law of 1840.

Had Jones been brought to trial between 1843 and 1851, he could have been punished under the old law of 1840.

In 1851 another entire new code of criminal law was passed for Iowa. This code repealed the entire 1843 law, but made provision for crimes committed but not tried while the 1843 act had been in force.

When Jones was brought to trial in 1855 for the murder he committed in 1840, he could not be punished under either the 1851 or the 1843 law because neither was in effect in 1840. But could he be tried under the 1840 law?

No. While the 1843 act provided punishment for offenses committed before it went into effect, the 1843 act was repealed by the 1851 act. The 1851 act reserved only the right to punish for those crimes committed while the 1843 act was in effect. The legislature had no left no provision for trying a murderer in 1855 for a crime committed in 1840!

Rather complicated you say? A lawyer's business is complicated—but one lawyer did find a holiday for murder. Jones's conviction for murder was reversed by the Iowa Supreme Court.[5]

I N 1893 AT MARION COUNTY, MISSISSIPPI, Will Purvis was sentenced to be hanged for the murder of Will Buckley. Buckley had died from a gunshot wound. At the trial, the brother of Buckley testified that he had been with the deceased when he was killed and had seen Purvis disappear into the woods after the fatal shot was fired.

Purvis maintained his innocence and produced an alibi witness who testified he had been miles away and Purvis had been with him at the exact time of the shooting.

But a conviction was affirmed upon appeal in a short two-page decision, the court saying, "proof of his guilt . . . rested upon the direct and positive evidence of an eyewitness," not on mere circumstantial evidence.[6]

Will Purvis stood upon the gallows trap and in full view of the hundreds who had gathered to see his neck broken, declared "You are taking the life of an innocent man!"

The rope was adjusted about his neck. A deputy sheriff stepped forward to cut the loose end of the rope extending beyond the hangman's knot. He did, then gave the signal to the executioner.

As a priest intoned "God save an innocent boy," Purvis fell through the trap—to the ground unharmed. The deputy had cut the rope too short to the knot and it did not hold.[7]

Mercurial mob sentiment quickly swung in favor of the pitiful boy whose hands and feet were still bound as he cowered beneath the gallows. The crowd refused to allow a second hanging and spirited Purvis into hiding. He was delivered up only when a new governor was elected who promised as one of the major planks of his platform to commute Purvis's sentence. The new governor kept his promise.

Two years later Buckley "allowed as how he might have been mistaken" in his identity of Purvis and shortly thereafter at a Holy Roller meeting, a conspirator confessed he was the real murderer under circumstances so compelling that Purvis was granted a pardon and in 1920 a $5,000 "indemnity." (The real murderer was never punished but God did "save the life of an innocent boy.")

Statutory notice is taken in most states that "to err is human" and that judges and juries are not divine. In these states, actual provision is made by statute to financially recompense those like Purvis, wrongly convicted. For example, California provides that if a prisoner proves himself to be innocent (of the crime for which he was convicted) by a pardon of the governor, he may make application to the State Board of Control for the "pecuniary injury sustained by him through such erroneous conviction and imprisonment."

However, damages in California may not exceed $10,000.[8] Wisconsin is liberal in rewarding its innocent prisoners; there is no limit to the amount it may appropriate.

Florida in one case ironically granted a "reward" of $2,500 to a prisoner wrongly convicted, calling the appropriation "for faithful service."

HOW DID WILLIAM HALL and John Dockery, never having been out of North Carolina, kill one Andrew Bryson in Tennessee?

The state prosecutor for North Carolina answered this question by charging both Hall and Dockery with murder for having stood on the North Carolina side of the state boundary and fatally shooting at Bryson who was on the Tennessee side.

Both were found guilty of first-degree murder and appealed to the Supreme Court of North Carolina. That court reversed the conviction, holding that since the shot had taken effect and the death had occurred in Tennessee, North Carolina did not have jurisdiction to try the defendants.

The court said that had the deceased, after being shot in Tennessee, staggered across the state line to die in North Carolina, at least part of the crime would have occurred there and the conviction could have been upheld.

Now it was Tennessee's turn. Its governor demanded that both defendants be rendered over to its laws, for had not North Carolina admitted the whole crime took place in Tennessee and it alone had jurisdiction?

But, said the governor of North Carolina to the governor of Tennessee, the United States Constitution (Article IV, Sec. 2, cl. 2) says only those may be extradited to the demanding state who "flee from justice" of that state.

The North Carolina governor was adamant: "How could defendants *flee* from justice in your state when they were never there?"

Extradition was denied, and Hall and Dockery were released though undeniably guilty of murder. They lived happily ever after, but they never ventured into the state of Tennessee for if they had, they would certainly have been tried for murder.[9]

Which governor was right? Both of them. The governor of North Carolina accurately interpreted the law of the time but the governor of Tennessee had the distinction, at least, of having some of his suggestions adopted in the doctrine of "constructive presence" in later law.

Today if any part of the act happens in a demanding state, that state can try the accused. Poisoned candy cases in which the candy goes through many states is an example.[10]

IF THE WORLD'S A STAGE upon which we all play our own small part, then sometime in our life we must all step onto that very busy little side show on that stage—the courtroom. When the curtain rises, we must all be dressed for the part. Form may be more effective than substance, the precise word must be used at the precise time, the exact entrances and exits will be closely watched. (In the past this was much more true than at present.)

We will have a peculiar audience. It will be small, only twelve people (now even tending to six), and it will be called a jury, but most peculiar of all, we will not know whether we act tragedy or comedy until after the show is over and on that the audience will give its verdict.

Charles Kitby and others, in 1894 in New Jersey, stepped into that busy little show with their tickets entitled, "Indictment—extortion".

For some reason peculiar to their own knowledge, then as now, those who pursue the juice of the grape, whether in the fields or in the bottle, often find themselves with one or more of these tickets. Kitby was charged, as a member of the New Jersey board of liquor license examiners, with having promised to give one Taylor a liquor license—for a consideration.

The district attorney did his little piece. It seemed to be just another of those plays run off daily in a thousand courts of a thousand counties. The prosecution said "t'is" and the defense "t'aint," but the "t'is" was more convincing for the jury.

But then the plot took an unexpected turn. It was discovered that the statute that created the office that Kitby "et al." (the other actors) held was unconstitutional. Therefore, in the eyes of the law, he never could have held such an office. What was plainer than no office, no officer?

Never before was a man so glad to lose a job for no longer could Kitby and company be guilty of extortion because New Jersey law provided that extortion was the taking of money under the color of authority of office: no office, no officer—no extortion.

Comedy, was the verdict of the audience. "Acquittal" wrote the clerk of the court as the busy little show went on for others not so lucky in "beating the rap."[11]

IN 1932 A LOS ANGELES JURY convicted three defendants of murder. A new trial was granted, but the district attorney appealed from the order granting the new trial. His appeal was denied and the new trial proceeded. Again all three defendants were convicted of first-degree murder, but—they could not be sentenced.

When a case is appealed, jurisdiction over that case passes to the (higher) appellate court, and only one court can have jurisdiction over a case at a time. After the case is heard in the appellate court it is sent back to the trial court with a formal order (remittitur) that a new trial is to be held.

In this case, a formal order had not accompanied the file when it was returned and retried, consequently the appellate court still had the case and the second conviction was void. A third trial was ordered.

After 1934 the case seemed to disappear from the law reports. Later I wrote to one of the attorneys who had tried the case originally. Came a laconic reply: at the third trial the case was dismissed for insufficiency of evidence (despite the fact that two juries had convicted the defendants for first-degree murder). The chief counsel was now dead.

What odds would defendants have given their attorney had they bet in 1932 on such a verdict of fate in 1938?

IN A SAN DIEGO TRIAL, defendant was placed on trial in a criminal action and the jury impaneled. After the jury had been selected, the judge noticed several procedural errors he had made that he feared would result in a mistrial.

On his own motion, he dismissed the jury and set the case for trial the next day before another jury. However, when he started to empanel the second jury, the defendant hollered "Double jeopardy!"

The California Supreme Court held that the first jury had been correctly impaneled, that the judge's error was immaterial. Therefore, the judge could and should have tried the case with that jury. Consequently, the defendant was "once in jeopardy." In dismissing that jury without the defendant's consent, the judge had made it impossible for the defendant ever to be tried again for the same offense. In the study that should be most predictable, the trial judge had had to guess; he guessed wrong.

Today the technicalities and formalities of the law are more form than substance. It's getting harder and harder to beat the rap.

Notes

1. "The dictionary definition of a term is frequently the mere air of the music which the accused has attempted to execute with variations. . . . It is something easier for an offender to baffle the dictionary than the penal code." *Minor v. State*, 63 Ga. 318 (1879).

2. Of course no woman could be a cleric and therefore no amount of "legit" could overcome this dilemma. As a poet of the age parodied: "the woman to the bough, the men to the plow."

   Benefit of clergy existed in the federal courts in the United States until abolished by Congress in 1790 (see *Commonwealth v. Stewart*, 1 Va. cases 114, 2 Va. Rep. 32), and was existent in England until as late as 1827.

3. *Regina v. Hartnett and Casey*, Jebb. Cr. and Pr. Cas. 302 (1840).

4. *In re Spier*, 12 N. C. 329, 1 Devereux's Reports 491 (1828).

5. *Jones v. State*, 1 Iowa 395, Cole's Ed. (1855).

6. *Purvis v. State*, 71 Miss. 706, 14 So. 268 (1894).

7. When Captain Kidd (who was really not a pirate but an officer in the King's navy and was not convicted of piracy but of murder by hitting a seaman with a water bucket) was strung up in 1701, the halter and scaffold broke. He was still alive so the question was put to the court if he could be hanged "again." He was.

8. California Penal Code §4900–4904.

9. *State v. Hall and Dockery*, 114 N. C. 909, 19 S. E. 602 (1894).

10. See *People v. Botkin*, 132 Ca. 231, 65 P. 460, (1901), where the accused sent poisoned candy through the mails from Califor-

nia to Delaware. She was convicted of murder in California though her victim died 3,000 miles away in Delaware and the accused had never been in that state.

11. *Kitby v. State*, 57 N. J. 320, 31 A. 213 (1894).

5

Studies in Murder

I N ALL THE CASES in this chapter, the defendant failed to beat the rap. But whether the verdict should have been "acquittal" instead of "guilty" involved much more than the rule of law at the court's command. Complex and mixed questions of morals and philosophy were involved—more so than in the usual case.

The word murder itself goes back at least 1,000 years. In early society, to facilitate crude administrative procedures of government, everyone had a definite group of people or clan to which he belonged. The *hundred* was such a group and probably consisted of one hundred families (or it may have defined the populated area of land that could be covered by one hundred hides).

Canute, the Dane, was not hospitably received by the English after his invasion of England in 1016 and many of his Danes, when separated from the body of the army, were killed and their bodies strewn upon the English countryside. To prevent further sniping of his Danes, Canute originated an ingenious system to make the actual murderer confess or his kinfolk deliver him up.

Canute decreed that for any Dane found killed within the territory or jurisdiction of the hundred, if the slayer were not immediately produced for punishment at the hands of the Danes, each member of the hundred would be assessed a sum of money called *murdrum* or murder fine.

Canute did not mind the killing of an Englishman, however, and so later by "presenting his Englishery" or proving that the deceased was English, the hundred escaped paying the murdrum. The English then disposed of the case according to their own laws. If the body was unidentified, however, it was presumed to be a Dane's.

By 1370 murdrum and presentment of Englishry had been abolished, but the word *murder* stuck.

If a killing was accidental or in self-defense, it was still considered murder. However, where the facts showed that the murderer killed by accident or in self-defense, the king issued a pardon. It was the custom at this time not to make fine distinctions when the law was strict, but to convict, then issue pardons wholesale as required.

Soon pardons were given so frequently in certain types of murders that a statute was passed to prevent convictions in these cases and it came to pass that accident and self-defense were recognized as valid defenses at trial and pardons in these cases were no longer necessary.

With the exceptions of self-defense and accident, all homicides were still considered murder and punishable by hanging. It was quite natural that Henry VIII, an expert in wives and the murder thereof, should redefine the crime of murder and a statute was passed in his reign preventing pardons for "wilful murder with malice prepense" (aforethought). The killings not wilful became *mansluder.* Basically the distinction prevails today.

Under present laws murder or homicide is the "unlawful killing of a human being with malice aforethought." Premeditation is only essential in first-degree murder. The degrees of murder vary among the states. For example, first-degree murder in California is either premeditated killing or killing done while committing another serious felony, such as arson, burglary, or robbery, whether intentional or not.[1] Manslaughter is unlawful killing without malice, as when provoked in a sudden quarrel or while committing a misdemeanor—like reckless driving.[2]

THOUGH JURIES CAN BE carefully instructed as to degrees and other elements of the crime of murder, they may still disagree and fail to return a verdict. *Regina (the Queen)* v. *Dudley and Stevens*[3] was such an unusual case that while an English jury in 1884 found that two men murdered another, the jury unanimously reported they were too perplexed to determine whether or not the men were guilty.

The case created so much interest that the best legal minds in the country searched the law reports for precedents but only two cases could be found to resemble it and neither was identical.

The two prisoners were indicted for murder on the high seas. Three men had left a sinking ship and huddled together against the elements in a lifeboat where they slowly starved. The youngest and weakest was likely to die first.

The judges reported that "the prisoners were subject to terrible temptation and to sufferings which might break down the bodily power of the strongest men and try the conscience of the best. Other details yet more harrowing, facts still more loathsome and appalling were presented to the jury . . . but . . . the prisoners put to death . . . the boy upon the chance of preserving their own lives by feeding upon his flesh and blood."

By a special verdict, the jury found that had the two men not fed upon the body of the youngest "they would probably not have survived; the boy being in a much weaker condition, was likely to have died before them. Under these circumstances . . . refer to this Court in the verdict if such killing be or be not murder."

The judges sentenced the two men to death but made the amazing confession that had they been so tortured and so tempted to save their lives, they would not have done otherwise: "We are often compelled to set up standards we cannot reach ourselves and lay down rules we could not ourselves satisfy. But a man has no right to declare temptation to be an excuse though he might himself have yielded to it, nor allow compassion for the criminal to change or weaken in any manner the legal definition of the crime."

Sentence of death was passed upon the two prisoners—but the queen granted a reprieve and commuted the sentence to six months without hard labor.

The first case at all analogous was reported in a medical treatise published in Amsterdam in 1641 and was passed aside as being "decided by a single judge of the Island of St. Kilts."

The next was an American case in which it was held "that sailors had no right to throw passengers overboard to save their lifeboat from swamping," but the court there intimated that had all participated in drawing lots (he that lost to be thrown overboard by the winners), it would not have been murder.

Put yourself in the sailors' shoes. Suppose you are the mate from the ship *William Brown* outward bound from Liverpool to Philadelphia in 1841. Your ship has just gone down with thirty-one hands. You are in command of a longboat with forty-one shivering and half-frozen survivors huddled about you. Your boat is sunk to the gunwales and is leaking. The sea is rising and you cannot bale fast enough. If you do not lighten your boat all will drown. Do you throw some of your passengers overboard to save the rest?

If you do you are a murderer. The United States Circuit Court actually gave such a ruling in 1842 when it decided this case.

Holmes, the mate, with the aid of the crew, threw sixteen men and women overboard to lighten his boat as each higher wave seemingly made it necessary. Those who were thrown overboard were first allowed to say their prayers.

The sisters Askin, to save their brother, willingly jumped overboard saying, "I care to live no longer." The brother, for whose murder Holmes was indicted, was later put overboard, though, unlike his sisters, he almost upset the boat in his violent struggles to spare himself. He had offered Holmes five sovereigns to save his life until morning, saying, "If God doesn't send help in the morning, we'll draw lots and if I lose I'll go overboard like a man."

Said the court, "Admitting then the fact that death was certain, and that the safety of some persons was to be promoted by an early sacrifice of the others, what law, we ask, gives a crew, in such a case, the right to be the arbitors of life and death—No! We protest against giving to seamen the power thus to make jettison of human beings, as of so much cargo."

The court then intimated that morally, at least, it was the duty of the crew to go overboard first: "Promulgate as law that the prisoner is guiltless, and our marine will be disgraced in the eyes of all civilized nations."

Holmes was sentenced to six months solitary confinement at hard labor and a fine of twenty dollars. Later, President Tyler refused to grant a pardon as the court was not unanimous in the petition, but the fine was remitted.

Did the court mean that legally if all couldn't live, all must drown? Probably not—the court suggested that *everyone* should have drawn lots to see who was to be thrown overboard, who to be saved.[4]

What would you—on Donner Pass, as a member of the Somer party in the Andes, or in this lifeboat—have done?

A S AN INTRIGUING STUDY in murder, consider the case of a rich old woman living the last years of her life in her lonely old house. A rascally heir, chafing at the years of her longevity, visited her one mournful winter evening. The next morning she was found—dead.

Superstitious neighbors told of the howling of dogs the night before. Several timidly confided to the district attorney after the autopsy surgeon reported "death by shock," that they had seen a tall, gaunt figure in a white robe floating about her house that evening.

The district attorney believed that the heir, without laying a hand upon his aged aunt, had connived to frighten her to death. But could the heir be indicted for murder?

Under the laws of the time, the answer was no. To be murder, the death had to result from a tangible body injury. The reason was a weird one: The courts did not want to encourage prosecutions for witchcraft.

In Idaho in 1910, one Heigho faced a more modern rule. Heigho, hearing that one Barton had made slanderous remarks about his character, went to the latter's home early one evening. He rang the doorbell. When Barton came to the door, Heigho abruptly started an assault upon his person.

Attracted by the screams, Barton's mother-in-law rushed to the door and saw the fracas. She screamed, "He has a gun," and fell to her knees in a swoon. As it was later described, "she began spitting bloody froth and a rattling was heard in her chest."

Despite the ministering of a physician, she was dead from shock within thirty minutes after Heigho had first knocked at Barton's door.

Heigho was indicted for manslaughter and immediately brought a writ of habeas corpus on the ground that he had not assaulted the mother-in-law. He further alleged that her death was unaccompanied by any physical blow.

Only two modern cases could the court find for guidance and both of these were from foreign jurisdictions. In _Queen_ v. _Duval_, a Quebec court had held it manslaughter where a son had brandished a knife over the head of his father until the latter had died from heart failure. In an 1874 English case, a man was convicted of manslaughter of a child who died from the shock of seeing the defendant beat the child's mother.

The Idaho court boldly stated a modern doctrine and held the facts of the case warranted an indictment for manslaughter even though the defendant had not struck the mother-in-law nor intended to harm her.[5]

In the civil law it has taken the courts of last resort a long time to allow recovery to one who has not been touched by a defendant but who has been visited with psychic shock or trauma. There are still restrictions before such a non-bodily-injured plaintiff can recover.

WHAT IS THE GREATEST murder trial of all times? The Knapp case, tried in Massachusetts in 1830, surely is a contender.[6]

Joseph White, a wealthy, kindly, and respected old gentleman of Massachusetts, was found one day in 1830, brutally murdered. There was no robbery and the authorities were at a loss to determine the motive.

Then one Richard Crowinshield, Jr., accused of the crime, confessed and implicated his brother, George, as well as Joe Knapp and Frank Knapp. The Knapps, alleged Crowinshield, had paid him to kill the old man because of property interest. All were indicted for murder.

Daniel Webster, then a United States Senator, was called upon to assist the prosecution, but before the trial got under way, a major blow was dealt the state: Crowinshield hanged himself in his cell.

Under the law at that time, an accessory could not be convicted before the principal. In this case, Crowinshield, the one who actually committed the murder, was the only principal, and since dead before trial, he could never be convicted. It appeared that the other three would go free because they were but accessories.

But Daniel Webster, as prosecutor, presented a point of law that was to remain in our jurisprudence to this day.

On the night of the killing, investigation showed that Joe Knapp, instead of remaining home as had been planned, was driven by morbid curiosity to go White's house and stand across the street while Crowinshield, inside the house, committed the murder.

Did this act alone make Joe Knapp a *principal* and as guilty as Crowinshield?

The first jury disagreed but Webster secured a conviction on the second trial and the Massachusetts Supreme Court upheld the conviction, ruling that, "If it is proved there was a conspiracy and one of the conspirators was in a situation in which he might have given aid to the perpetrators, then it is presumed he went there to help." Joe Knapp by his single act became a principal.

Whatever the reason to impel him to the vicinity of the killing, it caused Joe Knapp's death, for he was hanged a week before his brother was brought to trial. Too, it made possible the subsequent conviction and hanging of his brother for, a principal now having been convicted, Frank Knapp could be tried as an accessory.

Crowinshield's brother, George, the last brought to trial, was acquitted. Perhaps the juries had seen enough of murder and hangings; then again, it might have been because at this trial Webster did not prosecute.

THE HANGING OF A WOMAN who had killed no one once precipitated the impeachment of a President of the United States—Andrew Johnson, the only President against whom formal impeachment proceedings have been brought. (Nixon? You recall him. He wasn't impeached, he was pardoned.)

Mary E. Suratt, tried by a military commission for conspiracy in the assassination of Abraham Lincoln, and found guilty, had been sentenced to be hanged. Loath to hang a woman not one of the principal conspirators, five members of the commission addressed a petition to President Johnson recommending a commutation of her sentence to "life."

Yet, when General Hancock strode into the prison yard of old Washington Penitentiary and declared that the White House had failed to grant leniency to a woman, President Johnson had not seen the petition. A few moments later in that prison, Mary Suratt fell through the gallows; her three conspirators separately fell with her.

The President, criticized for refusing to sign the petition he had never seen, sent for the full records of the case. Tucked away in the file was the petition, which someone had placed there apparently with the intent of having him look it over—or more probably, overlook it.

The President immediately sent for his minister of war, Edwin M. Stanton, whom he believed responsible for this, and demanded his resignation. Stanton refused.

Now Johnson, after the Civil War, had pursued a liberal policy toward Southern sympathizers. Stanton and Congress opposed him. To restrict the President, Congress had, in 1867, passed the tenure-of-office act, preventing a president from removing any officer approved by Congress without its consent.

Under this act, Stanton defied Johnson's demand for resignation and refused to give up his office to Johnson's appointee, a man who later became president himself—General U.S. Grant. Johnson again demanded the resignation; Stanton again refused and called for congressional aid. It came in the form of impeachment proceedings against Johnson.

On May 11, 1868, the vote in the Senate stood thirty-five for impeachment, nineteen against. But the vote for impeachment of the only U.S. President so tried, and because he had not saved a woman from hanging, had failed by one vote: The Constitution requires a two-thirds majority.

ABOUT THE TIME of the San Francisco earthquake, one William Kauffman had fallen in with bad companions. Perhaps it might be more appropriately put that good companions had fallen in with him. (How many times have I had a mother come to me to say, "John was a good boy—he was led by bad companions.")

Of an evening in San Francisco we find William Kauffman and five others arming themselves with the implements of the profession used in the burglary of a cemetery vault. Each of the five others carried a revolver. Kauffman carried none, a fact that he was later to urge upon the Supreme Court of California as grounds for reversal of his conviction of murder.

Arriving at the cemetery, the conspirators were dissuaded from their original purpose by the sight of an armed man. Since the night was young and burglars make loot while the moon shines, it was suggested they rob a coal yard. With this in mind, the band divided, Kauffman and another in the lead. As they walked down the sidewalk, Kauffman heard a yell and a shot. Kennedy, another conspirator, ran toward them and disappeared.

The five remaining members of the band were continuing their walk when Officer Robinson came up and demanded, "Who's got that gun?" Conspirator Wood answered by reaching for his gun and shots were exchanged. Officer Robinson was killed.

The band now rapidly dispersed and the next we hear of Kauffman is in Fort Williams, Canada, whither he had escaped.

Extradited to San Francisco and indicted with the other five for the murder of Officer Robinson, Kauffman alleged as a defense that, first, he had had no gun that evening, therefore, he had not intended to shoot under any conditions; secondly, the original burglary had been abandoned; and, thirdly, when Officer Robinson came up, Kauffman had held his hands above his head and had taken no part in the shooting.

But the Supreme Court held him as guilty as the other five conspirators, saying there had been a conspiracy to commit an unlawful act (robbery) and to the success of this venture, the conspirators armed themselves: "Pistols are used by burglars not for breaking into safes but for preventing interference with the criminal design."

By going with the others, Kauffman condoned their acts and made himself a part of everything done by any of the five. It was not necessary that he carry a gun or that he actually pull a trigger to make him guilty of murder.[7]

This is called the "felony-murder rule" and is under vigorous dispute in state supreme courts. A robber does not intend to kill, but he's committing a felony and if a homicide results by someone else, even unintentionally, for his originally wrongful act he could be held guilty of murder.

What about a hunter shooting at a deer out of season, a felony, and accidentally killing a nearby farmer? Murder under the felony murder rule? Generally no, because it was not a sufficiently aggravated felony. But technically it could be.

MR. AND MRS. TURNER and Rhoda Carter were ardent spiritualists. Into their esoteric circle they introduced one J.D. Farrell who became so proficient in the art of calling up spirits from the other world that two years later we find him acting as a medium for the other three.

One day in 1913, Pike County, Arkansas, was startled to hear of the death of the two women and the near death of Mr. Turner. The decedents had committed suicide by taking an overdose of morphine and it was only the ministrations of a physician that saved the life of the third mystic.

Farrell became the first person in the state's history to be indicted for first-degree homicide under a one-hundred-year-old Arkansas statute providing that anyone assisting another in the commission of a suicide was guilty of murder.

When asked what had made him tired of living, Turner stated that Farrell, in his capacity as a medium, had gotten messages from Robert, a deceased son, "asking us to come over on the other side." The witness further testified that the three had contemplated suicide for more than two years and were anxious to go over. Farrell's assistance in the suicide was recounted by a druggist who testified he had sold the defendant a quantity of morphine about ten days before the deceased had taken it.

Farrell acknowledged the purchase of the drug but stated that he had bought it at the request of one of the decedents for a toothache. When the court intimated that there must have been many aching teeth, judging from the quantity he bought, all that remained necessary to convince the jury was a motive.

Did Farrell, who had learned of his hidden power of reaching into the other world through the teachings of his friends, out of gratitude, assist them over to the "other side"? If he had, the application of the old law might have been harsh.

What determined the minds of the jurors was the further testimony of Turner, that the afternoon he took the morphine he deeded his property to Farrell. Innocently he said, "I suppose because we were fixing to go over on the other side."

The verdict of guilty against Farrell reflected a jury's wonderment that he should remain behind with his newly acquired home when he too could have accompanied his friends to the much more beautiful land he had so vividly and enticingly pictured.[8]

OFTEN CRUEL, sometimes capricious, but always relentless is the way fate plays the game of law called "man wanted—murder."

It may be an old photograph or the scribbled part of a name that brings about an arrest. Or routine checking with FBI records in Washington for fingerprints, taken when a man is arrested on another charge, may bring the flash—"wanted."

In 1939 I received a telegram that read: "By reading papers you will know my case. Beg you to interview me. William J. Smith." I've received many such telegrams in the almost fifty years since then, but none with such a dramatic and tragic story behind them.

The wire had been sent from San Quentin Prison. Father George O'Meara, prison chaplain and one of the kindest and most humane men in the world, asked me to see Smith. In the interview room at the prison the terrified boy whispered the details of his case to me.

He was in prison because of a conviction on burglary in Los Angeles and his five-year sentence was about up. But that was not the crime worrying him. He was wanted for murder and, up to that time, he alone in all the world knew he had done it.

In 1936 he had shot and killed a postal employee in Sacramento while engaging in a burglary of the Sacramento post office. After this offense he had made a successful escape; the police had lost his trail. It was after this escape that he was picked up for the Los Angeles burglary.

He described to me how his fingerprints had been taken in Los Angeles, how he had waited to learn that they had traced the former murder to him, for he was sure he had left fingerprints at the scene of the killing. His fingerprints were sent to Washington, the routine check was made, but in some inexplicable manner the fingerprints of the man wanted in Sacramento were not matched with his.

Found guilty on the Los Angeles burglary, he was sent to San Quentin. There he was fingerprinted again and daily he waited for the report from Washington that his fingerprints matched and he was the one wanted for murder in Sacramento.

As the days went by and no call came from the warden's office, the anticipated relief did not come to him. Instead, there was the wretched stomach-churning suspense of waiting: It was far worse than being caught.

He wanted to run, to hide, but he couldn't. He was in a cell; a rat in an iron trap. With each tick of the clock he played the game of fate. He seemed to be winning. But still he never could be sure when some clerk might, as a further routine matter, compare fingerprints of men wanted with his. Every day he waited for "They want you at the warden's office, Bill." Then it came. They did—or so he thought.

Bill was called to the warden's office and there sat two Los Angeles, not Sacramento, policemen! This momentarily puzzled the prisoner but his doubts were dispelled by the first words of the officer: "Well, Bill, you thought you could get away with it, didn't you? You might as well confess. We've got the goods on you!"

Bill jerked upright and opened a dry mouth to blurt it all out when the officer interrupted: "Just tell us who was with you on that Beverly Hills job."

Bill sat stunned. The Beverly Hills job! He'd never done a job in Beverly Hills. The officers were mistaken and what is more, Bill convinced them that they were mistaken. Seeing how white and trembling the boy was, the officers even apologized for the scare they had given him. But as they left, Bill sat watching them go. He was so shaken that he was tempted to call after them to get the thing over with. He had to tell. He couldn't keep it bottled up any longer.

That night in his cell Bill couldn't sleep; he tossed and sweated and shook. Was that visit an omen that his luck was holding—or was it proof that it was running out? He didn't have much longer to go for parole. Could he make it?

If only he could tell someone, that might take part of the weight off his mind. Bill did. He woke his cell-mate. He swore him to silence and confided in him.

But this was the trump card fate had held. The cell-mate, seeing a chance at currying executive favor, went straight to the warden with the story.

Then came the real call to the warden's office. Called up, Bill now almost gladly blurted out the whole story. The fingerprints long overlooked were sent for and compared; they checked beyond a reasonable doubt. Bill Smith was the man long wanted for murder in the Sacramento post office.

The trial was held in Sacramento. I told Father O'Meara that if he would come and sit in the front row of the courtroom each day, I'd represent Bill and try for life imprisonment. The father couldn't and I turned Bill down.

The verdict of the jury was murder in the first degree. Sacramento, with Folsom Prison nearby, is a hanging town. On September 8, 1939, William Smith paid the extreme penalty on the gallows of San Quentin Prison because he couldn't withstand the suspense of "man wanted—murder."

Just before he was hanged, Bill sent me a letter in which he said, "my case didn't turn out so well but for that, of course, I can blame no one but myself. I wish to thank you for your kindness in dealing with me and the time you wasted, at your own expense, in my behalf."

I had never been so ashamed in my life. Could I have taken just a little more time to arrange my calendar, I've no doubt I could have made a jury see the punishment Bill had already suffered in the terror of the thousand hangings this boy had endured while waiting for the real call and perhaps gotten him life imprisonment, a verdict I had hoped for and felt probably just under the circumstances.

A GATHA CHRISTIE COULD NOT write a scenario more suspenseful nor a plot more convoluted than the story that unfolded at the murder trial of William Archerd in California in 1967.[9]

Archerd was on trial for the murder of two of his wives and a nephew, and evidence of three other murders (a third wife, a friend, and a wife's ex-husband) of like design was introduced. The six murders had occurred over a twenty-year period, and are the only *known*, reported cases of murder by insulin poisoning in the United States. (Only one other occurred worldwide—in England in 1956.) Others? They're hard to detect.

Each of Archerd's victims was a close friend, relative, or wife who became unwanted—or not as valuable to Archerd as the insurance proceeds from their deaths.

Archerd had been trained as an attendant in insulin shock therapy at a state mental hospital, and became an expert in the benefits of the controlled coma that results from therapeutic insulin injection. But, too much insulin or too prolonged a coma means irreversible brain damage and death.

Beginning in 1947, Archerd began luring his victims into his web. His modus operandi was fiendish and effective: Archerd talked the victims into allowing him to kill them!

The victims were close to Archerd, and Archerd preyed upon their trust. To each he proposed a plan to fake an auto accident and split the insurance proceeds. (Archerd, of course, was the beneficiary of all the policies.) He told his prey of his expertise in administering insulin, harmlessly and painlessly, but at the same time producing temporary symptoms of apparent shock or concussion. Each victim, unsuspecting and enticed by the prospect of making money, would allow Archerd to inject him or her with insulin. At the onset of the symptoms, Archerd would whisk the "accident victim" to the hospital. Thereafter, the victim's symptoms would mysteriously worsen, eventually leading to coma, convulsions, and death. Cause of death was undetermined or misdiagnosed.

No one seemed to connect these deaths with the ever-present figure of Archerd, sitting patiently by the hospital bedside, the dutiful relative—waiting for a chance to be alone with the victim and to inject him with massive amounts of insulin.

No one noticed the minute puncture marks on the arms of the victims after Archerd's visits. And, even if they had, Archerd's crimes still would have eluded detection, since there was no effective method of detecting insulin in the body until 1967—twenty years after the first murder occurred.

Police had suspected Archerd since 1956, but they knew that before they could file any charges, they had to establish the *corpus delicti* (the body of a crime, built of substantial, factual evidence that a crime has actually been committed, not the literal "body"). In 1956 medical authorities couldn't establish that the cause of death in these cases was linked to criminal activity, and there were no eye-witnesses to Archerd's injections still alive.

In 1967 police heard of the insulin research being conducted at UCLA by Dr. Edward Arquilla. Dr. Arquilla was able to identify the type of brain damage shown on brain tissue slides of some of the victims. Hospital and autopsy records were reviewed and physicians re-interviewed. The pieces of the puzzle were finally fitted together with the aid of modern medicine.

Archerd was indicted, convicted, and sentenced to death by a judge who called him "more evil than any I have ever seen before." (Archerd tried to attack his conviction on the grounds that he had been denied a speedy trial, but the court was not sympathetic.)

Abolition of capital punishment (recently restored) in California saved Archerd's life as it saved the life of another grisly killer, Charles Manson. But those who say capital punishment is a deterrent should note that these two most aggravated killers *committed* their homicides while capital punishment was in full force and effect in California.

Notes

1. California Penal Code §189.
2. California Penal Code §192.
3. *Regina* v. *Dudley & Stevens*, 14 Law Rep., Q.B.D. 273 (1884).
4. *U. S.* v. *Holmes*, 26 Fed. Cas. 360, 1 Wall Jr. 1 (1842). This drama was the subject of the movie *Souls at Sea*—Gary Cooper played the mate.
5. *Ex Parte Heigho*, 110 P. 1029, 18 Idaho 566 (1910).   Similarly, in civil law, a mother was allowed to recover for the mental anguish of seeing her child hurt, whereas the old rule had required that the mother fear the assault on herself in order to recover.
6. *Commonwealth* v. *Knapp*, 26 Mass. 505, 9 Pick. 496 (1830).
7. *People* v. *Kauffman*, 152 Cal. 331, 92 P. 861 (1907).
8. *Farrell* v. *State*, 111 Ark. 180, 163 S.W. 768 (1914).
9. *People* v. *Archerd*, 3 Cal. 3d 615, 477 P. 2d 421, 91 Cal. Rptr. (1970). This is the California Supreme Court's opinion on appeal. Archerd was indicted and tried in 1967.

6
Black Date

PUNISHMENT DETERS, is the theory, so absolute punishment must deter absolutely. And on the Black Date, as San
Quentin prisoners call their date of doom, punishment
becomes reality.

Does man want to be "good" or is he only because of the
restraints running all the way from teacher's reproval to capital
punishment? On the other hand, is a retributive and punishing
penology as effective as a rehabilitative and educational one?

Some of us will be good regardless, more every day, I like to
think. But most of us, the unfortunate, who would not otherwise
be good are so because of punishment instead of rehabilitation. I
suppose, because it has been so since the world began, that man
must demand and expect some punishment, retribution. Unfortunately, those punished return the punishment in recidivism.

It is the rule of law that if an act is made criminal by statute, but
the legislature inadvertently fails to assess a punishment, the act is
then not unlawful!

Behind every civil law there is punishment; the judge maintains order in court by his theoretical, and many times practical, weapon of contempt; judgments can ultimately be executed by the sheriff and interference therewith is likewise contumacious.

Law does not rely upon the goodness in man's nature; it must expect his recalcitrance and wickedness. Even those moral souls and righteous citizens who would "never think of disobeying the law" may intuitively be impelled to this piousness by an inherent dread of law's ability to enforce its dictum.

But for the brutal and hideous punishments meted out since time began, the law is not to blame. As in other instances cited in previous chapters, but particularly so here, punishment is according to the will of the people. Even the Ku Klux Klan's lynchings are the will of the majority of the people involved.

A law is a standard of determining guilt or innocence for one's conduct. The punishment of the guilty, and its form, is the responsibility of every citizen. For each prisoner hanged, there has been placed an individual responsibility upon each surviving citizen of the state. He made that law and he may change it. The hangman is the citizen's employee, for the citizen's taxes pay the salary.

It should be a revelation for the taxpayer actually to witness what he has willed rather than to say, ostrich-like, "That's too morbid for me." (A bill was introduced in the Nevada State Legislature in 1937 making it compulsory for all district attorneys to serve a prison sentence so they could appreciate the punishment they asked of juries. The measure was defeated in the Senate, 12 to 3.)

Sheriff Richard Hongisto of San Francisco recently served five days in jail for contempt (the refusal to carry out an eviction), and recommended the experience for the edification of all corrections officials.

It would serve little to recount the diabolical punishments meted out to various races through the ages, to describe the cries of anguish and the cracking and wrenching and avulsions of bones upon medieval torture machines. Yet, amid all this brutality, it is a paradox that more men were generally sincere in their purpose to expiate, to fix responsibility, and, by example, to make a better world. We've seen that law is fashioned by people, that in a democracy the law is the tool of the citizens rather than they its. Just how modern (humane) is criminal punishment today? Perhaps it is not as corporal, but I've had more than enough prisoners tell me that enforced idleness is just as bad. "Doing time" is the toughest part of punishment. The magnificent human mind and body, if stalled, is like the best machine: It rusts away.

In ancient times, the most usual and dreaded punishment was dismemberment. King Canute of England, an "enlightened" ruler for his times (early eleventh century) provided: "Let the offender's hands be cut off, or his feet, or both, according as the deed may be. And if he have wrought yet greater wrong, then let his eyes be put out and his nose and his ears and his upper lip be cut off, or let him be scalped, whichever of these shall counsel those whose duty it is to counsel thereupon, so that punishment may be inflicted and also the soul preserved."

L ET US CONSIDER but three incidents of punishment as horrendous as any in the annals of man. The first:

> He was encased in a coffin-like box, from which his head, hands, and feet protruded, through holes made for that purpose; he was fed with milk and honey, which he was forced to take, and his face was smeared with the same mixture; he was exposed to the sun, and in this state he remained for seventeen days, until he had been devoured alive by insects and vermin, which swarmed about him and bred within him.[1]

The second: Because Tom Price, a black, threatened a white man for advances made to Tom's attractive wife, Tom was dragged from his bed, abducted, and finally wired to an upright post.

> The first step in the execution was the whipping which raised crimson gorged weals on the negro's naked body. Then a match was set to the straw and sticks—but not too many of these; the flame was not intended to kill. As the flames reached his flesh, the negro

writhed and screeched in agony but only now did the real torture commence. So tightly was Price wired to the post that his tense body could not shrink when one of the white men advanced with a brace and bit. Into the muscles of the groin cut the biting tool. Time after time he fainted to be revived again as the torture was stayed.

From the crowd came again and again that animal growl—lustful and cruel. The game was nearly over. A slash of knives and another form of medieval torture had been revived. The fire was now kicked out and the unconscious, but still living negro was dragged to a tree at the side of the square. As his limbs barely jerked and danced at the end of a rope, his body was... [further tortured].

And the last:

Immediately after the head was severed and dropped into the basket, I took charge of it. The facial expression was that of great agony, for several minutes after decapitation. He would open his eyes, also his mouth, in the process of gaping, as if he wanted to speak to me, and I am positive he could see me for several seconds after the head was severed from the body. There is no doubt that the brain was still active... His decapitated body, which was previously fastened by a strap upon a bench, was in continuous spasmodic and chronic convulsions, lasting from five to six minutes, also an indication of great suffering.

Which is the most barbaric? Since barbarity is a term relative to the age and the supposed enlightenment of the people living in that age, we should know when these punishments occurred. The first was current at the time of Christ, the second occurred in 1924 in America, and the last is a description of a guillotining in present-day France.

We have seen how law has modernized itself. Has man humanized his punishment, the end result of law? Let Nicola Tesla, who invented the electric chair, tell us:

I am opposed to capital punishment in any form; I do not think it deters crime.... For the sufferer, time stands still; and this excruciating torture seems to last for an eternity.... We call ourselves a civilized people. Yet this infliction of death by the electric chair is the most cruel form of torture ever invented by man. It is the destruction of human flesh by a process which induces the maximum amount of pain which the human mechanism is capable of feeling, to say nothing of the mental anguish caused during the lengthy process by which the electroplates, etc., are arranged.[2]

I N THIS DAY OF CARNAGE, when murder is often glorified as an act of heroism, politics, or revenge, the words of George Manley, spoken from the gallows in 1738, are appropriate:

> My friends, you assemble to see—what? A man leap into the abyss of death!...I acknowledge the just judgment of God has overtaken me. My Redeemer knows that murder was far from my heart, and what I did was through rage and passion, being provoked by the deceased. Take warning, my comrades; think what would I now give that I had lived another life. Courageous? You'll say I've killed a man. Marlborough killed his thousands, and Alexander his millions. Marlborough and Alexander, and many others, who have done the like, are famous in history for great men. Aye—that's the case—one solitary man. I'm a little murderer and must be hanged.
>
> Marlborough and Alexander plundered countries; they were great men. I ran in debt with the ale-wife. I must be hanged. How many men were lost in Italy, and upon the Rhine, during the last war for settling a king in Poland? Both sides could not be in the right! They are great men; but I killed a solitary man![3]

Unfortunately there is a certain grotesque gallantry to the gallows that thirteen steps cannot erase: The last meal, with all its trimmings; the phonograph scratching out an ancient tune for the macabre walk, the flick of a cigarette, and the last speech before the black cap is set—all given to the man who is to die because he *is* about to die.

But if the purpose of punishment is to deter crime, then the most ignominious method should be used and, furthermore, it should be inflicted in such a manner that the public has notice thereof. In line with these requirements, the old ducking stool was about as effective a means of punishment as has been invented by man. One does not make a speech of bravado with his mouth spluttering bubbles, his hair stringing seaweed, his pants ballooning water. Impressionable children could find nothing of the romantic rascal about such an individual.

That the ducking stool and other means of public ridicule were efficacious is attested by seventeenth-century writers. I feel that, in this respect, law was further advanced than at the present time when our punishment is meted out behind prison walls in a very secret manner. The only notice given to the public it is intended to *deter* is by lurid press accounts that have usually played up the bravado of the condemned. Such accounts create a result the exact opposite of that which the law intends with punishment. The recent Gary Gilmore extravaganza is a perfect example of glorification instead of deterrence.[4]

The peripheral incidents of capital punishment today have become more spectacular than humiliating. In Massachusetts, under an old law, the sheriff presiding at a murder trial appeared in top hat and tails and wore a sword. In Germany the executioner had to be formally attired. The English judges, until recent captial punishment abandonment, symbolically wore black wigs when pronouncing judgment of death and the Canadian Supreme Court, when affirming a death sentence, appeared in resplendent scarlet robes reserved especially for the occasion. The later and ultimate extravaganza was thus preliminarily heralded.

Such mystical, symbolic elements of capital punishment are common. It is still thought among the illiterate of many countries that any part of the body of an executed murderer exerts a magical and protective power or brings good luck. It is not uncommon among the peasants of Europe to put the finger of a dead thief under the threshold in order to protect the house homeopathically against theft. In 1894 a farmer was convicted of grave robbing in Bavaria. He had dug up the body of a condemned man and taken out one of the eyes that he would be "rendered invisible to mortal sight."

CAPITAL PUNISHMENT WAS the cure for witchcraft and sorcery throughout the ages. The executioner's axe somehow seemed to dispel all imagined evil forces. The cry of "Witch!" rang out, a charge was made of turning the barber into a toad, and the capital cure was sure to follow.

The following account of the learned Lord Hale's charge to a jury trying two women charged with witchcraft may warn us today to beware the intellectual witch hunt.

> Gentlemen of the jury, I will not repeat the evidence unto you, lest by so doing, I should wrong it on the one side or on the other. Only with this I will acquaint you, that you have two things to enquire after; first, whether or not these children were bewitched? Secondly, whether the prisoners at the bar were guilty of it?
>
> That there are such creatures as witches, I make no doubt at all, for, first, the Scriptures have affirmed so much; secondly, the wisdom of all nations hath provided laws against such persons, which is an argument of their confidence of such a crime; and such hath been the judgment of this kingdom, as appears by the Act of Parliament which hath provided punishments proportionable to the quality of the offence.
>
> I entreat you, gentlemen, strictly to examine the evidence which has been laid before you in this weighty case, and I earnestly implore the Great God of Heaven to direct you to a right verdict. For to condemn the innocent and to let the guilty go free, are both an abomination unto the Lord.

The jury, having retired for half an hour, returned a verdict of guilty against both of the prisoners on all the indictments; and the judge, putting on his black cap, after expatiating upon the enormity of their offense, and declaring his entire satisfaction with the verdict, admonished the witches to repent, then sentenced them to die.

The bewitched children immediately recovered their speech and their senses, and slept well that night. Next morning Sir Matthew, much pleased with his achievement, departed for Cambridge, leaving the two unhappy women for execution. They were eagerly pressed to confess, but they died with great constancy, protesting their innocence.

There were some bedeviled children in those days, wretched little monsters whose lying testimony sent more than one innocent person accused of witchcraft and more to his death. But today their legacy still lives. I've seen children give conniving lying. Innocent defendants are frequently saved by discerning jurors remembering perhaps more than anything else the child perfidy in the early witchcraft trials.

THE WORD *lynch* has an interesting history. One Mr. Lynch, a Virginia planter, had found the errant path of a thief leading to his hen house, and catching him red-handed, lashed him to a tree to give him a thorough flogging. It became parlance to speak of any summary punishment as *lynching*.

Justice in California in the earlier days was procedurally as crude as the cooking. There were no condemned rows and the accused was often summarily tried and the rope thrown over the nearest tree.

It is recorded that "Irish Dick," despite his hasty temper and the trouble it brought him, was a lovable fellow and was granted his last request, to arrange his own lynching. With a noose about his neck he climbed a tree, secured the other end of the rope, and upon the sheriff's signal, with a wave to the crowd, gracefully leaped from the limb and "broke his neck as clean as any in the crowd had ever seen done."

ONE OF THE MOST BIZARRE customs of the gallows which lasted until colonial America was the gallows marriage: "...and you shall be here and now hanged by the neck until dead. What say you, John Smith, have you any last words?"

Had he a mind to utter them, the bitter words would have been constricted in a throat paralyzed at the ghastly sight of an ominous rope, that last earthly reminder of a revengeful world.

But in the crowd below, a maid in search of a husband had both mind and spirit to cry out. Carefully appraising the piteous mortal upon the gallows she came to the decision that he was her husband-to-be. "I claim him for my husband and will willingly marry him," she cried. "By all that is legal I demand you stop the execution."

No more weird yet romantic custom in all ancient law can be found than the right to a gallows wedding. Some authorities classify it as a "vulgar error" in history based upon pure fancy. Yet, as one old English periodical chronicles: "It seems doubtful if such a queer idea could have taken possession of the popular mind unless there was some foundation for it in the law."

There are actual instances in France in the fifteenth century of condemned men being saved from the gallows at the last minute by enthusiastic husband-seekers marrying them on the spot.

In 1725 a woman petitioned King George I for the pardon of a convicted felon that she might marry him under Tyburn Tree, the old gallows. The pardon was granted and the couple lived happily ever after.

The procedure followed in claiming the husband was as weird as the custom of the gallows marriage itself. The maid claiming the condemned man had to be stark naked at the time she cried, "Stop the execution." Sometimes the law conceded her a light smock.

In New York in 1784, a "smock gallows marriage" actually saved the life of a condemned man, the only recorded instance of the custom in this country.

What sort of woman would marry sight unseen a condemned man to save him from the gallows? Perhaps only a woman little better off than the prisoner would accept such a mate. Yet consider the hundreds of amorous letters randomly sent to condemned men by complete strangers. A romantic fascination remains with these men.

In France and Italy the custom grew that if any notorious strumpet would beg a convicted man about to be hanged to be her husband, her plea would be granted in order that their joint lives might be bettered by so virtuous an action.

SINCE GALLOWS WEDDINGS are no longer a way to escape the hangman's noose, how does it feel to get a last-minute reprieve

from execution? In 1934, just after having graduated from law
school, I defended Joseph Kristy and Alexander Mackay for
violation of California's "Little Lindbergh Kidnapping Law." The
San Quentin Prison Board had been kidnapped as hostages by
Kristy and Mackay, but the prison break failed. Since Mackay was
a Canadian, the English government entered the case and I was the
recipient of numerous transatlantic telephone calls from London.[5]

One Friday morning (Black Date was always on Friday morning) when all hope for a reprieve was exhausted, I was advised that
a reprieve had been secured from the governor of California. The
warden still hadn't heard of it and the clock approached the fateful
hour of ten. At about fifteen minutes to ten the cat-and-mouse
reprieve came through.

Father O'Meara, the prison chaplain, was in the "bird cage"
next to the gallows room and both boys were "ready to go." They
were brought into the office of captain of the yard Ralph New as
the clock struck ten, the exact moment of their postponed
execution. Each looked at the other and Mackay whispered to me,
"The hardest thing I have ever had to do was to come back."

Later "Mac" sent me the following letter describing the last
hours.

San Quentin
April 24/36

Dear Melvin,

I feel a little better tonight, did not go to bed, as I slept good
last night, something I know you did not. I am told Joe and I came
nearer to the scaffold, without actually arriving there, than any
man or men in the history of the prison.

Naturally, we are deeply grateful to you . . . we can never repay
our debt to you. I imagine you want to hear what transpired.

On Wednesday, in going "up" [to the holding room], we did so
without hope. The treatment we were accorded cannot be too
highly praised, we more than appreciated that.

Did not sleep much Wednesday night, being too busy enjoying
"tailor mades" and cigars, and real good food to boot. We conversed
with the guards until quite late.

On Thursday morning, we heard from the father that the
governor had reserved decision, we, of course, knowing you had an
appointment with the governor in Sacramento.

On Thursday afternoon, Father O'Meara informed us that our writs had been denied, but that the United States Secretary of State had requested a stay from the governor, and such news turned our minds to better things. We entertained much hope, as did everyone we saw. We actually thought it only a matter of a few hours before coming back to the row.

Six o'clock rolled around and we began to get skeptical. At seven we were worrying. At eight we were more than worrying. Just the least bit of hope can change a calmly resigned man beyond human comprehension.

At 9 P.M. we were sinking into despair, we were, at first, resigned but we had been given good cause to hope, and the disappointment hit me hard.

When at 11 P.M. we had heard nothing we gave up and went to bed, and settled down to brass tacks. I awoke at 5 and wrote two letters. Joe slept until 6:30, at which time Father O'Meara came in and gave us both confessions and communion.

The Father told us to get set to go, which we were. We then ate a large breakfast, and between playing the phonograph and talking to the Father, we whiled the time away. At 9 A.M. I began to "get set." I never realized or felt a thing this morning until then. I thought mostly of my mother. I was determined to put up a "good front," and at 9:15 had reached the point where I knew I could "make the grade." Joe was getting a kick out of listening to Mae West's recordings and, I'm sure, was in better form than I—of course, we never did get what one might call sentimental, so I don't know what feelings the Hunky did get.

At 9:20, Father O'Meara left to answer the phone, and I continued to pace back and forth. He came back from the phone, stood and looked at Joe and me for a moment, and quietly said, "Boys, get ready! You are going back to the row."

I said, "Stop kidding, Father," and he answered, "You know I would not kid you, Mac!"

I was lost for a minute. One of the guards made me sit down, and I'm telling you the truth, that news at that time was harder to withstand than walking to the gallows. That is hard to believe, but it is the truth. I would have gone to the scaffold feeling much calmer than I did after hearing the good news.

I'm glad I'm alive. I never thought I'd be alive to write this letter. . . . Being somewhat tired, I'll stop and write you tomorrow. In the meantime, best regards . . .

Sincerely,
Mac[6]

Both Mac and Joe ultimately were hanged after our appeal to the United States Supreme Court was unavailing.[7]

Has there ever been such a terrible thing as a mistaken hanging? We shall never know how many there have been. But years ago, a black man, the youngest man ever to walk the thirteen steps, was hanged at San Quentin Prison. After the execution, that which everyone who lives under capital punishment fears, was discovered: An appeal had been pending and by law the execution should have been stayed until after the appeal had been heard.

The man himself didn't know there was an appeal pending. Whose fault was it? Everyone's, no one's. So tedious, so lengthy and official is the path to appeal, so many different sign posts and detours on the way up, so many hands through which the papers must pass, that the responsibility never was fixed.

Yet the boy's death did more to remedy a defective criminal procedure than any efforts he could have exerted in a none too noble life. California's legislature passed a law making appeal automatic in all cases before execution.

Would the appeal have reversed the conviction? I read some lecture notes of a talk given by the boy's attorney in Los Angeles. Speaking of his client's case on appeal, the attorney said that in the murder trial the prosecution had introduced evidence proving his client's gun had been obtained in a former robbery. He wrote, "In my opinion, such evidence was wholly incompetent and grievously prejudiced the rights of the defendent."

Of course, the Supreme Court never passed upon the point. It was moot; the boy had already been hanged, hadn't he?

A few days after the hanging, a letter from the Los Angeles County Clerk was found. It had been buried at the bottom of the warden's files. It carried the terse notice, "The case is now on appeal." Had it been found two days sooner, the execution would have been stayed.

The warden had telephoned the governor's office the morning of the execution; he had also telephoned the clerk of the California Supreme Court. Neither office had heard that an appeal was pending.

Law is only as infallible as her servants, and only as humane as the society that drafts it.

Notes

1. The common pillory was described this way:

    > This well-known instrument was made of all shapes and sizes, and varied from a forked post or a split pillar to what must have looked like a penal dovecote made to hold several prisoners. The convicted were sometime drawn thither on hurdles, and might be accompanied by minstrels on the way. The hair of the head and beard was shaved off, and sometimes the victims were secured by being nailed through the ears to the framework, and might also be branded. With faces protruding through the strong beams, and with hands through two holes, secured and helpless, they were made to stand defenseless before the crowd as targets for any missile that might be thrown. To those who were hated this was a serious ordeal, for they would be so pelted and knocked about by the mob as to be badly wounded, if not actually done to death. On one occasion two informers were killed in the pillory for getting certain lads hanged for the sake of the reward. At length those who had stood their time were released, and those who had had thier ears nailed would be cut free, and then they might slink away from the scene of shame, or be carried back to prison to endure additional punishment.

    It was a felony at common law for the sheriff to behead one who was sentenced to be hanged. *Year Book*, 35 Henry VI, 58.

2. *New York World*, November 17, 1929.

3. An excerpt from a letter sent me by one of the men on the "row marked C" (condemned row) at San Quentin, in which he describes his fellow tenants: "When I was in the yard I used to think that only the hardest guys were on condemned row, but my education was sadly neglected, most of the real tough ones manage to get life on murder. Most of these fellows up here are nice fellows who got a little peeved with their girl or wife and she, as the case might be, was suddenly deceased.

I'll venture to say that the biggest part of them never stole a dime in their life."

4. A Charles Peace, one of the most notorious murderers in English history, himself subsequently hanged, in his early career was drawn to the gallows and stood under them fascinated many times while watching other outlaws hanged.

5. But it was the English government that unintentionally hindered, rather than helped, the defense as the California newspapers immediately resented the interference of a foreign government in the case.

6. Mackay also sent me the following poem of his own composition:

MELANCHOLIA

A convict in a death cell sat,
So mournful, sad and blue,
He knew that soon he might depart
This world of wondrous hue.

He wandered back to childhood days
With melancholy gloom
He thought of all those honest ways
Discarded: for a shameful doom.

He thought of schooldays free from care,
When worry sat so light,
The home he left, where he did share,
In family life so bright.

He thought of his mother, sister and brother
And was weighted down with shame.
Those dear ones he knew, would try to smother
The ignominy of his name.

He had worldy ambitions, as all of us do,
He wanted to get ahead,
But destiny tripped him, it knocked him askew,
And his fate? Well! He might soon be dead.

That old, old story, the one we oft' hear,
A woman, a drink, and a song,
The bright lights, money, and so-called good cheer,
Were the things which helped him go wrong.

The money comes easy, a gun in his hand,
Night spots and good times galore,
And fair weather friends who thought he was grand,
Forget! Now he's paying the score.

So, thievery is not a good business at best,
The money goes fast as it comes,
And, reader, be honest, and heed my behest,
The Law always collects in large sums.

7. *People* v. *Kristy*, 4 Cal. 2d 504, 50 P. 2d 798 (1935), cert. denied, 297 U.S. 712, 565 Ct. 593.

7

Happily Ever After

ANKIND HAS ALMOST ALWAYS recognized some procedure for perpetuating a fleeting romantic relationship
in a more permanent union. In the early common law,
one could become married by a very simple process—by merely
agreeing to be married: "If a man say to a woman, 'I promise to
marry thee and if thou are content to marry me, say I do or kiss
me,' if the woman do, say, or kiss, spousals are contracted." No
consummation (sexual relation) was necessary in the old days.

By the year 700, the pope had made marriage so simple that all
could contract it, this being his purpose: "Better to marry than to
burn." No ceremony, no license, no banns were required, merely
that a man and woman state that from a certain time forward they
were married. This is what was and is known as a *common-law
marriage.*[1]

This is the prescribed form of marriage for Scotland (where
from the manner of contracting the marriage, there must always
be a considerable number of persons who could not say offhand

whether they were married or not!). A very few states still have common-law marriage.

In states where the common law has been changed by statutes requiring a license and solemnization, the common-law marriage is no marriage at all. Of course, if a common-law marriage is contracted in a state authorizing such marriage, the couple are considered married everywhere, even in states where such marriage might not be lawfully contracted originally.[2]

THE CAPTAIN'S WORD may be "law" at sea, but he makes a poor sea lawyer of Cupid when he performs a marriage, for often it is not legal. There are many who still think erroneously that the captain is a marrying man. It is only when a husband or wife, after they have been living together many years, brings suit for divorce, or when one spouse seeks to inherit by law that the couple are amazed when informed that they were never legally married on shipboard.

Many sea marriage couples living today as husband and wife would be still more amazed to know that the validity of their marriage may depend more upon the residence of the owner of the vessel than upon the vessel they were married on.

Bud Fisher, the creator of "Mutt and Jeff," was married on the *Leviathan* on his way to England. There is no law of marriage, strictly speaking, on the high seas. Therefore, the boat, wherever it goes, is followed by the law of the nation or state wherein the owner of the boat resides. The *Leviathan* was owned by the United States, therefore federal law followed the vessel and a common-law marriage, or a marriage without license or ceremony, would suffice. Even the words spoken by the captain were superfluous.

IF A CHURCH WEDDING is too expensive, or if, as groom, you are too timid to face the preacher, you may have your best friend stand in for you. However, before executing such a *proxy* marriage, the groom should inquire carefully into the laws of the state in which he intends to marry. The requirements as to license, ceremony, or merely an agreement to marry, vary greatly even between neighboring states.

A proxy marriage is sometimes the only way around circumstances. In June 1981, Nobel Peace Prize winner Andrei Sakharov's stepson Alexey Semyonov married Yelizaveta Alekseyeva by proxy. Semyonov was in Montana for the wedding; Alekseyeva was in the Soviet Union and not allowed to leave. It took a seventeen-day hunger strike on the part of Sakharov and his wife, Yelena Bonner, before the Soviets permitted Alekseyeva to join her husband in Boston.

In early English law, wedding presents were not only demanded from the wedding guests, but, when pledged, were considered a legal debt.

Several weeks before the marriage, a *bidder* was paid to carry invitations to all the friends of the couple about to be married. He usually carried a long stick, with ribbons flying, and, standing in the middle of the guests' rooms, he invited them, usually in rhyme, to attend the wedding. He also bade them to be sure to bring their presents. In exchange he promised them good entertainment.[3]

In less practical communities, wedding gifts were returnable in kind if the donors themselves were married and gave a bidding. In some instances the wedding gifts were payable upon demand. If repayment was refused, the donor went to a court of law to collect his wedding gift.

In more recent times, the late great Supreme Court Justice Cardozo, sitting then on the New York Court of Appeals, ordered an American to pay $2,500 a year to a count, and this ten years after the marriage.

In 1902 Miss Schweizer was engaged to Count Alberto Giacomo Giovanni Francesco Maria Gulinelli of Italy (as is said in legal documents, "hereinafter called 'Count' for short"). After the engagement, her father agreed to pay to the count's bride $2,500 annually. The money was to be paid in lire and the agreement was written in Italian—further evidence of father Schweizer's desire to appeal to European good will.

On the day of the marriage, father paid $2,500. In fact, every year father made his payments—until 1912. On that date, when no check was forthcoming from father-in-law to son-in-law, summons and complaint traveled in the other direction.

In court, defendant father-in-law wanted to know what "consideration" (a legal term meaning "what's in it for me?") he got out of the annual $2,500.

To this Justice Cardozo in effect said: Hadn't the father ever heard of broken engagements?

> The defendant knew that a man and a woman were assuming the responsibilities of wedlock in the belief that adequate provision had been made for the woman and for future offspring. He offered this inducement to both while they were free to retract or delay.
>
> An ancient judge has beautifully said of marriage: "Marriage is attended and followed by pecuniary consequences; happiness or misery to the parties; by life to unborn children; by unquiet or repose to the state; by what money ordinarily buys and by what no money can buy, to an extent which cannot be estimated or expressed, except by the word *infinite!*"

To make certain that the father was sufficiently impressed, the court added that he must live up to his "honorable engagement."

A S RECENTLY AS 100 years ago, married women in the United States and England could not own their own property. Upon marriage a woman's real property (and the rents and profits therefrom), money, jewels, and household articles became the husband's property forevermore. Even her personal clothing belonged to him. If the wife worked, her earnings belonged to her husband, to squander or save as he saw fit.

Under the early common law, when a woman married, she legally ceased to exist. Once the husband slipped the ring upon her finger, she whom he celebrated in song and verse for her wisdom and to whose superiority of judgment he knelt as a pagan to his idol, became legally an imbecile and a slave, unable to judge for herself and utterly unresponsible for anything she might say or do. The law recognized but one person after marriage, and that was her husband.

A wife could not make a contract or agreement, for after marriage she was no longer a legal person. If a child was born to the union, the husband had exclusive control over it. Married women couldn't vote because legally they didn't exist. For the same reason they couldn't hire an attorney or an agent. They couldn't even make a will. If the wife was injured, her husband brought suit for her and collected and kept the damages.

Blackstone attributed the rule of evidence that a wife couldn't testify against her husband to the fact that a man couldn't be forced to testify against himself!

If a wife committed a crime, the law presumed she was coerced by her husband. Consequently he, not the wife, was the criminal.

One of the best examples of the dead hand of the past ruling the law of the present is the California case of *People* v. *Miller:*[4] The defendant and his wife were tried and convicted of criminal conspiracy under a penal code section providing for conviction when the act is committed by "two or more persons." The Supreme Court of California reversed, holding that the act was committed by but *one* person, not "two or more," for, as we have seen under the common law, as soon as a woman marries she lost her legal identity. In the eyes of the law their identities had merged and she and her husband were forevermore regarded as "one person." There weren't the "two or more" required for a conspiracy.

Since the wife ceased to exist after marriage, the husband was responsible for all her civil wrongs after marriage—and all her prenuptial debts.

Guests at an eighteenth century wedding would not be shocked or surprised at seeing the bride appear clad only in her birthday suit or at most, a "shift" or a "smock." The custom of the bride being entirely naked or clad in a single sheet at the time of marriage was based upon the law of the times.

Under the common law, the community property of both the wife and the husband was liable for the wife's pre-nuptial debts—unless she came to him destitute. From early Saxon days into the eighteenth century, a debtor-bride often came to the wedding clothed only in a plain white smock or shift. This was a public declaration of warning to her creditors that she took no property to her husband, and therefore that he could not be charged with any responsibility for her debts.

The notion that a bride, who lacked modesty as well as money, could throw off her debts with her dress was even observed in the colonies for a time. In 1784 in Pennsylvania, a bridegroom, acting with the proper spirit of chivalry and to save the appearance of his bride, not to mention his credit, met his bride in her scant drapery, halfway between her house and his. Here he provided her with warm garments, but only after formally announcing in the presence of the assembled guests that the wedding clothes he placed upon her belonged to him and were only "loaned" to the bride for the occasion.

It is also recorded that the Widow Mary Bradley claimed her Maine husband in 1774 while clad only in her smock. It was a cold, wintry day, and the gallant clergyman threw his cloak about the shoulders of the shivering widow to protect her from the icy blasts of the biting wind.

THIS UNENVIABLE POSITION of the married woman under the common law continued until the middle of the nineteenth century. While the transformation is not quite complete in some states even today, at that time was begun one of the most complete reversals in policy in all law. Today, in most jurisdictions, a wife stands the equal of her husband in the eyes of the law.[5]

This emancipation of the married woman was brought about by courts of equity and statutory changes. To complete title to his wife's property, it was often necessary for a husband at common law to seek redress against the wife's debtors in court. The chancellors in equity courts looked at the husband, standing before them stuffing his pockets with the property of his wife, and said, "Mr. Husband, you would pull a little harder upon our heartstrings and we would be more inclined to aid you in collecting from your wife's debtors if you would first promise to settle some of that money on your wife."

It was not long before equity courts [6] made it their particular problem to see that married women were financially protected.

Legislatures in the United States and England took up the fight for "equal rights for married women," and soon politicians began to incorporate this as a plank in their platforms for re-election. "Married women's acts" were the result.

MANY CHANGES HAVE TAKEN PLACE in the laws regarding marriage. Just as many changes have taken place in the law regarding divorce. In the early common law there was no provision for divorce, except when two infidels were married and one later became a Christian. In this case only the church would grant a full divorce. As marriage grew more complicated with the requirements of licenses and ceremonies, the law made divorce easier to obtain.

The church was the first to relent and grant a "limited divorce" from bed and board *(mensa et thoro).* This did not mean that either party was single or free to marry again; it only gave the husband the right to keep the wife from his home. It was not until 1858 that one could get a divorce in an English court. Before this time, the few divorces granted were passed as special acts of Parliament in each case.

During the hundred years before the American Revolution there were no divorces in New York and after it became a state, there was no provision for divorce. Until recently there was only one ground for divorce, as in England: adultery, and the guilty party could never remarry in that state.

As late as 1890, the subject of divorce was so new that in some American jurisdictions there was no procedure to obtain a divorce. In South Carolina, until recently, one had to petition the legislature for a divorce.

A DIVORCE COURT IS a court of equity and one must come into equity courts with "clean hands." Formerly, this meant that one spouse must be innocent and one guilty, otherwise equity would not hear the case. (There are no juries in equity cases.)

Therefore, if a husband deserted his wife, she could obtain a divorce, but if the wife also deserted the husband, although this established grounds for both, both were guilty. Equity would not hear the case and both had to remain married. Holy wedlock became unholy deadlock.

This was the law everywhere in the United States until recently. Now there are "no-fault" divorce laws, like California's, which routinely grant divorces upon the request of one spouse, so long as that spouse is even briefly a resident of the state. "Divorce court" scenes of domestic recrimination no longer occur over who got caught doing what to whom; they're now about who gets to keep the station wagon.

In the somnolent republic below the Rio Grande, one great American institution moved with singular rapidity—divorce.[7] Why did Americans head for Mexico or Reno when wedded bliss ended? There were two reasons: the speed of obtaining the decree and the number of grounds available.

A New York husband could get a divorce only on grounds of adultery, and he might be reluctant to publicly charge his spouse with that. If he lived in California, while there were more grounds available, he had to wait one year after securing his *interlocutory* decree before remarrying.[8] Other states had similar restrictions.

So one chose a more tolerant jurisdiction, Reno, where a final decree is given after six weeks residence, or Mexico, where the decree is obtainable almost at once. (Paris, Haiti, and several other jurisdictions are just as liberal.)

After returning to one's home state, however, is the divorce valid there? The answer depends upon two things: First, you must have complied with the law of the foreign state and, second, you must have given up your former home and actually acquired a bona fide residence in the foreign state before the divorce was granted, so that you really were subject to the jurisdiction of its laws.

Although the United States Constitution provides that each state must give the judgments (and a decree of divorce is a judgment) of sister states "full faith and credit," some of the judges do not like to see the "home folks running off to Reno" and swearing in court that they have established permanent residence there, when the judges and "those back home" know full well the expatriates can just wait out the six weeks to get back home again. There is therefore no assurance that the foreign decree will be given "full faith and credit" in the state in which the divorced person particularly wants it to be good (especially when the foreign residence requirements are very brief and subject to judicial suspicion).

It may be said generally that divorces by mail, where neither party leaves the home state, are invalid because neither party has come under the jurisdiction of the foreign state.

T HE FOLLOWING INCIDENTS prove that someone had been at least very whimsical in setting aside what God had joined together.[9] There are actual Los Angeles court cases under the old "fault" laws in which plaintiffs asked for decrees of divorce on grounds of extreme cruelty: because the husband slept in the chicken house instead of the bed, because "he blew smoke in the goldfish bowl making the fish sick," because "he became intoxicated and wrung the necks of two pet monkeys," because "he stuffed the piano with chicken feathers."

For the men: "She laid down in the driveway so I couldn't back the auto," "she insisted her pet dog sleep in the same bed with me," "she called me names in three languages, two of which I understood," "she put beer bottles, knives and forks in my bed," "she jumped on me from behind and bit me in the shoulder," "she took out her false teeth at the table and picked them with a fork."

Hugo Zacchini, one of the "human cannonball" brothers daily shot from a cannon, had nerves of steel but could not stand the nagging of his wife. He told the judge, "my home life has so upset me that the safety of my brothers and myself is seriously jeopardized." Divorce was granted on grounds of extreme cruelty.

Cornelius Price, of Columbus, Ohio, filed complaint for divorce, alleging extreme cruelty in that his wife, after stating she had prepared a rare dish for him, placed on the table a plate of boiled automobile tires and inner tubes. His wife, in defending the action, alleged that she did it as "an object lesson."

A New Jersey plaintiff sought to have her marriage annulled because after five years she remained a virgin. The defendant insisted his reason for abstinence was the the fact that sexual intercourse was painful and distressing to his wife. Of the defendant's allegations the New Jersey Court of Chancery said: "Such solicitude of a groom is noble, of a husband, heroic. Few have the fortitude to resist the temptations of the honeymoon. But human endurance has its limitations. When nature demands its due, youth is prodigal in the payment. Men are still cave men in the pleasures of the bed."

This court thereupon advised the annulment.[10]

DIVORCE OFTEN RESULTS in alimony, or as today's euphemism would have it, "spousal support." But what if you don't pay your alimony? You can go to jail, as Mr. Politano of New York did. When he finally petitioned the court for release, he "enjoyed the unique, if unhappy, distinction of being the senior inmate of the sheriff's alimony colony."

But to go back to the start of the trouble: Mr. and Mrs. Politano became such in 1927. Husband expended his entire savings of $3,000 in fitting up and supporting a home. "As their union was blessed with no children, the wife atoned for this by installing her mother and sister as permanent members of the household."

After the divorce, husband couldn't make the payments the court had ordered. When one doesn't pay in accordance with court decree, he is adjudged in contempt of court; the punishment can be jail. However—and here is the oddest part of this jail sentence—it is for no definite time, but until the defendant *complies* with the court's order to pay.

How could Mr. Politano earn money to pay the decree while he was in jail? He fell more hopelessly in debt and consequent contempt every day. When he finally got the ear of Justice Bonynge of the New York Supreme Court, Mr. Politano had been in jail over two years because he couldn't pay his alimony.

Said the justice:

> Punishment for contempt is a deserved and salutary rebuke to one who has affronted the dignity of a court. If an evil-doer invades my courtroom and reviles me or my ancestors or my country with indecent or blasphemous utterances, a penalty of thirty days is the strait-jacket [limit] of my righteous wrath.
>
> Can I truthfully say that this defendant, who, through poverty or misfortune, omits to pay alimony to a vindictive and relentless wife, has offered my court an affront more than thirty-fold greater?

Saying that an extension of petticoat government in the home to petticoat justice in the court was not always expedient, the court freed Mr. Politano.

For those ordered to pay who *can* pay and don't—in jail they stay until they do comply with the court's orders.[11] But doesn't this sound like a debtor's prison? How can a hapless spouse be thrown in jail?

The answer, saith the courts, is that they are *not* imprisoning to enforce payment of support; they are punishing disobedience to a court order: to pay support. But the righteous need not fear; only a spouse that is financially able to pay and refuses to do so can be adjudged in contempt (unless the spouse has *intentionally* brought on his poverty to avoid payment).

A NEW VENTURE in matrimony, something with which Henry VIII did not have to contend, is *palimony*. Michelle Marvin, plaintiff, versus Lee Marvin, defendant, decided by the Supreme Court of California in 1977,[12] called our attention to this windfall for the emerging sex (now the emerged sex).

In this case the plaintiff got very little from the wealthy screen actor with whom she had lived for seven years through thick and thin under the belief she was to get half the property if ever they split. Most of the meager award she got from the Los Angeles trial judge went to lawyers' fees and costs.

Palimony is an award or settlement for one of the unmarried spouses made when they split after they have lived together. A couple doesn't have to live together as husband and wife in order for there to be a palimony award. Indeed, if the sole reason for the relationship is to live together sexually and as husband and wife, the agreement might be illegal and neither putative spouse would get anything upon dissolution.

In the Marvin case, Justice Tobriner of the California Supreme Court wrote: "During the past fifteen years there has been a substantial increase in the number of couples living together without marrying.... Such nonmarital relationships lead to legal controversy when one party dies or the couple separates. Courts of appeal faced with the task of determining property rights in such cases have arrived at conflicting positions."

What then is the majority court view of palimony and what is the present state of the law generally throughout the United States?

First, if the couple enters into a nonlegal "marriage" in good faith and not because one has a prior spouse living or another invalid reason, courts will give relief upon petition by an innocent "spouse" or upon death and the property generally will be equitably divided.

However, if the principal consideration is a meretricious and sexual relationship and the property rights are only incidental, the courts look askance at any attempt to enforce palimony by court action. One looking forward to palimony in the future should be careful that the "immoral relation" was not made a principal consideration of any agreement.

Palimony is property given by the court to the petitioning putative spouse based upon a contract—written or oral, express or implied—that the parties will share their property or their earnings. Oral contracts in most fields of the law are just as valid as written ones; written ones just happen to be more certain.

An implied contract is different from an express contract in that the activity shows that the parties intended a division of the property had they stopped to think or had they "contracted," i.e., written it down.

Thus, it will be seen that the basis of the palimony suit is some sort of an agreement or contract for property. It isn't the living together and indeed, as seen above, if the consideration for the palimony is principally the living together, palimony will probably be denied.

Justice Tobriner suggested that "Adults who voluntarily live together and engage in sexual relations are nonetheless as competent as any other persons to contract respecting their earnings and property rights. Of course, they cannot lawfully contract to pay for the performance of sexual services, for such a contract is, in essence, an agreement for prostitution and unlawful for that reason." Many financial arrangements can be agreed upon, from pooling earnings to forming a partnership. But I would suggest having a written contract drawn by a lawyer.

I presently have a typical palimony suit between Nick Nolte, the prominent film star, and the beautiful model Karen Luigi Eklund. The couple lived together for seven years and property was taken in both names. Neither wanted to marry but they did live together as husband and wife and Nolte told many film personalities, who will testify at trial, that he treated Karen as his wife, and that she had half his property and half his earnings.

When Nolte walked out, he took all of the property that he had promised to Karen. He did, soonest thereafter, marry someone else. Now Nick doesn't want to share the not inconsiderable property and Karen has sued for palimony and the economic peripherals of court costs and attorneys' fees.

IS THERE PALIMONY after death? A former French model, Genevieve Gillaizeau, thirty-five, claims she was the late Darryl F. Zanuck's mistress and has challenged the movie mogul's will in a Riverside County court. Madame or Mademoiselle Gillaizeau is contesting Zanuck's will, saying that it is not his true will; she also wants damages and property.

This may not be a true palimony case, although there is nothing in the new law that is being made on palimony that says one cannot test his or her right to palimony after death as well as during life.

Generally, these suits by the "faithful housekeeper" contend that the aged and decrepit testator had promised to leave half his estate to the patient housekeeper provided she stayed with him and kept his house for X number of years. There is nothing of putative marriage or sexual favors at all here and again it is solely a question of whether there was an agreement, express or implied. Sometimes the faithful housekeeper wins on the express or implied agreement; sometimes the court awards her an "equitable amount for her services," what the forgetful testator would have had to pay someone else to have taken care of him.

SINCE THE BASIS of palimony is the express or implied agreement, written or oral, *not* the consideration for living together, obviously the parties to the agreement would not necessarily have to have the qualifications of a husband and wife. This raises a very interesting question. Can there be palimony between male homosexuals who live together and similarly between lesbians?

While I know of no appellate decision yet, cases are being brought in the lower trial courts that will ultimately reach the appellate level, and I feel these cases will be decided in favor of palimony unless the justices find an "overriding meretricious relationship."

The protection of individual rights, sexual as well as ethnic, has come a long, long way. The unmarried "spouse" today is in a far better legal and economic position than was the legal wife who, under the early common law, legally did not exist.

Notes

1. Dr. Myrtle McGraw, child psychologist, and Rudolph Mallina, research engineer, who, according to the New York papers, signed a contract before Justice Samuel I. Rosenman on December 18, 1936, and "went home as thoroughly married as if they had held hands in a religious ceremony," would have been surprised to know that they could have been legally married in a fashion even more simple: Had they gone to a state where the common law prevailed, all that would have been required for a valid legal marriage was that they *consider* themselves and act as if married!

    Almost as simple is an old Montana law providing that a couple may be married merely by filing a declaration of marriage for fifty cents.

    But according to most courts, mere agreement is no longer enough to create a common-law marriage; there must be agreement *plus* consummation (and consummation must include at least cohabitation as husband and wife). So merely saying "I do" won't always do.

2. However, a temporary visit to a common-law state won't always give rise to a valid marriage upon return to the home state. There should be some indication that more than a romantic vacation was intended before some courts will consider the common-law marriage valid.

3. The following is an example of what the well-written wedding invitation of the nineteenth century contained:

    Carmarthen, August 19, 1828.

    We beg leave respectfully to acquaint you that it is our intention to enter the matrimonial state on Tuesday, the 23d day of September next; and from the encouragement we have received, by the kind promises of our friends, we purpose making a bidding on the occasion, which will be held the same day, at the Old White Lion, in Queen Street, where we hope to have the pleasure of your company and influence; and whatever favors you may then think proper to confer on us will be gratefully acknowledged, and repaid with thanks whenever required on a similar occasion, by your humble servants,

> *Dennis Woods*, Currier.
>
> *Eugenia Vaughan*,
> Servant at the Ivey Bush Hotel

4. *People* v. *Miller*, 82 Cal. 107, 22 P. 934 (1889).
   Until 1976 in California, a married woman was legally incapable of committing any misdemeanor if it was at her husband's command. California Penal Code §26(7)

5. Until 1975, a husband in California was legally designated head of the family. He had the right to choose *any* "place or mode of living" and the wife had to obey him.

6. Equity courts are different from law courts, though in America they are now merged. The chancellor sat in equity without a jury and gave a less rigorous and more "equitable" justice than the judge in the law courts by the rigors of the common law.

7. Some time ago I received a letter on the stationery of the "Pan-American Office—Mexican Legal Matters Exclusively—Cable Address Panoff," from Señors Minardes, Rosas, Dis, Despero, and Grinol. The letter informed me that "we have open [sic] this office—specializing in Mexican divorce." A divorce could be secured "when both parties agree to the divorce"—in ten days.
   American lawyers could not send such letters because they could not advertise. To have sent such a circular letter would have meant disbarment until a recent Supreme Court nod of the head on that issue.
   A Colorado attorney once (1893) inserted in a Denver newspaper the following advertisement: "Divorces legally obtained very quietly; good everywhere. Box 2344 Denver."

The next day instead of a client's letter in the box was a summons to court. Said the court:

The advertisement published by respondent says in effect: "If you are dissatisfied with your partner in life—if you desire a divorce—communicate with me, and your desire shall be gratified. Everything will be done very quietly, and you will be able to sever the disagreeable marriage tie without public scandal and hence without reproach."

Such an advertisement is against good morals, public and private. It is a false representation, and a libel upon the courts of justice. Divorces cannot be legally obtained very quietly which shall be good anywhere. Public hearings are required.

The lawyer was ordered suspended temporarily.

8. California Civil Code §61 (stats. 1903, p. 176).

Today, California spouses must still wait six months to remarry, California Civil Code §4514. The rationale for postponing entry of a final "dissolution" (the modern euphemism for that distasteful "divorce") for six months is to prevent hasty divorces without time for "reflection and reconciliation." A noble idea, but in a state with a divorce rate approaching 50 percent, also one of dubious effect.

Even if his state had such a "cooling-off period," the spouse who couldn't wait to make the same mistake twice could marry in another state without a waiting period. If the marriage were valid in that state, California had to honor it.

9. Justice Ragan of the Nebraska Supreme Court once said in the case of *Cochran v. Cochran*, 42 Neb. 612, 60 N.W. 942 (1894), divorce laws "are not designed for, and must not be used for, the purpose of enabling even preachers to 'off with the old love and on with the new.'"

10. *Tompkins v. Tompkins*, 111 A. 599, 601, 92 N. J. Eq. 113 (1920).

11. "An able-bodied man can earn ten cents a day, and can afford to pay his divorced wife three dollars a month as alimony." *Muse v. Muse*, 84 N.C. 35 (1881).

12. *Marvin v. Marvin*, 18 Cal. 3d 660, 683–84, 557 P. 2d 106, 134 C.R. 815 (1977).

8

Where There's a Will,
There's a Lawyer

F EW THINGS SHOW the human character in a more
ridiculous light than the circumstances of will-making. It is
the last opportunity we have of exercising the natural perversity of the disposition, and we take care to make good use of it.[1]

The marriage choice of his son or his daughter, the yearly
moaning at his grave of bagpipe dirges, the disposition of his entire
estate to a family of cats, burial in a Ferrari, all are examples of
testators' perversity.

Edward Wortley Montague's will was after his death the portrait
of his character in life:

> To my noble and worthy relation the Earl of ——— I do not
> give his lordship any further part of my property because the best
> part of that he has contrived to take already. Item, to Sir Francis
> ——— I give one word of mine, because he has never had the good
> fortune to keep his own. Item, to ——— the author, for putting
> me in his travels, I give five shillings for his wit, undeterred by the
> charge of extravagance, since friends who have read his book
> consider five shillings too much. Item, to Sir Robert Walpole, I

leave my political opinions never doubting that he can turn them into case, who has always found such an excellent market in which to change his own. Item, my cast-off habit of swearing oaths, I give to Sir Leopold D —— in consideration that no oaths have ever been able to find him yet.

(Note: The testator's mother, Lady Montague, had disinherited him.)

Just after the Franco-Prussian war, a Capuchin monk, noted for his charity, thus bequeathed his entire property, consisting of breviary, frock, cord, a volume of M. Thiers, and a wallet: "First, to the Abé Michaud, my breviary because he does not know his own; secondly to M. Jules Favre, my frock to hide his shame; thirdly, to M. Gambetts, my cord, which will one day prove useful around his neck; fourthly, to Mr. Thiers, his own work, that he may read it again; and fifthly, to Frances, my wallet, because she may shortly have occasion to collect alms."

I N THE LAW OF WILLS, the layman sees, prima facie, further corroboration for his contention that "the law's a ass." But, as in some of the ridiculous specifications that were grounds for divorce, it is not the lawyer at all who is to blame. The will is the act of the layman himself. It can be his monument or his folly. And, as one court said, few men pinched by the messenger of death have a disposing memory. Had the unadvised lay author of a ludicrous will gone to the lawyer instead, his devisees would have found particularly apt the expression "law is the rustic curb of old father antic," as Shakespeare's Falstaff put it.

However, no lawyer could have improved upon the will of the battle- and bottle-scarred old veteran who left "to the nurse who kindly removed a pink monkey from the foot of my bed, $5,000; to the cook at the hospital who removed snakes from my broth, $5,000."

Pink monkeys? Snakes? This doesn't sound much like "being of sound mind." Yet any inmate of an asylum, even though certifiably psychotic, can make a valid will. All that is required is *testamentary capacity*, the standard formula that requires a testator to know—at the time he makes his will—the general nature of his property, his relationship to those who might claim a right to inherit his estate (his relatives), and a general idea that the practical effect of what he's doing is to dispose of that property to certain fortunate recipients. It doesn't matter what sort of fantastic delusions may cloud one's mind, so long as he understands the effect of making his will and it is not written as the product of that delusion.

That's a fairly generous standard, which most of us, even in our worst moments, can usually meet. And that's fortunate, since the ravages of time take their toll, and often at the time a will is needed most, the mind is struggling with senility, eccentricity, and failing memory.

The law recognizes the frailty of the human mind in its winter years, and pursues the testator's *intent* despite obstacles of confusion and mental weakness.

It's often said that mere belief, no matter how absurd it may be, is not a sufficient delusion to invalidate a will. No matter how speculative, how unacceptable, how occult or arcane, the testator has the right to his or her religious, personal, or political beliefs, even if the folks cluck their tongues about old gramps and his seances. We all have the right to leave our estate to Reverend Moon—or Reverend Sun.

But delusions that are so pervasive and irrational that the court cannot find testamentary capacity mean that the will can't be separated from the delusion, and the will fails. Thus, one who saw snakes in her bed, pigs on her floor, and elephants on her ceiling was not adjudged competent to write a valid will.[2] Poor Richard Turpin, saw men climbing through closed windows, his wife rising from a ditch in the yard, and feared people were trying to take his ranch away from him. His will was set aside by his son, who inherited the entire estate, thereby proving the last of his father's delusions to be true.[3]

Personal eccentricity and aberrance are forgiven to some degree. In 1929 an Illinois court held that simply because a woman drank liquor and used "improper language," she didn't necessarily lack the competence to make a will.[4] (Intoxication, alcoholism, or drug use won't invalidate your will, either—unless you were so drunk at the exact time you wrote the thing that you didn't know the object of your bounty and the amount of it.)

Each case makes its own law on its own facts. Mrs. Johnson wasn't considered incapacitated just because she felt wheels grinding in her head, ate any sugar cubes she could find, and bit the heads off matches and placed the stems in patterns on her coffee table.[5] But Mr. Pessagno's will was set aside as incompetent because he saw the Virgin Mary once too often, frightened little children on the street by striking at them with his cane, cut his lawn with a pair of scissors, and left a large portion of his estate to someone who had just embezzled from him.[6]

Courageous Louisa Strittmater, an ardent feminist, had her will set aside due to "feminism to a neurotic extreme" and "a morbid aversion to men," because she left her estate to National Women's Party. The court found from the evidence that she "regarded men as a class with an insane hatred. She looked forward to the day when women would bear children without the aid of men, and all males would be put to death at birth."[7]

I HAVE FOUND over the years of many will contests that there's nothing better a jury likes to do than remake a will. They can give away a lot of money and it doesn't cost them a dime.

The strange case of Howard Hughes's multiple and mysterious wills exemplifies the conflict between intent and capacity. Debate over Hughes's mental state, and the authenticity of the various *holographic* (solely in the testator's own handwriting) and printed wills attributed to him, will no doubt rage for years. Whether Melvin Dummar, the unassuming gas station attendant named as heir to one-sixteenth of Hughes's fortune will ever see a penny remains to be seen.

The following will was offered for probate:

In the name of God, Amen:
My featherbed to my wife, Jen;

Also my carpenter's saw and hammer;
Until she marries; then, God damn her.

Seeking to accomplish in death what he could not in life, a testator gave his estate to a single woman of fifty, who disliked theatricals, on the condition that she engage a theater and perform there for a week.

A Frenchman, by profession a cook, decreed upon death that a new recipe be posted on his tombstone every day for eternity.

A lawyer made a will that was both confession and testament. He left $200,000 to a lunatic asylum declaring that many of his clients who paid him the exorbitant fees he asked should be inmates!

A French court, to the praise of justice, held a French testator sane, and admitted to probate his will, which declared that France was a "nation of bastards," and he, therefore, left his entire fortune to the poor of England and ordered his body thrown into the sea a mile from the English coast!

These ludicrous wills are not necessarily the result of a mind normally given to folly, since some of the greatest minds of each age left wills of monumental absurdity. These wills show the caprice and the perversity that is in the best of us, and law's problem here is again one of human nature.

For example, Jeremy Bentham, a man of gifted intellect, made elaborate plans for his cadaver after death. He bequeathed his body to a hospital with instructions that it would be embalmed and preserved entirely and that he should, when thus preserved, preside at meetings of the hospital directors and be present at the banquets of his old friends. (His body actually was preserved in the hospital museum for years.)

The amazing will of Solomon Sanborn of Medford, Massachusetts, left his body to Professor Oliver Wendell Holmes to be used for anatomical research, with but one condition: that two drumheads be made of his skin! Upon one of these drumheads, Sanborn desired that Alexander Pope's "Universal Prayer" should be inscribed, and on the other, the Declaration of Independence. The drumheads were to be presented to the testator's friend, the drummer of Cohasset, on further condition that on June 17 each year the drummer should beat "on the drumheads at the foot of Bunker Hill the stirring strains of 'Yankee Doodle.'" Holmes declined the bequest.

Though Patrick Henry may have said "Give me liberty or give me death," in death he was not willing to accord even the smallest quotient of that commodity he, at least forensically, so dearly valued. When he died, he left a will that provided that if his widow remarried, she forfeited all the estate he had bequeathed her. The wife was more loyal to her husband's ideal of freedom than he was—she remarried and forfeited her late Patrick's estate.

The will of the late Marshall Field covered sixty pages; that of John William Mackay of the Postal Telegraph Company was set forth in but one page. Edward Harriman, the builder of railroad empires, disposed of his property in what would be a short telegram: forty-eight words. All had millions of dollars, made in different ways, and left in different kinds of wills.

George Washington executed a long will. In one clause he endowed a university of the District of Columbia, because, he wrote, "it has always been a source of serious regret with me to see the youth of these United States sent to foreign countries for purposes of education [and to learn] principles unfriendly to republican government."

What a turn about would he see, living today, when so many foreign students are learning republican government in our universities.

William Shakespeare bequeathed "unto my wief my second best bed with the furniture."

The wills of the great, as well as the humble, may still be seen, as they were written, in the archives of the probate courts of the counties and countries where they died: Napoleon, Lord Nelson, Van Dyke, Mark Twain. (Of course, the wills of members of the royal family are not probated like ordinary mortals.)

One will not find the will of one of America's great: Abraham Lincoln. When the assassin's bullet found him he had drawn no will. More than anything else this may disprove stories that he expected death when it overtook him; otherwise, smart lawyer that he was, he would certainly have drawn a will. (Or would he? Some people are quite content to let their property go as the law provides when they die *intestate*—without a will.)

Admitting then that it is the layperson, not the law, who is to blame for ludicrous wills, are not the cases legion in which the law has actually thwarted the plain intent of the testator because he overlooked some "silly technical" rule of law?

I recall the will of a deceased man brought to me by two of three surviving brothers. During his lifetime the deceased had said in no uncertain terms that he desired that his estate go to these two brothers solely, that he wanted, specifically, that the third brother take absolutely nothing. Furthermore, the deceased had gone to a stationery store and bought a form will. He had dated it, filled in the blanks in unambiguous language, and signed it in his own handwriting. His intent was manifestly precise.

Yet, the third brother took one-third of the property—exactly what the deceased did not want him to have. His intent was clear but the homemade will violated the "technical" rule of law that in a holographic will the *entire* contents must be in the handwriting of the *testator* (or *testatrix* if the will-maker is a woman). Had the brother but copied the form and his insertions entirely in his own handwriting, the third brother would have been excluded as he desired. Or, he might have made the instrument an *attested* will by merely having the signatures of two witnesses on it, and the third brother would still have been excluded.

But isn't the law "a ass" here when the intention of the testator is so obvious? The answer is that the right to the enjoyment of property by one's legatees, or the right to a will, is not an inherent right.[8] It is a right specifically granted by the state under which one lives, and that law has seen fit to impose "technical" restrictions that must be minutely followed. These restrictions are not imposed for hardship, as the two brothers may well have thought in the case just cited, but are the result of deliberate considerations in imposing safeguards to prevent forgery, fraud, undue influence, and careless wills—to make certain of the intention of the testator in the great majority of cases.

Rather than cynically saying "where there is a will there is a lawyer," we should say perhaps there *should* be a lawyer. It is safe to say that any lawyer could have improved upon the document offered for probate in Anderson County, Texas, in 1934, as the last will and testament of one Herman Oberweiss, yet it may be doubted if any lawyer could have as eloquently pictured the misgivings of the testator as to some of the recipients of his bounty:

> I am writing of my will mineself that des lawyir wand he should have much money he ask to many answers about the family. First think i want done i dont want my brother Oscar got a durn thing. I got he is a scallywag he done me out of four dollars foreteen years since.
>
> I want it that Hilda my sister she gets the north sixtie akers of at where I am homing it now I bet she dont get that loafer husband of hers to brake twenty akers next plowing. She cant have it if she lets Oscar live on it i want i should have it back is she does.
>
> Tell mamma that six hundret dollars she has been looking for ten years is berried from the bakhouse behind about ten feet down. She better let little Frederick do the digging and count it when he comes up.
>
> Pastor Licnitz can have three hundret dollars if he kisses the book he wont preach no more dumhead talks about politiks. He should a roof put on the meeting house with and the elders should the bills look at.
>
> Mamma should the rest get, but I want it so that Adolphy should tell her what not she should do so more slick irishers sell vaken cleaner, they noise like hell and a broom dont cost much.
>
> I want it that mine brother Adolph be my executor and i want it that the judge should please make Adolph plenty bond put up and watch him like hell. Adolph is a good busniess man but only a dumkoph would trust him with a bested pfenning.
>
> I want durn sure the shclemial Oscar done nothing get tell Adolph he can have a hundret dollars if he prove Judge Oscar don't get nothing; that dur sure fix Oscar.
>
> (signed) *Herman Oberweiss*

THERE ARE THREE types of wills: *holographic*, *attested*, and *nuncupative*. None of these is nearly as formidable as the names imply. The holographic will, as we've seen, is a will written entirely in the hand of the testator, and dated (it does not have to be correctly dated) and signed by him or her. One of San Francisco's great trial judges, presiding in the probate department, beloved Judge Frank T. Dunn, left a short holographic will.

The attested will may be typewritten (the holographic obviously cannot) or made in longhand, but must have the signatures of two disinterested witnesses, witnesses who are not named in the will, and it must be dated. Thus the witnessing of a will may turn it from a holographic to an attested will. (Usually, however, a court will rule that the witnesses' signatures are "surplussage," disregard them, and allow the will to stand—or fail—as a holograph.) Some states require more than two witnesses and have other requirements. Louisiana has a system unique to that state.

The nuncupative will is an oral will but it's rarely used, since most jurisdictions reserve it for soldiers and sailors who are in fear of impending death, and then only a limited amount of property may pass by it. The dying serviceman must orally make his will in front of two or more witnesses.

The holographic will may be written with pencil or pen on paper or inscribed on any substance capable of receiving a written impression.

There was rumored to be a "well authenticated" case of a will being written in chalk upon a barn door, but no one has been able to find a report about it in the law books. However, there *was* a will chalked by a man on a corn bin and another inscribed on a bedpost, both filed in *Doctor's Comments* in London.

An odd will was once written in the handwriting of the deceased: "17–1925 Mag. Everything i possess. J. B."

The testator was a sailor and "Mag" found this written on an eggshell placed on top of a wardrobe in the room where the testator died!

The court did not find fault with the substance upon which the will was inscribed, but refused its admission to probate upon grounds that the sailor did not *intend* this to be his last will and testament. (The testator's intent is the guiding rule.)

However, a microscopic will engraved by a sailor upon a navy identification disk has been admitted to probate.

A Pennsylvania court stated that since the "Ten Commandments were written with the finger of God on tables of stone," a will could be written on any substance. Yet a Philadelphia court, feeling that perhaps an eraser might be guided by the hand of the devil, held that a will could not be written on a slate with a slate pencil.

There is something pitiful about the person who leaves a hastily scribbled, absurd, or erratic holographic will. Perhaps it's the last defiant gesture of a person shaking off the coils of a too normal life, his monument to the flamboyant life he would have liked to have lived. What solitary and yet lonely pleasure he must have had in drawing the will that laughs last. Of course, there's always a chance that the fanciful will may be "broken." But to some, it's a chance worth taking.

A wealthy old California recluse had drawn up the usual sober, formal will, and placed it in the equally sober, formal safe deposit box. He died and the bank presented the will for probate. But two nurses, who had taken care of the old gentleman in his last illness, presented another will—written on a petticoat!

While he had left the bulk of his estate to a relative, the "petticoat will" bequeathed $10,000 each to the two nurses. Although it had hung half forgotten in a closet for months, the court accepted the petticoat over the formally executed bank will that had been put in the strongest safe deposit box by the biggest banker with the most expensive pocket watch in town.

Yet, by a peculiar quirk of the law, the nurses could not take their $10,000 under the will. If a will bequeathes anything to a witness, the witness is suspected of being "interested" and perhaps might be tempted to commit a little fraud. So the law disqualifies interested witnesses. The nurses were witnesses to the will, and so lost their bequests.

In a California will there was more forgery than eccentricity. A nurse brought a stepladder into court with a will written upon it. The love of the deceased for her, she claimed, was as great as his will was unusual. What she couldn't explain, however, was why the handwriting exhibited none of the German characteristics that the testator always employed in his other writings. The "will" had been forged.

"Dear old Nance, I wish to give you my watch, two shawls, and also $5,000, your friend, E. A. Gordon."

That was all there was. No formal "I, being of sound mind and body," no gold seals or expensive parchment, no other will was found. Could this note be a will? The Supreme Court of

California held it to be as valid a will as any ever probated in that state.

It is not necessary that the language itself be in any particular form and the words in which the testator expresses his intention are immaterial. No magic words or legalese is necessary. It is only necessary that it appear from the writing that the testator was *intending* to make a disposition of his property, and to whom, to be effective after his death.

In a Vermont case, a signed statement, "Everything is Lous," on the front page of a record book was held not to be a will in favor of the testator's widow, Lulu. It failed to be a valid will not because of its brevity or form, but because it did not appear that the testator had *intended* it to be his will.

In Maryland, however, a testator wrote on the back of a business letter (addressed to a man and his wife) the following, all in his own handwriting: "After my death you are to have $40,000. This you are to have will or no will. Take care of this until my death." There followed the deceased's signature and the date. The $40,000 passed to the addressees; it was held to be a valid will.

Then there was the New Hampshire will where the deceased had endorsed on the back of a note: "If I am not living at the time this note is paid, I order the contents to be paid to A. H." He died before the note was paid. The New Hampshire Supreme Court ordered the money paid over to A. H. It was as valid a will as could be drawn.

Entries in a diary have been held to be a will. But again the primary question for the court's consideration is "Did the deceased *intend* it to be a will?" A maxim of law in interpreting wills is that *intent* be the "polestar of interpretation." Courts seek to do only what the deceased actually and finally intended.

The following, written by the deceased on a leaf of a timebook kept by him was received as a valid will: "March 4 will my property to my wife my death John Sullivan." No greater tribute could be left by this brakeman, thundering to his death atop a flying boxcar, than that his last brief thought was of his wife and to provide for her after he was gone. No more legal document could be achieved by a hundred lawyers.

SHOULD A LAWYER, then, be employed to draw a will? His charges are generally quite nominal since the average legal draftsman hopes that he will later probate the will and be paid amply for the latter service.

In the complicated will with trust provisions, contingencies, and "remainders," the lawyer should be consulted. But what if it's a simple will?

We have seen what has happened to some simple wills, but then the layperson has been known successfully to perform such simple operations upon himself as pulling teeth. (At least the lawyer would put a stop to the practice of leaving one dollar to undeserving heirs. He knows that to "cut them off," they need only to be *mentioned* and need not be given *any* sum of money, even if the bequest leaves change from a dollar. We're still not quite sure that the leaving of one dollar cuts off the one the testator wants most to omit.)

Lawyers really are generally inclined to assist the layperson *out* of a labyrinth of legal difficulties rather than invite him in as this lyric points out:

> You had better employ a lawyer's hand
> Than encounter the risk that your will shouldn't stand.
> From the broad beaten track where the traveler strays,
> He may land in a bog or be lost in a maze;
> And the law, when defied, will avenge itself still,
> On the men and the women who make their own will.

But the layman may answer with the greatest glee: What about the case of Samuel Tilden?

Samuel Tilden was one of America's so-called greatest lawyers. Statesman and reformer, he was also a one-time Democratic candidate for the presidency of the United States. In his practice he had pompously drawn thousands of wills and had probated many more.

When he died he left an estate appraised at over five million dollars (four million of which was left to found a New York public library). He provided in the will he drew himself that that was how his property should be disposed.

Yet, the will of the great lawyer Samuel Tilden was set aside because it was improperly drawn. And that even though the contested clause was one he drew himself and recommended in his teaching at law school in his class in wills and trusts!

If you want someone else to draw your will for you, only a lawyer may do it. Anyone else drawing a will would be practicing law without a license and in most states this is a criminal offense. Decidedly, a bank cannot draw a will for its clients for two reasons: It is not a lawyer and a corporation cannot practice law.

I T IS GENERALLY necessary as a matter of law that a lawyer be employed for the probate of a will. Practically, a layperson cannot do this any more than he can perform an appendectomy, although he may make a stab at it, if it is not illegal.

The majority of states have statutory fees for the lawyer for probating an estate, which are the same as for the executor of a will (or the administrator if there is no will). The fees are usually graduated downward according to the size of the estate.

Laws regulating these fees were passed because probate lawyers, hired to probate and protect, were regularly taking too big a slice from the estate pie. Probate lawyers from time immemorial have been the striped-pants establishment, firms spending more time at wakes and burials than in law libraries. Generally, the real probate work was principally done by the probate lawyer's skilled secretary. Now it is almost all done by the paralegal.

The following is the revelation in the will (offered for probate in 1939 in Akron, Ohio) of such an eminent lawyer as the late chief counsel for the Goodyear Tire & Rubber Company: He forbade the appointment of a trust company as executor of his will on account of his "unfortunate experiences with so-called trust companies as institutions wholly incompetent to transact the business they claim superiority in."

Upon the death of the testator the will is presented to the safekeeping of the probate court and (though the practice may vary somewhat in each state) notices to creditors and heirs are published and mailed. After some statutory period, such as California's six months, the estate may be distributed. Usually it takes a little longer than the minimum time before the probate file is closed. For example, in California the average probate time is fourteen months.

The administrator must make his accounting and, if the court approves, distribution is ordered—unless a will contest intervenes and a jury remakes the will—knowing better the testator's intent than he himself did.

Before these six months are up, an estate cannot be distributed; nevertheless, widow's allowances may be given, and if the estate is not large, some states permit that it may be set aside for the widow upon affidavit, free of any claims of creditors. Of course, it is entirely unnecessary to write in one's will "After all my just debts are paid, I distribute...," because the estate cannot be distributed until all "just debts" are paid. Probate is the collection agency's last reward.

Of course, the period of probate may run well over the six months. In fact, for business or tax reasons it may be profitable to keep the estate of the decedent open indefinitely and whole businesses are run, nominally, under the dead hand of "estate of John Smith."

It is said that an English lawyer took his son into practice with him and, it being necessary for the father to leave town for several days, advised the son to familiarize himself with the cases in the office and settle any that were not too complicated.

When the elder member of the firm returned, the son gave an account of his activity and particularly that he had taken the file of the Estate of Morehead over to the probate judge, had the estate distributed, and the file closed.

"The case had been going for fifty years and all that was needed for the last thirty-five was to have the judge sign the order. The judge agreed to, though for some reason I can't understand, he seemed quite amused that the estate should be closed," concluded the son.

The father sank into his chair and clapping his hand to his forehead replied, "Good Heavens, son, that estate started and supported your grandfather, it educated you and kept your father and mother. It would have sent your children and your children's children to college and you in a morning of folly settled it!" (This incident took place in Dickens's *Bleak House.*)

TO CONCLUDE this chapter with a moral: About the year 1906, Hodson Burton of Buchanan, Michigan, made ready to die. He made the normal will with all the flowery (and generally unnecessary) legal language. But in this will there was one odd item.

The old man had a large pile of gold. The location of this gold, said the will, would be divulged by his lawyer five years after the old man's death.

The old gentleman died, and five years passed. The lawyer called the heirs together and announced that he would now divulge the secret hiding place of the gold. Could the heirs imagine where the testator had hidden his fortune? None could.

The lawyer chuckled then grew very solemn. "The dead man himself will now tell you," he said.

Everyone was greatly impressed. So was the lawyer. Shaking with emotion he left the room, the creaking of a safe door was heard, the lawyer reappeared, then unwrapped and carefully broke the seal of a large package. It was a phonograph record.

He advanced toward the phonograph, but his foot slipped, the record flew into the air and splintered into a thousand pieces upon the floor. Supposedly, the gold was never found.

Recently I was called to contest the last will of Sally Stanford, a good friend of mine in life and one of the last great madams of a tolerant city—San Francisco. (Interestingly, I had played the part of the mayor of San Francisco in "Sally of the House," the TV life story of Sally.) I think Sally is sitting up there laughing at us, for she left not one will but six, and four different trusts to dispose of her estate of twenty million dollars.

Moral: Beware of the whimsical will!

Notes

1. Hazlitt, William, *Table Talk* (1821–22).
2. *Estate of Morgan*, 225 C. A. 2d 156, 37 Cal. Rptr. 160 (1964).
3. *Estate of Turpin*, 222 C. A. 2d 57, 34 Cal. Rptr. 812 (1963).
4. *Applehans v. Jurgenson*, 336 Ill. 427, 168 N. E. 327 (1929).
5. *Estate of Johnson*, 62 C. A. 2d 41, 144 P. 2d 72 (1943).
6. *Estate of Pessagno*, 58 C. A. 2d 390, 136 P. 2d 644 (1943).
7. *In re Strittmater's Estate*, 140 N. J. Eq. 94, 53, A. 2d 205 (1947).
8. In early English common law, property could be devised in only one way: primogeniture, or descent to the eldest son. The intricate selective bequests of modern wills were unheard of; it was either the eldest or the crown in the "good old days."

9

Puck's Court

THE DECISIONS OF THE CASES in this chapter might seem wrong at first. But if they do, ask yourself how *you* would have decided them. All the facts necessary to make your award are here. You be the judge, so you may hereafter better appreciate the difficulties of judging.

One admonition: "Everyone is presumed to know the law," you, as well as dissenting Supreme Court justices—and perplexed Warden Edgar.

In 1897, Warden John C. Edgar of California's San Quentin Prison was given the choice of committing murder or of going to jail for contempt of court, and he had just one hour to reach his decision!

One Joseph Ebanks had been convicted of murder. The Superior Court of San Diego, California, sentenced him to San Quentin Prison, there to be "hanged by the neck until dead" on the eighth day of October, 1897.

Came that date, and, as Warden Edgar was preparing for the execution, he was served with papers by counsel for Ebanks showing that an appeal had been taken to the federal courts. However, no judge had made an order staying the execution.

Literally, in one hand, Warden Edgar held the order from the California court to execute Ebanks on that very day, and in the other, a notice that an appeal had been allowed to the U.S. courts. While the notice of appeal did not state that the U.S. courts necessarily wanted a living defendant before them on appeal, the warden surmised that it would be preferred.[1]

The attorney for Ebanks warned, "If you hang my client and it is later determined that his appeal automatically operates as a stay of execution, you are guilty of murder." The San Diego court advised him, "If you ignore my order for execution on this day, you will be in contempt of court."

As the Supreme Court of California later said, "He was placed in a most trying and difficult position; in this clash of judicial authorities there was no court to which he could look for direction."

Someone was wrong, but for the warden "ignorance of the law is no excuse." He chose the lesser of the possible penalties to himself and delayed the execution. The San Diego court immediately declared him in contempt of court and ordered him to pay a fine of $200 or go to jail.

To determine exactly what the law was that everyone was "presumed to know," the warden brought a writ of habeas corpus to the California Supreme Court.

The warden had "presumed" correctly.[2] The Supreme Court decided the appeal to the U.S. courts had operated as an automatic stay. Warden Edgar was released from jail and sent back to his own prison.

THE HISTORY OF MAN is written in his lawsuits. Pertaining to an unsavory bit of English history, that of the slave trade, there is the 1783 case of *Gregson* v. *Gilbert*.[3] It tells of a voyage of an old sailing ship that for horror is unequalled in the annals of the sea.

The ship picked up a cargo of slaves on the coast of Guinea and set sail for Jamaica, a six weeks' voyage. Mistaking Jamaica for Hispaniola, the captain sailed on and on until water and provisions ran low.

Sixty slaves died from thirst and forty more became frenzied from the tortures of sun and parched throats and cast themselves overboard. To preserve the remaining water for the crew and to save part of the slave cargo, 150 more blacks were deliberately cast overboard. When the ship finally reached Jamaica after eighteen weeks, thirty more slaves were found dead in the hold and seven of the seventeen members of the crew later died from the rigors of the voyage.

As was common in those days, the owners of the ship had insured the human cargo with an English insurance company. They sued on the policy to recover the value of the slaves and claimed that the loss was due to a "peril of the sea."

Said the English court, "It has been decided, whether wisely or unwisely is not now the question, that a portion of our fellow-creatures may become the subject of property. This was therefore the throwing overboard of goods to save the rest of the cargo and crew."

However, the court denied the claim for insurance saying that it was the ignorance of the captain and not the "peril of the sea" that caused the loss. Further, there were still several butts of water left when the blacks were drowned and the "necessity" was therefore only apprehended, not imminent. It was also proved that the day after the slaves were drowned a rain came up and the water casks were filled.

Further evidence was given that even after the rain more blacks were put overboard. This caused the court to remark, "The truth was that finding they should have a bad market for their slaves, they took this means of transferring the loss from the owners to the underwriters."

Shortly after this case was decided, a statute was passed prohibiting the collection of insurance on slaves thrown overboard for any reason. Slave insurance against other risks still went on.

A S THE ANCIENT MERCHANT PRINCES of the Mediterranean, greedy for profit, stocked their ships to the gunwales, and beyond, with rich treasures and slaves, they made them unmanageable and top heavy. In storms it was often necessary to jettison part of the cargo to save the rest.

To save the time-taking deliberations of whose cargo should be jettisoned, the custom grew that the captain, if ship and cargo were in peril, decided what cargo to cast into the sea, and the owners of the cargo saved must contribute or divide theirs with the owners of that which was jettisoned. Everyone shared in the loss proportionate to the value of his cargo.

This is still the law of the sea of all nations today and is called *general average*, but oranges, not slaves, became the subject of a unique "general average" case before the Supreme Court of Massachusetts.

The *Fredonia*, loaded with oranges, fell in with another ship bound from Liverpool to New York with a cargo of 350 passengers. The other craft had done badly in a storm the night before and her captain requested the skipper of the *Fredonia* to take her passengers aboard. The *Fredonia* herself was full and though she could take the passengers aboard, she could only navigate thereafter by jettisoning part of the cargo of oranges.

As the court later said, there was no legal duty for the *Fredonia* to save the passengers but the court did commend her skipper for jettisoning part of his cargo to make room for them. The other craft went down and later the consignees of the oranges asked for general average. They were denied.

The court said the *Fredonia* and her cargo were in no danger; the oranges were not thrown overboard to save the rest of the cargo but to save and make room for the rescued passengers. In fact, the court found that the oranges were thrown overboard *before* the passengers came aboard. However (and two judges dissented upon this, thinking the distinction too subtle, and with those judges you may agree), had passengers been *first* taken aboard the *Fredonia* one by one to the number that their weight made that craft unnavigable, *then* the oranges thrown overboard, the jettisoning of cargo would have been to save and navigate the ship and general average would have applied.

The captain had made the mistake of jettisoning the oranges *before* the passengers came aboard instead of casting a crate of oranges overboard as each passenger came aboard.

Ironically, the name of the other ship was the *Gratitude*!

THIS NEXT CASE should please commuters all over the world. However, it proved very embarrassing to the Southern Pacific Railroad.

One day in 1891 W.H. Robinson bought a through ticket from San Francisco to Alameda, across the bay. When he presented his ticket he asked for a stopover privilege in Oakland, on the way to Alameda. He was refused. But Robinson *did* stop off in Oakland, and upon boarding the next train for Alameda was asked for another fare. This he refused to pay and was immediately put off the train.

Four years later, after passing through the lower courts of California, Robinson finally reached the California Supreme Court which, in a thirty-three page opinion, affirmed his award for damages based upon California Civil Code Section 490, which provided $200 damages against any railroad company "refusing a stopover privilege desired by a passenger."

But Robinson did not stop here. While the Supreme Court was deciding Robinson's first case he and his friends were assiduously engaged in a daily commute to Alameda and upon each trip demanding a stopover privilege and being daily refused.

By 1901, *ten years* after the original trip, Robinson and friends had made over 3,000 trips and now, armed with the judgment in the first case, sued the railroad for $600,000.

This time in the California Supreme Court, the railroad was plaintiff and brought suit for an injunction against Robinson and company to prevent them from bringing any further suits and to declare his $600,000 claim invalid.

By this time the suit had attracted the attention of most lawyers in California, since Robinson already had a judgment on the precise grounds against the railroad.

Said the same Supreme Court of the second case, "No case is found in the law books where an undertaking of this character ever assumed such proportions, and where the spirit of speculation was carried on daily for weeks, months, and even years, with all the method and system of a great business undertaking."[4]

Ten years of Robinson's life had been wasted and his original $200 long since spent, for the Supreme Court enjoined him from bringing any further suits on the basis that they were not brought in good faith. The code section provided $200 damages for passengers refused a stopover privilege when they "desired" one.[5]

Said the court, when Robinson applied for a stopover privilege, he did not "desire" one; on the contrary he hoped and expected to be refused. Thus was the Southern Pacific, a force of tremendous political potency in California in the early days, saved $600,000.

E IGHTY-THREE-YEAR-OLD Mary Washington, the mother of George Washington, was laid to rest in a spot of her choice, near Fredericksburg, Virginia, in 1789. In 1831 an "association" was organized to erect a monument to her memory over her grave.

Years later the land upon which the grave was located was bought by George Shephard, the deed designating the lot as the "monument lot" but stating that the monument of Mary Washington was specifically excepted from the sale.

Shephard later gave an option on the land to a real estate firm in Fredericksburg, which immediately published the following advertisement in the *Washington Post:*

On Tuesday, the 5th inst., at 4 o'clock P.M., at the Capital of the United States of America we will offer for sale, at public outcry, about 12 acres of land, situate within the Corporation of Fredericksburg, embracing the grave of Mary, the mother of General George Washington, and also the material of her unfinished monument. At the same time and place we will offer, to the highest bidder, the house in which she lived and died, and within eight squares of the tomb.

Colbert & Kirtley,
Real Estate Agents,
Fredericksburg, Virginia.

Mr. Shephard indignantly wrote to the realtors saying the deed expressly reserved the grave and monument from sale. The realtors brought suit for breach of contract claiming the option was upon the grave and monument and the case came before the Virginia Supreme Court of Appeals in 1892.

Justice Fauntleroy dismissed the realtor's suit saying "The record in this case presents for review by this Court the sacrilegious and shockingly shameful spectacle of a controversy and traffic over the grave and sacred ashes of Mrs. Mary Washington.... It was dedicated to public and pious uses forever. From that day to this no right or claim of private ownership has ever been exercised over it, or made to it."[6]

So while the Brooklyn Bridge, Grant's Tomb, and city hall may have been sold many times over to country visitors, it actually took a decree of court to hold invalid an option on Mary Washington's grave and public monument.

COURTS HAVE PUNISHED litigants and even lawyers for contumacious conduct and presentation of fraudulent claims, but in the annals of all law no more audacious and contemptuous case can be found than the "Highwayman's Case".

So strange a case it was that for years it remained a romantic legend, part fiction, part fact, and still is regarded as "legal romancing" by many members of the bar.[7] Two highway robbers, unable to divide their spoils, appealed to a court to aid them!

It happened that John Everett and Joseph Williams in 1725 were partners in "business.". Everett filed a bill in equity for an accounting and in the bill set forth that an oral partnership existed between the plaintiff and defendant, that defendant was "skilled in dealing in several sorts of commodities," that the parties had "proceeded jointly in the said dealings on Hounslaw Heath, where they dealt with a gentleman for a gold watch."

Further recitals show how the parties "dealt" with several gentlemen for "divers watches, rings, swords, canes, cloaks, horses, bridles, saddles, and other things to the value of 200 pounds and upwards," and how there was a gentleman at Blackheath "who had several things of this sort to dispose of, which defendant represented might be had for little or no money in case they could prevail upon said gentleman to part with the said things," and how after some small discourse with the said gentleman, the said things "were dealt for at a very cheap rate."

The bill or complaint further recites that the parties' joint dealings were carried on at Bagshot, Salisbury, Hampstead, and elsewhere to the amount of some 2,000 pounds and upward, and that "defendant would not come to a fair account with the plaintiff touching and concerning the said partnership." The bill was signed by one Jonathan Collins as counsel.

When the court finally recovered its composure, a sergeant of the court moved that the bill be investigated. Two weeks later, the bill was dismissed as "scandalous and impertinent," and messengers were dispatched to bring both robber plaintiff and defendant into court to answer for contempt. Plaintiff's lawyer was also summoned.

Fines of fifty pounds each were assessed and it was "ordered by the Court that Jonathan Collins, Esq. (the lawyer), whose hand appears to be set to the said bill, do pay the defendant such costs as the deputy shall tax, and the court declares the indignity to the court as satisfied by such fines."

John Everett, the plaintiff, is supposed to have been hanged at Tyburn in 1730 and Joseph Williams, the defendant, at Maidstone in 1727.

THE MAN WHO INVENTED the most universally accepted system of criminal identification, a system that has (probably legitimately) sent thousands of guilty to jail and the gallows, once, by his own testimony, helped convict for treason the most innocent man of all time in the cause célèbre of France—Captain Alfred Dreyfus of the French General Staff.

The man who testified against Dreyfus was Alphonse Bertillion, after whom Bertillionage, the international system of criminal identification, is known.

By counterespionage, a French spy had found in a wastepaper basket at the German embassy a crumpled note of military information. It was so secret that it had obviously come from a general staff officer.

Dreyfus, the only Jew on an anti-Semitic staff, was immediately called to the war office. There, ignorant of the purpose of the call, he was directed to write a note. It was the language of the note found that was dictated. The handwriting was hastily compared; Dreyfus was clamped into solitary confinement and kept there for fifteen days without even being apprised of the charges against him.

Then he was charged with treason and the trial that rocked the French government into the twentieth century began. For the state, Bertillion was called as the ace handwriting expert. Very carefully he compared the writing on the exemplar letter that had been found with the writing on the letter that Dreyfus had written. Solemnly he announced his decision. Little did he know that his testimony contributed to one of the greatest miscarriages of justice in man's history. He testified that the same person wrote the two notes; it was the link connecting Captain Dreyfus with the treason.

Despite his anguished screams of innocence, Dreyfus was publicly degraded; with pomp and ceremony his orders were stripped from his uniform on parade. The rest is history known to every Frenchman; how Dreyfus was sent to the horrendous Devil's Island; how he spent four years there in solitary confinement.

How the Germans must have laughed all this time. They had daily proof of the error of vaunted French justice; French Commandant Esterhazy, the real traitor, was still stealing French military secrets for them.

Not until 1906 was Dreyfus proclaimed entirely innocent and then only after the intervention of Emile Zola, who for his trouble was himself sentenced to a year in prison.

But Bertillion? Despite his colossal error, the criminal identification system bearing his name is still used all over the world—a mocking monument to man's efforts to administer justice impartially through the "Blind Goddess" with her scales evenly balanced.

IN ALBERTA, CANADA, one Booker had been accused of the fatal shooting of four people. Lodged in jail, Booker would not confess nor could the police find the gun that the prisoner allegedly used. These two elements of proof were essential to the crown's case.

However, before trial, the services of a Dr. Langsner, criminologist and hypnotist, were secured with remarkable results.

The prisoner was brought into the guardroom and left alone for half an hour with the doctor. Though he claimed he had no conversation with the prisoner, the doctor immediately left the guardroom and after a short search of an area previously covered by police, the doctor uncovered "Exhibit A for the Crown"—the missing rifle.

Again the doctor went into the guardroom with the prisoner and, after sitting with him in silence for half an hour, came out and said to the police, "Gentlemen, you may expect a complete confession in half an hour." Half an hour later the prisoner sent for the police and finally confessed the murder.

The crown's case was now complete. But before the confession could be admitted into evidence, counsel for the defense, upon appeal to the Supreme Court of Alberta in 1928, succeeded in having it excluded.

Doctor Pope, professor of medicine at the University of Alberta, testified that it was his opinion that a subject could be so hypnotized as to reveal information which, if acting under his own will, he would suppress. Further, he testified a subject could be so hypnotized that the effects would continue even after the hypnotist had left the subject's presence—for a half hour perhaps, he added significantly.

The hypnotist testified that he had not spoken a word to the defendant nor the defendant to him and further that hypnosis was not employed (despite a retainer for professional hypnotic services).

However, the Canadian high court found that hypnosis was indeed employed, for how else could one account for the doctor finding the gun and how could he foretell a confession "within a half hour"? The Canadian Supreme Court suppressed the confession, since a confession must be free and voluntary and a man in a true state of hypnotism talks and acts not from his own will but from the suggestion of another.

However, "Exhibit A," the gun, was allowed to remain in evidence because there could be no doubt as to the authenticity of the lethal weapon.

This is the first hypnosis case I know of like it in the law books.[8]

CAN YOU IMAGINE a prisoner serving a 25-year term in a federal prison refusing a pardon from the President of the United States?

Gerald Chapman did. But then Mr. Chapman had good reason, very good reason. Not only did he refuse a pardon but he brought a writ of habeas corpus to keep himself *in* prison.

In 1922 Gerald Chapman was convicted of a federal offense and sentenced to twenty-five years' imprisonment in the federal penitentiary at Atlanta, Georgia. He escaped.

While at large, Chapman shot and killed a policeman in New Britain, Connecticut. He was later caught and by the time a murder indictment had been brought against him in a Connecticut State court, he was back in the federal penitentiary. There he definitely wanted to stay, for a death sentence awaited him in the state court.

In 1922 a person in federal custody could not be tried or punished by the state courts until Uncle Sam had released him from federal custody. Federal officers were willing to release Chapman, but, after all, a warden can't just kick prisoners out of prison before their terms are up. His job is to keep them *in* prison.

An old decision by John Marshall of the United States Supreme Court was found that said a pardon is like a deed or a gift, and not valid until accepted. Chapman wasn't accepting any pardons today, thank you.

Attorney General Harlan Stone and President Calvin Coolidge had a solution. President Coolidge drew an executive order commuting (not pardoning) the prisoner's sentence to time served. The commutation was read to Chapman in his cell and, although he refused to accept it, he was carried out of the prison by force.

Tried in Connecticut and sentenced to death, Chapman brought a writ of habeas corpus to be taken back to the federal penitentiary to be allowed to serve out his twenty-five years before being executed by Connecticut.

The writ was refused on the ground that he hadn't been pardoned but commuted. While a pardon "liberates the prisoner" and must be accepted by the prisoner to be valid, a commutation merely "withdraws the restraining jurisdiction"; it can be effective even though not accepted.[9]

Today, federal prisoners are routinely transferred to state facilities for court proceedings upon request of state authorities. To do otherwise would undermine the chances of successful state prosecution, because prisoners too have a right to a speedy trial. If a prisoner were required to do all his federal time before being shipped off for his reckoning with the state, he could easily beat the rap by yelling "speedy trial!" The U.S. Bureau of Prisons and the attorney general wish to avoid this loophole.

WHEN A MAN, conscious that he is dying, accused another as his murderer, that "dying declaration," either written or oral, can be used as evidence against the accused. But suppose a man on trial for murder wants to introduce the dying declaration of another man that the dying man, not the man on trial, is the murderer. Is that confession admissible?

One Chickasaw, an Indian on the Hoopa Valley Indian Reservation in California, had been murdered. James Donnelly, a white man, was accused of the murder and brought to trial.

At his trial, Donnelly offered evidence that tended to prove that Joe Dick, another Indian, was the real murderer of Chickasaw. The court allowed him to prove that Joe Dick knew Chickasaw and was familiar with his habits. Chickasaw had been murdered on a sandbar and the court further allowed Donnelly to prove that the tracks leading from the sandbar were those of Joe Dick. These tracks led to Dick's acorn camp.

Donnelly further proved that Dick had consumption and was short of breath, that the tracks from the sandbar to the acorn camp showed the impression of a man sitting down at short intervals, the tracks of a man short of breath. After laying this foundation and pointing the finger of suspicion at Joe Dick, Donnelly announced that Dick had died shortly after the murder but that he, Dick, had fully confessed the murder of Chickasaw.

But when Donnelly sought to read Dick's confession to the jury, the confession that would have freed him, the trial court excluded this evidence as hearsay (a statement made out of court not subject to corroboration, and offered in court as true). James Donnelly was found guilty of murder and sentenced to life imprisonment.

On appeal to the United States Supreme Court, the conviction was affirmed and the murder confession held inadmissible as hearsay.

Justice Holmes in an amazing dissent said the confession "would have a very strong tendency to make anyone outside a court of justice believe that Donnelly did not commit the crime."

While the Holmes dissent later became the law in a good number of states, in the Donnelly case "rules of evidence have matured by the wisdom of the ages and are now reserved from their antiquity and the good sense in which they are founded."[10]

That hearsay rule, although riddled with exceptions, still stands.

DESPITE THE LATE J. Edgar Hoover and federal laws against kidnapping, there is one type of "snatching" that still goes unpunished and is even considered "due process of law."

Sometimes a governor will refuse the request of a governor of a sister state for extradition of a fugitive from justice. The peace officers, upon such a refusal, have often kidnapped the fugitive from the sanctuary state into the state where he was wanted. Not only does such kidnapping go unpunished, but the fugitive is placed on trial the same as though he were brought into the state by legal process. The court asks no questions about how the prisoner ended up in front of it.

In the case of *Mahon* v. *Justice*,[11] allegorically named, the governor of West Virginia demanded extradition of a fugitive from justice living in Kentucky. While the two governors were exchanging correspondence, a body of armed men from West Virginia, chafing at the law's delay, crossed the state line into Kentucky and kidnapped the fugitive. They brought him back to West Virginia for trial.

On a writ of habeas corpus to the United States Supreme Court, it was held that a state has the right to punish anyone within its borders and once he is within those borders, the law will not inquire as to the manner in which he got there. A similar decision was rendered by the same court in *Ker* v. *Illinois*,[12] where the defendant was kidnapped in Peru by Illinois peace officers and brought back to Illinois for trial. Thus, in one instance, kidnapping was not inconsistent with "due process of law" by decision of the Supreme Court of the United States. Remember, also, how Eichmann was kidnapped by the Israelis from South America and tried in Israel.

In 1905 formal complaint for the murder of Frank Steinberg was filed in Idaho against one Pettibone. Pettibone, at the time, was in Colorado and claimed that he did not commit the murder. He said he was not a fugitive from justice because he had not been in Idaho at the time of the murder.

One must be a *fugitive* from the demanding state to be eligible for extradition. If he wasn't there, no extradition. Indeed, that is supposed to be the sole issue, was he a fugitive, in an extradition hearing.

On a Saturday night at 11:30, Pettibone was arrested in Colorado. He was refused an attorney and placed in an armored car. By next morning he had been shuttled across the state boundary into Idaho.

Clarence Darrow, for the defendant, went to the United States Supreme Court and alleged that there was a conspiracy between the governors of the two states to return Pettibone to Idaho without a hearing in Colorado. That court held with Senator

William Borah, who appeared for the people of Idaho, and said the kidnapping was with "due process of law".[13]

I N KINGSTOWN, JAMAICA, in 1908 earthquake and fire destroyed the whole town. The damage ran into thousands of dollars.

Most of the people carried insurance. Yet the region is so subject to earthquakes that premiums for earthquake insurance are too high; as in San Francisco, only fire insurance is usually carried.

If the fire came first, the insurance carriers would be required to pay; if the earthquake came first, no insurance would be paid.

When the case came to court, plaintiffs produced two officers of Port Kingston who were on a boat in the harbor at the time of the catastrophe. They both testified they had noticed a pillar of smoke at 3:30; at 3:35 the earthquake struck. The captain of another ship corroborated this testimony.

But what won the case was the curiosity of a third witness who lived on a hill in back of the town. He had noticed the pillar of smoke, had taken angles and measurements of it, and testified it was precisely 255 feet high *before* the earthquake struck.

The case went through the highest courts in England and the insurance companies had to pay.

W HAT A PITEOUS BATTLE man wages. His tools are but a scant few years of life, yet he seeks to build for all eternity. But if there be an everlastingness to man, it is in his laws and lawsuits. Even as old wines gather bouquet with the years, so suits at law are given new reference with the passing of time.

In the year 999 all the men of Naples, in accordance with the apocryphal prophecy, dreaded the anticipated coming of the end of the world in the year 1000. They looked to the safety of their souls.

Between Salerno and Naples is a mountain rich in forests and pasture lands. The owners of the mountain waited until December 999, then, judging the signs inauspicious for the continuance of the world, and wishing to fortify their chances for the hereafter, deeded the entire hill to the Convent of Saint Trifone.

That the year 1000 passed without cataclysmic disturbance, either material or spiritual, we can now attest. Those good men who had sought to buy into the Kingdom of Heaven by giving up their material wealth felt that with the passing of the year 1000, they were doomed to an earthly existence. What is more, they knew that in the material world they would be provided for as they provided. Consequently, they sought a return of their lands. They waited, however, two years more to allow for any miscalculation in time. The basis of the suit they finally brought was that they had granted the land only upon the implied condition that the world end at the year 1000.

Since 1002, the legal fight has been handed down by heirs of the original owners from generation to generation. Thousands of processes have been filed and the case has been before innumerable judges.

Recently historical briefs were revived and the convent again forced to defend its title.

Notes

1. "Commutation after the death of a prisoner will do him no good!" *In re McMahon*, 125 N. C. 38, 34 S. E. 193 (1899).
2. *People v. Ebanks*, 117 Cal. 652, 49 P. 1049 (1897).
3. *Gregson v. Gilbert*, 3 K. B. 232, 99 Eng. Rep. 629 (1783).
4. *Southern Pacific Co. v. Robinson*, 132 Cal. 408, 64 P. 572 (1901).
5. The code section was subsequently amended to provide for payments of a passenger's actual damages only (Public Utilities Code §7658) and later repealed.
6. *Colbert et al. v. Shephard*, 89 Va. 401, 16 S. E. 246. (1892).
7. *European Magazine*, May 1787, Vol. 1, p. 360.
8. *Rex v. Booker*, 4 D. L. R. 495 (1928) (Alberta).
9. *Chapman v. Scott*, 10 F. 2d 156 (1925), aff'd on appeal, 10 F. 2d 690 (1925).

    The modern rule, based on a prisoner's right to have a speedy trial even while in custody, was stated by the Supreme Court in *Smith v. Hooey*, 393 U. S. 374, 89 S. Ct. 595 (1969).
10. *Donnelly v. U. S.*, 228 U. S. 243, 33 S. Ct. 449 (1913).
11. *Mahon v. Justice*, 127 U. S. 700, 8 S. Ct. 1209 (1887).
12. *Ker v. Illinois*, 119 U. S. 436, 7 S. Ct. 225, (1886).
13. *Pettibone v. Nichols*, 203 U. S. 192, 27 S. Ct. 111 (1906).

10

Guardians of the Constitution

B ACK IN 1936 I had the privilege of being admitted to practice before the United States Supreme Court. It was on the day the Wagner Act (the National Labor Relations Act) was held constitutional. The right to union organizing was affirmed.[1] My notes for that day paint the following picture before the bench.

Someone raps sharply and white curtains part behind a huge, dark bench. An old man in a black silk robe appears and quickly takes his seat. I am looking at the Chief Justice of the United States, Charles Evans Hughes.

A crier solemnly and slowly intones, "Oyez! Oyez!—God save the Supreme Court and the Constitution of the United States." No hurried clerk's mumbling here.

It is Monday, admission day for new candidates to the Supreme Court. I sit inside the rail with some twenty other young applicants for admission. We have been properly instructed, warned, and awed. The preparation begins to take effect.

If we hear Chief Justice Hughes ask, "Are there any applicants for admission?" it will mean there are no decisions today. Instead, he nods to Justice Roberts. It must be a decision. The Wagner Act! The case will be history.

Justice Owen Roberts speaks. He presents the entire decision of the Court, word for word, without looking once at the written opinion before him. Reporters write furiously and stuff notes into pneumatic tubes leading to an elaborate pressroom in the basement. While the courtroom awaits the decision, in all parts of the world editors are already being handed it and presses roll with the headline "Wagner Act Upheld!"

As Justice Roberts speaks, I look about the court. The hushed crowd represents only a fraction of the number of people that stood in line since early morning to gain entrance. They are tense and reverent; they know history is being enacted before their eyes. One feels they are thinking, "I can tell my grandchildren that I was there the day the unions won their right to exist."

I look intently at the Chief Justice. He leans toward Justice Roberts; now and then his lips move to repeat a word or phrase. Behind me sits Mrs. Hughes. She follows her husband's every word when he later speaks; he, in turn, seems to gaze often in her direction.

Nine old men, as President Roosevelt so disparagingly said. That is plainly evident, their age accentuated by the huge bench. But there is the grandeur of strength and individuality in each face, an individuality echoed in the choice of seats: each justice sits in his own odd, comfortable chair. Justice Louis Brandeis's old gooseneck lamp strikes a sharp angle in front of him.

Justice Roberts finishes. There is a moment of silence, then the Chief Justice gives a dignified nod to the then most conservative justice on the bench, Justice George Sutherland, from Utah. Of course, he will dissent.

"I take a different view." A little man, with the snow of seventy-five years in his beard, adjusts his rimless glasses and leans forward to speak these words.

The case involves the right of the Associated Press to discharge an editorial writer for union activities protected by a labor act passed in 1935. Justice Roberts has just given the majority opinion. It is now the law. But Sutherland's dissent will stand by its side, as principle and precedent for future arguments.

"Congress shall make no law abridging the freedom of the press," says Sutherland. At the words, "no law," the old man seems to gain new vigor. He draws himself from his chair and up to the bench. He is no longer judge but advocate, sincerely, earnestly, simply pleading with his audience, the members of the press and the world, to understand the danger he sees in the majority's opinion.

To hold that the editor may not be discharged, as holds the majority of the court, he says, may not of itself destroy freedom of the press; however, "a little water trickling here and there through the dam is a small matter itself, but it may be a sinister menace to the security of the dam, which those living in the valley below will do well to heed."

No need to strain for his words now. They come with force and resolution. He finishes: "Let them [the people] withstand all beginnings of encroachment, for the saddest epitaph which can be carved in memory of a vanquished liberty is that it was lost because its possessors failed to stretch forth a living hand while yet there was time."

Sutherland has made his stand, alone against the President, Congress, and the Court.

A recess follows, then the Chief Justice asks, "Are there any applicants for admission?" My name is the second called and my sponsor clears his throat to read from a slip of printed paper. The Chief Justice waves me to the far side of the courtroom, where the oath is taken before the clerk attired in a frock coat. Then, single file, we march to the clerk's office to sign the register. Back, way back in it, are names like Daniel Webster and John Marshall. Quill pens are provided; they effectively bridge the gap of years.

We pay fifteen dollars and the spell is broken only when someone whispers in my ear, "You can have your certificate engraved for a dollar extra!"

B UT LET US GO BACK even farther to the court of Daniel Webster's time.

Chief Justice John Marshall's tall, gaunt figure was bent over as if to catch the slightest whisper, the deep furrows of his cheeks expanded with emotion and eyes suffused with tears; Mr. Justice Washington was at his side, his small emaciated frame like carved marble. Daniel Webster was arguing the great Dartmouth College case in 1819—the last time in Supreme Court history it is said tears have been seen to come to the eyes of the justices in open session.

With his eyes fixed upon the chief justice, Webster concluded in the deep tone the audience loved to hear: "Sir, I know not how others feel [glancing at his opponents], but for myself, when I see my alma mater surrounded like Caesar in the Senate House by those who reiterating stab upon stab, I would not, for this right hand, have her turn to me and say, 'You, too my son!'"

Back in 1769 the English crown had granted a corporate charter to Eleazar Wheelock to found a free college for the Indians. This became Dartmouth College, and years later the New Hampshire Legislature passed an act taking over the supervision of the college.

Webster, for the college, was arguing that a corporate charter was a contract and that the sovereign state was bound by the crown grant. Since the United States Constitution prevents a state from impairing the obligation of contracts, the act of the New Hampshire Legislature was argued to be unconstitutional. The Supreme Court agreed with Daniel and constitutional history was made. From that time forward states could not reverse or change the charters of corporations that they had granted.[2]

History cannot detract from his deserved fame, yet the fact is that Webster's whole argument in this case was taken from that delivered by now unknown lawyers Smith and Mason in the lower court. But "The God-like Daniel" breathed life and color into the words as only he could.

Webster's associate counsel on the case was Joseph Hopkinson, the author of "Hail Columbia."

THE SUPREME COURT had been provided with one of the finest kitchens in Washington, yet the justices who ate in that most exclusive dining room often have had their food brought from home and used their own china and silver, disdaining the governmental issue. Some justices even refused to eat together.

In the days of John Marshall it was different. The justices not only ate together, they drank together. In fact, criticism reached the ears of Chief Justice John Marshall of the court's custom of having "a cup together" before going on the bench, so the great justice made a "rule of court" that the court would not drink together (or singly) before going on the bench except on rainy days, and then only to dispel the gloom of clouded skies.

Several weeks later, not a drop of water having fallen in the meantime and the skies giving no promise of rain for days to come, the justices were gathered together in chambers. One of the associate justices looked at his chief who in turn went to the window through which the sunlight was streaming. The chief justice gazed far off into the distance. There was not a hint of a cloud anywhere. After a moment of thought, he turned and with a twinkle in his eye said: "Gentlemen, our jurisdiction extends over the *whole* United States. This is a vast nation. Undoubtedly *somewhere* in our vast land at this very moment it is raining. I think you'd better fill the glasses."

IN THE OLD DAYS, the court convened at noon. Lunch was an interesting occasion. It became customary, as a justice's appetite prompted him, to step behind the curtains in the back of the bench and there take the noonday meal still within hearing, yet out of sight, of the courtroom. The attorneys had to continue their arguments to the court even though the particular judicial mind to which they sought to address their remarks might at that time be otherwise engaged in the solemn deliberative effort of choosing between the delicacies of a leg of fried chicken and a peck of steamed oysters from Harvey's.

When the crowds throng the Supreme Court now it is to see the justices perform, not the attorneys. But time was when the attraction was solely the lawyers as they presented their cases before the court, performing in their finest hour.

William Pinckney of Maryland was an exquisite dandy, wearing corsets to diminish his bulk and cosmetics to smooth a skin wrinkled with age. Yet he was a profound lawyer and had once finished an argument before the great court when Mrs. Madison and some other ladies appeared. Ladies in court were, in those days, a rare sight and of course never more than spectators to the battles of men.

Recognizing their presence, Pinckney recommenced his argument for their benefit and though using fewer legal arguments, he scattered more histrionic flowers. Finishing his performance, he stated he would not cite further cases to prove his argument as it might prove fatiguing and inimical to the laws of good taste, which on the present occasion (bowing low), he wished to obey.

Visiting the Supreme Court today it seems hard to believe that such an era ever existed.

While Henry Clay was Speaker of the House, the State of Kentucky retained him as counsel to present that state's argument in a claim against the State of Virginia before the United States Supreme Court. The great orator was to appear before the court for the first time and a curious concourse had gathered to determine whether the lawyer of the West would be able to sustain his reputation in this new forensic arena.

Clay arose; there was some slight agitation in his manner, but he soon recovered his customary composure and as usual wove a charm of words that held spellbound both audience and court.

In their black robes, the judges sat very sedate and attentive. Justice Washington, his eyes following Clay's every gesture, unconsciously took a small snuffbox from under his robe. Clay, perceiving the box, broke off in the middle of his argument and advanced gracefully to the bench.

There, where he and the justice were perhaps the only unembarrassed spectators in the whole courtroom, the lawyer helped himself to a pinch of the justice's own snuff. As he applied the pinch, Clay observed, "I perceive Your Honor sticks to the Scotch." He then returned and resumed his argument where he had left off as though it were the ordinary custom for lawyers to help themselves to a justice's snuff while the court was in session.

So distant must judge and juror be from lawyer in the courtroom that Clay's action was received with astonishment and indeed admiration. One of the justices afterward remarked he did not believe "there was a man in the United States who could have done that but Henry Clay."

The gesture was so natural it made the incident all the more delightful. There was not a trace of impropriety on the one hand nor patronage on the other.

I F ANY SINGLE FACTOR precipitated the Civil War, it was the Dred Scott decision.[3] The Supreme Court held unconstitutional in that case an act of Congress prohibiting the keeping of slaves in certain northern territory (Illinois, a "free" state, was the state in question), declaring that slaves were not citizens entitled to the same rights as free men under the Constitutuion.

This shameful decision, unrivaled in sheer injustice and inhumanity by any other Supreme Court decision (except perhaps the decision upholding the constitutionality of Japanese citizen relocation camps during World War II) is yet another indication that even constitutional law mirrors its own time. As in most law, the prejudice and passion of every age are preserved in the great court's annals, and the court has often followed the heights and nadirs of our own social and economic history.

Justice Taney, who handed down the decision, had been refused confirmation to the Court by the Senate when nominated by President Jackson. Several years later his nomination for the vacancy created by the death of John Marshall was confirmed by a then Democratic Senate.

Taney continued to act as chief justice although his country was fighting its Southern brothers over the opinion he had rendered. As long as Charles Sumner sat in the Senate, a bust of Taney was refused its appropriate place in the Supreme Court.

U PON THE BENCH of the United States Supreme Court now sit justices who, in thought and opinion, are as different as the geography of the country over which they decide. And now, for the first time, a woman sits at the bench among "the brethren." We will have the opportunity to see how Justice Sandra Day O'Connor's background and views shape her judicial opinions. For the mountains of the West, the cotton fields of the South, the urban areas of the East, the Constitution becomes what these justices say it is.

Sitting upon the bench at one time were two justices who had actually shot at each other. Their respective opinions were those of the divergent factions of a warring people: Justice Horace Lurton and Justice John Harlan had been on opposite sides in a battle in Kentucky in the Civil War.

Today justices divide into liberal, conservative, and moderate camps and the court shifts slowly, very slowly. At one time there was another division. In 1895 when Chief Justice Fuller sat upon the bench, by coincidence the justices who sat on one side of him had children and grandchildren (Field, Gray, Brown, and White) while those on the other side were childless (Harlan, Shiras, Peckham). Chief Justice Fuller himself was very fond of his grandchildren; on one occasion a grandchild sat upon his lap while the court was in session.

I N ITS MANY DECISIONS the Supreme Court has time and again upheld the constitutional rights of the individual. In 1886 the Court protected the right of a San Francisco man to carry on a lawful business.

Yick Wo had opened a laundry. Soon there were 240 Chinese laundries in San Francisco, so many that white competitors began to talk of "coolie labor." The San Francisco Board of Supervisors passed a seemingly harmless but cunningly restrictive ordinance that provided that all laundries in San Francisco had to be maintained in brick buildings except under special permit.

Police soon began to appear at the doors of the Chinese-owned laundries and Yick Wo scurried to the city hall for his permit to operate his frame-building laundry. It was summarily denied.

Other Chinese owners told him that their permits were likewise being denied. After taking a count, it appeared that by a strange coincidence only Chinese laundries were operated in *frame* buildings so that only Chinese owners were refused permits to operate laundries.

Yick Wo suddenly found himself in jail with 150 of his fellow-Chinese laundrymen for violation of the ordinance. On a writ of habeas corpus he marched into the state supreme court. The California Supreme Court held the ordinance valid, however, and ordered Yick Wo back to jail.

Yick Wo had heard that in Washington, D.C., there sat another court that passed upon every law in the land whether it be enacted by Congress, a state legislature, or a board of supervisors. But Washington was a long way away and would the Supreme Court consider the case of an insignificant Chinese laundryman from California?

They did. Yick Wo's writ of habeas corpus was granted, he was freed from jail, the California Supreme Court and the San Francisco Board of Supervisors were reversed, and the United States Supreme Court held that Yick Wo, and the other Chinese laundrymen, by the passage of the ordinance and the operation thereof, had practically been deprived of the "equal protection" of the laws under the United States Constitution.[4]

THE SUPREME COURT INTERPRETS the Constitution when it decides that an act of Congress is unconstitutional. But where does it get the power to make such judgments? Since Congress is elected by the people, doesn't congressional legislation represent the will of the people? The Supreme Court justices are not elected; rather, they are appointed by the president with the approval of Congress. Suppose the executive branch of the government, the president, declares a law to be constitutional. Why isn't *his* decision final? Members of Congress and the president take the same oaths to support the Constitution as do Supreme Court justices.

The Constitution provides that "the judicial power shall extend to all cases" and that it shall be "vested in one Supreme Court." Some authorities say this is the key language granting to the Supreme Court the power to review acts of the executive and legislative branches. Others point out that nowhere in the Constitution are there the words "the Supreme Court alone may declare acts of president and Congress unconstitutional."

It's an intriguing game. Read the Constitution. You may find some language you firmly believe grants the power; others will just as vehemently disagree.

If the constitutional fathers had wanted the Supreme Court to have this power, why didn't they definitely say so?

They did. Thomas Jefferson said: "The Judges would consider any law as void which was contrary to the Constitution." George Washington regarded "the judicial system as the chief pillar upon which our national Government must rest."

Colonial judges had held acts of colonial assemblies unconstitutional. English judges had held legislative and executive acts unconstitutional or against "natural law". When the sovereign Elizabeth created a playing card monopoly for one of her favorites, the Judges held it "unconstitutional"—although England has no *written* constitution Elizabeth's action was considered *contra de rerum natura* (against natural law).

The constitutional fathers were familiar with these doctrines of judicial review, the right of courts to hold legislative and executive acts unconstitutional, since courts of their times were doing it. They did not, by any language in the Constitution, curb this power, yet they did not by any express language set forth the power, because, as one said, it would be an insult to the intelligence of the judges to set forth a judicial power so generally established. To provide for justices and a Supreme Court was sufficient to provide them with all ordinary, established judicial powers.

The exercise of the power under the Constitution to hold acts of Congress unconstitutional is not new. The Supreme Court has held laws unconstitutional since *Marbury* v. *Madison*,[5] the great decision of John Marshall that specifically declared the Court's right to do so. That was 1803. The power has been too well established, desired, and customary to admit of controversy, the Court said then.

Chief Justice Pemberton, one of the judges of the despot Charles II, and not the worst even for those times, often boasted, "I've outdone Parliament a thousand times in making law!"

When, in old England, the judges came upon an act of Parliament that was of doubtful validity, they moved, robes, wigs, and all, over to Parliament to ask the members thereof what was meant by the law.

What would happen today if Chief Justice Burger, after looking at a draft of new legislation, availed himself of the ancient privilege and moved over to Congress with the eight other judges in tow to ask the majority leader what was meant by a bill?

It is recorded in England that upon one occasion Chief Justice Thorpe, accompanied by Brother Sir Hugh Green, marched into the House of Lords, where there were assembled twenty-four bishops, earls, and barons, and asked them, "as they had lately passed a statute of jeofails what they intended thereby."

A later chronicler reflects, as might some today: "If the Lords were still liable to be interrogated, they would not unfrequently be puzzled and the revival of the practice might be a check to hasty legislation."

IT IS SOMEWHAT DIFFICULT to amend a constitution to make it say what it already says. In 1793 the United States Supreme Court, in the case of *Chisholm* v. *Georgia*,[6] declared that the Supreme Court had jurisdiction, under the Constitution, to try a suit against the state of Georgia by a citizen of another state.

A sovereign cannot be sued except by permission; he is above the law. Suits against the United States, likewise, can be brought only by its statutory consent. States believed they, too, enjoyed this privilege of sovereignty.

In addition, it was feared that allowing suits against states would lead to numerous prosecutions from the various claims of refugees, Tories, holders of state paper, and Loyalists to recover confiscated property after the American Revolution. "Every State in the Union will be thrown into the greatest confusion," it was said.

In the year after the decision, a resolution proposing what became the Eleventh Amendment passed both houses of Congress. Ratified as a constitutional amendment in 1798, it was construed to terminate all suits then pending against any state and preventing any future ones.

The amendment reads: "The Judicial power of the United States shall not be construed to extend to any suit in law or equity, commenced or prosecuted against one of the United States by Citizens of another State, or by Citizens or Subjects of any Foreign State." (Note the word "construed".)

Ninety years after this amendment, a smart lawyer brought a suit in the Supreme Court against a state on behalf of one of its own citizens. He pointed out that the amendment was so drawn as to apply only to suits brought by citizens of a different state or foreign country.

The Supreme Court decided against him in *Hans* v. *Louisiana*,[7] saying that the Constitution, as it was originally written (in spite of its prior decision to the contrary), did not authorize a suit against a state by any private citizen without the state's consent.

T HE PEOPLE OF THE USSR were granted a constitution that in guarantees and promises may be as ideal an instrument of government as is the American. Yet the average Soviet citizen has no freedom of speech, no right to vote, no right to impartial trial, no right to religious freedom, and no guarantee that he will not be placed under arbitrary arrest, all recognized as basic human rights in our Constitution.

Why not? All the fine language is present in the Soviet instrument. Yet one thing is lacking. There is no independent, impartial judiciary with the power to declare void legislative and executive acts that abrogate these rights. The Supreme Soviet is in all respects supreme.

At least three times Congress passed bills of attainder (a legislative act directed against one individual that punishes him for alleged wrongdoing without trial), although such bills are expressly prohibited by the Constitution. Numerous times since the Civil War, Congress has attempted to violate human rights of the citizen guaranteed by the Constitution. The Supreme Court has eventually said no to these excesses in most cases. State legislatures have repeatedly passed laws undermining constitutional guarantees. They were held unconstitutional.

Judicial review, then, is necessary to guarantee "constitutional guarantees" by checks and balances upon other sometimes wayward branches of our government.

Seldom have issues in a national controversy been as clearly defined as in President Roosevelt's New Deal legislation. Yet rarely has the question of policy and interpretation been as bitterly disputed.

Since the Supreme Court held the National Recovery Administration unconstitutional, all New Deal legislation was tested by that court by two questions: Has Congress invaded the field of states' rights, and has Congress improperly delegated its legislative power to an executive agency? These were the two issues and the only two. For every unconstitutional New Deal bill, at least part of the Court answered yes to one or both of these questions.

To confuse still further the question of policy, a Democratic president and, consequently, a Democratic Congress, advocated strongly centralized or federal power and control in purely internal affairs of the states, or to use the historically significant phrase, "usurpation of states' rights" by the federal government. (In the past this was always claimed as a Republican principle; the Democrats until that time had fought for states' rights.)

As to states' rights: In the United States today, one lives under *two* governments, state and federal. Granted to the federal government, in the Constitution, are certain definite rights and powers, while the states keep the residuum of power. Power to regulate interstate commerce, the mails, declare war, and the like, were functions appropriately reserved and delegated to the central government. The power to define, regulate, and provide for purely local, city, county, and state questions, such as licensing a certain local business, or regulating marriage and divorce, was left to the several sovereign states, which accounts for the diversity of domestic relation laws.

So when the federal government stepped into the state field to regulate purely local business under the NRA, the Supreme Court said "unconstitutional." How far the Congress may invade the purely local field in legislation is one of degree and, under the *Wagner* decision, the Supreme Court went further than it had ever gone before.

Today the concept of states' rights is very limited. The Court confirmed Congress's power to regulate even purely local and intrastate businesses, including pricing, wages, and hours, so long as there is even the remotest effect on interstate commerce.

For example, a small farmer in Wisconsin can be told how much wheat to grow, even if he never sells it on the market and only uses it himself, since the amount he grows means less will be bought in interstate commerce.

The penetration of federal regulation has reached deep into all aspects of individual life, and state economics, politics, and social welfare now all exist within federally prescribed rules.

As to the delegation of power by Congress, "We the people" gave the Congress, in the Constitution, power to legislate. "We" tacitly prohibited Congress from delegating that power to a president, a board, or a commission unless, of course, only the administrative, working details of a bill were left to be ironed out within certain definitely ascertainable limits. (The Supreme Court here again held the New Deal in error for having delegated an amorphous power.)

President Reagan ran on a program of decentralizing the federal government, returning more power to state and local governments. He embodies the conservative mood of the country in the early 1980s. With the appointment of Justice O'Connor and the possible appointment of other justices with conservative leanings, we could see changes in the way the Constitution is interpreted. For example, a number of liberal laws regarding state and federal funds for abortion and welfare programs may be repealed. Probably the greatest change, however, is the likely return of much power, much government, to the states—and this change will be held constitutional.

Throughout our history the Supreme Court has been the guardian of the Constitution. And that Constitution is what the justices say it is.

Notes

1. The case was *National Labor Relations Board* v. *Jones & Laughlin Steel Corp.*, 301 U.S. 1, 57 S. Ct. 615 (1936), and it held that Congress had the power to provide by that act that employees have the right to collective bargaining procedures and union organizing without fear of losing their jobs.
2. *Trustees of Dartmouth College* v. *Woodward*, 17 U. S. [4 Wheat.] 518 (1819).
3. *Dred Scott* v. *Sanford*, 60 [9 Howard] U. S. 393 (1856).
4. *Yick Wo* v. *Hopkins*, 118 U. S. 356, 6 S. Ct. 1064 (1886).
5. *Marbury* v. *Madison*, 5 U. S. 137, 1 Cranch (1803).
6. *Chisholm* v. *Georgia*, 3 U. S. 419, 2 Dall. (1793).
7. *Hans* v. *Louisiana*, 134 U. S. 1, 10 S. Ct. 504 (1889).

11

Search and Caesar

The right of the people to be secure in their persons, houses, papers, and effects, against unreasonable searches and seizures, shall not be violated; and no Warrants shall issue, but upon probable cause, supported by Oath or affirmation, and particularly describing the place to be searched, and the persons or things to be seized.

—Amendment IV
The Constitution of the United States

FREEDOM FROM RANDOM and harassing searches seems fundamental to any democratic system of government. When Daniel Ellsberg's psychiatrist's office is ransacked by the FBI, when the Democratic National Headquarters is bugged, when Martin Luther King's room is wiretapped, our sense of justice is shocked and even the government has to answer for such gross invasions of our privacy.

Yet this fundamental freedom is a relatively new one in common-law history, and the American Revolution had to be fought to win it.

The *search warrant*, a document authorizing and describing items to be seized, was unknown in early common law. The monarch's agents were free to search and ransack when and where they pleased for evidence of crime, treason, or heresy. "Have you got a warrant?" was an unintelligible question. Anything found, though originally unsuspected, was good evidence usable in court later on. Not so now.

T HE CROWN'S BROAD POWER to search and seize at will became a tool of political and religious oppression.

Each succeeding regime in sixteenth and seventeenth century England used the search and seizure power to suppress Catholic and Puritan literature. If the crown's ecclesiastical judges considered a writing "heretical, schismatical, and seditious," "offensive to the state," or "scandalous and lying," the printers and their presses would be quickly seized. Tudor censorship was effective— and permanent.

In 1662 the practice of issuing *executive warrants* began. These were documents of the most general and discretionary nature and empowered an agent of the crown to search anywhere for seditious books and to seize anything unlicensed (unapproved) by the Tudor censors.

Eventually, the crown began to prosecute those unfortunate heretical authors for "seditious libel," and *general warrants* were used to seize all of the accused man's property and arrest anyone in any way connected with the disfavored literary work. A bad review from the crown meant worse things than losing royalties; it could mean losing one's head.

The abuse of general warrants spread to the American colonies, but colonists were not as docile as Tudor printers. The crown's revenue officers had been given blanket authority to use *writs of assistance* to search for goods smuggled in violation of British tax laws. Waving these writs, officers of the crown ransacked colonial homes with impunity. The colonists began to complain of these indiscriminate abuses, and the first seeds of the Revolution were sown.

The turning point came in 1761. James Otis, a noted orator, challenged the validity of the hated writs in public debate in Boston.[1]

Otis denounced the writs as "the worst instrument of arbitrary power, the most destructive of English liberty, and the fundamental principles of law that ever was found in an English law book," because they placed "the liberty of every man in the hands of every petty officer." His English counterparts were beginning to agree with him, although too late to prevent the coming Revolution.

IN 1763 JOHN WILKES, a member of Parliament and a champion of popular causes, anonymously published *The North Briton*, a writing that was "esteemed heinously libelous" for its bold criticism of the government. Lord Halifax (secretary of state) promptly issued a general warrant to search for its author, and four of the king's messengers were dispatched. It was later reported that "Armed with their roving commissions, they set forth in quest of unknown offenders; and unable to take evidence, listened to rumors, idle tales and curious guesses. They held in their hands the liberty of every man whom they were pleased to suspect."[2]

Eventually, Wilkes's house was ransacked and all his personal papers were seized. But Wilkes was not to be so easily intimidated. He sued Lord Halifax and recovered 4,000 pounds from him—and 1,000 from one of the men who had searched him.[3] The court called this warrant "a ridiculous warrant against the whole English nation."

Lord Halifax may have been insulted, but his power to issue general warrants was fast declining.

In 1762 John Entick had published *The British Freeholder* and a specific warrant, naming him and his papers, was issued for this "seditious" work. The king's messengers rummaged through Entick's house for four hours and carted away all his books and papers.

In 1765 Entick sued for trespass, and Lord Camden rendered a decision that is called "one of the landmarks of English liberty." Not only did Entick recover for trespass, but the general warrant, which allowed the seizure of all of a person's papers, was declared invalid and contrary to the spirit and history of English law.[4]

A year later, the House of Commons passed a resolution condemning general warrants. When the battle for individual liberty in the colonies was over, the colonists determined to prevent the kind of warrant abuses they had suffered under English rule. Their recent struggle against oppression and revulsion against general writs were motivating factors behind the Fourth Amendment.

The Fourth Amendment was fashioned to protect against the midnight knock on the door, to protect against invasions of the sanctity of one's home from random, indiscriminate searches. To colonists still smarting from the whip, the Fourth Amendment was soothing relief.

TWO HUNDRED YEARS have passed and the struggle between government authority and individual privacy still goes on, although now amid a myriad of electronic, telephonic devices and snooping techniques never dreamed of by John Adams. Law, in this area as in all others, has flexed with, adapted to, and incorporated the conditions of each age.

Today, not only must there be a *specific* warrant to search for *specific* property issued by a neutral magistrate (not by the sometimes overzealous police whose job it is to discover evidence), but it must be based on actual facts suggesting that the evidence will be where the policy say it is when they get there. Even with all these safeguards, the manner and time the police search must also be considerate of citizens' rights. (If contraband is actually found *without* a warrant, it is "poisonous" and can't be used in court as evidence. Does this make of law a game?)

For example, in California, a warrant has to be served between 7 A.M. and 10 P.M., unless the police get specific permission from a magistrate to search at night.[5] If a warrant isn't served within ten days after issuance, it is void since there is no assurance that the evidence will still be where the warrant says it is.[6]

During Prohibition, police in Lewiston, Maine, broke into one E. W. Buckley's house to hunt for bootleg liquor. They weren't armed with just a warrant; they brought axes, picks, and crowbars and when a search of the house proved fruitless, they set to work with their tools, determined to find the booze they just knew was hidden somewhere in the house.

While the anguished Mr. Buckley stood proclaiming his innocence, the police proceeded methodically to tear out a two- to four-foot strip around the walls of every room in Buckley's house. They didn't find a drop, and left a despairing Mr. Buckley up to his knees in plaster, wallpaper, and dirt.

Mr. Buckley sued the police for trespass. Even though the police had a legal warrant, the court agreed with Buckley:

> The general principle however, is that, while the officers should search thoroughly in every part of the described premises where there is any likelihood that the object searched for may be found, they should also be considerate of the comfort and convenience of the occupants, should mar the premises themselves as little as possible, and should carefully replace so far as practicable anything they find it necessary to remove.[7]

Mr. Buckley was awarded damages and Messrs. Entick and Wilkes smiled down upon him.

D OLLREE MAPP IS another unknown name that became a landmark in search and seizure law. On May 23, 1957, Cleveland police officers arrived at Dollree Mapp's house to look for the pornography they'd been informed Ms. Mapp had stockpiled. But Dollree knew she had rights, or at least she thought she did. She refused to let the police in without a search warrant and called her lawyer. More police arrived and when it became apparent that Dollree was intransigent, they broke down her door.

Dollree was outraged and demanded to see a warrant. An officer waved a piece of paper and Dollree snatched it out of his hand and shoved it down her ample bosom. A free-for-all ensued and the police retrieved the "warrant" and handcuffed Dollree, because she'd been belligerent in resisting an official rescue of the warrant from her person. The police wouldn't let Dollree's lawyer in when he showed up, and while Dollree sat handcuffed and furious, they searched every inch of her house. The pornography was eventually located.

The U. S. Supreme Court took Dollree's dim view of this affair. If police can use illegally seized evidence once they get it, reasoned the court, the Fourth Amendment will become merely "a form of words, valueless and undeserving of mention in a perpetual charter of inestimable human liberties."

Such police abuse called for a deterrent of some kind. Civil suits for trespass wouldn't be enough, because the police could still get their convictions despite the most outrageous and harassing searches. (Furthermore, plaintiffs generally have a pretty tough time prevailing in such suits against the cops. Juries are sympathetic to the officer who was "only doing his job," and if the plaintiff is in jail it makes things even tougher.)

So the Court proclaimed from that day forth an *exclusionary rule* would prevail among the states. Anything seized by an unlawful search would hereafter be inadmissible in state and federal courts. Thereby, the Court compelled respect for the Fourth Amendment by removing any incentive to disregard it.

The Court decided that there was no proof that the piece of paper Dollree had attempted to preserve in her décollatage was a warrant. No warrant, no admissible evidence. Dollree's conviction was reversed.

Justice Cardozo, like many others, thought it a disgrace that "the criminal is to go free because the constable has blundered." But Justice Clark addressed this view eloquently:

> The criminal goes free if he must, but it is the law that sets him free. Nothing can destroy a government more quickly than its failure to observe its own laws, or worse, its disregard of the charter

of its own existence.... Our Government is the potent, the omnipresent teacher. For good or for ill, it teaches the whole people by its example. ... If the Government becomes a lawbreaker, it breeds contempt for law; it invites every man to become a law unto himself; it invites anarchy.[8]

Since Dollree Mapp's case, the exclusion of evidence and reversal of convictions because of improper searches have become commonplace.

After the exclusionary rule, as pertaining to the Fourth Amendment, was debated, the most hotly contested question became "What is a search?" Is looking through someone's garbage a search? What about fingerprinting and drawing blood? Bugging? Looking in an open window with a flashlight? Using metal detectors at airports? Using any of the other modern electronic privacy invaders?

The answer came down from the nine esteemed justices on high: A search occurs when someone pries, peeks, or listens in an area where we *reasonably expect to have privacy,* and *that* entirely depends on the circumstances, as we shall see.

The California Supreme Court, among many other courts, has held that we have a reasonable expectation of privacy in our garbage.

Police had Edward Krivda's house under surveillance in Los Angeles. When they saw a garbage truck approaching, they had a flash of investigative brilliance. They asked the trashmen to empty their truck *before* they picked up Krivda's trash, so that the police could sort through it afterward for marijuana debris. This the civic-minded trashmen did. But the court reversed Krivda's conviction and elevated the right to privacy in trash to new heights. The court explained:

> We can readily ascribe many reasons why residents would not want their castaway clothing, letters, medicine bottles, or other telltale refuse and trash to be examined by neighbors or others, at least not until the trash had lost its identity and meaning by becoming part of a large conglomeration of trash elsewhere. Half truths leading to rumor and gossip may readily flow from an attempt to "read" the contents of another's trash.[9]

Once your private trash joins the common stash, however, the law says it's fair game.

After Robert Kennedy was assassinated, Los Angeles police set up a security detail around Sirhan Sirhan's residence to keep the morbidly curious away. Officer Young was drinking a cup of coffee in Sirhan's backyard one afternoon, and walked over to the trash to throw the cup away. As he dropped in the cup, he noticed an envelope with writing on it and retrieved it.

This was the damaging envelope that established premeditation and helped convict Sirhan of first-degree murder. On it was written in Sirhan's hand: "RFK must be disposed of properly. Robert Fitzgerald Kennedy must soon die die die die."[10] (Sirhan was saved from execution later when the California Supreme Court held capital punishment unconstitutional. He is still in prison but can't be executed even though the same supreme court has recently held, under certain circumstances, capital punishment is now legal.)

Sirhan tried to hide behind his Fourth Amendment rights, but the court wouldn't agree. Since Sirhan's mother and brother shared his house, the court decided he had no right to expect his trash to be private. (This is a good example of close questions making bad—or good—law. The court *had* to draw a fine line of difference between Sirhan's trash. Perhaps the crime was too enormous, sentiments were too high to do otherwise—but it's obvious the distinction was the judicial splitting of a hair.)

The Fourth Amendment applies to the archcriminal and the petty offender alike. The FBI and the Los Angeles Public Library once teamed up to catch a woman who was checking out library books and selling them to bookstores. A maid searched the woman's trash at police request, and the court approved the search since the FBI had given the police prior information that constituted probable cause that evidence of the heinous offense would be there. The enterprising bookworm was convicted of grand theft—$200 worth of library books.[11]

ALTHOUGH THE CROWN'S AGENT can no longer search without a proper warrant, what happens when the crown's agent inadvertently stumbles upon evidence by, say, noticing it through an open window? The courts are sympathetic to the trials and tribulations of police work and don't expect an officer to leave the murder weapon lying on the porch for six hours while he gets a warrant.

So the "plain view" doctrine provides that, even if you have an expectation of privacy in your home, backyard, or car, police can seize any evidence they see in plain view without warrant if they have a right to be in the area. If police are walking by and your window is open, or if you invite the officer in to purchase tickets to the policemen's ball, you are also inviting him to seize the marijuana you have lying openly on your desk.

This actually happened in the home of a California appellate justice: His wife had called the police for assistance but when they came they also noticed "in plain view" marijuana plants being cultivated. He lost his job. Now he's back practicing law.

The plain view doctrine led to abuses. In a recent case, a sheriff and his deputies hired a helicopter and flew it back and forth over a suspect's backyard twenty feet from the ground looking for marijuana. The suspect claimed it was corn, but the sheriffs discovered otherwise.

At the trial, the sheriff cried, "Plain view!" But the court said that not only did the rancher have a right to expect privacy in his own backyard, the sheriff had no right even to be there. Furthermore, the court pointed out that flying a helicopter at that altitude was itself illegal.[12]

Although the naked eye, and what it sees in plain view, is fair game for seizure, a police view must really be *plain*—unaided by sophisticated visual aids like telescopes. The courts consider a visual intrusion into a private place to be a search. When the FBI used an eighty-millimeter telescope a quarter-mile from an apartment building as part of a gambling investigation, the court said that all the evidence the officers saw inside was the product of an unlawful search, and inadmissible in court.

Plain view means plain, unaided view, although the court made clear it wasn't concerned about "the extent to which an agent may crane his neck, or bend over, or squat ... so long as what he saw would have been visible to any curious passerby."[13] (There *have* been cases in which police have been allowed to use common devices like flashlights and binoculars, but not sophisticated modern devices that give a plain view from a mile away.)

Not only can evidence be seized if it is in plain view, it can also be seized if it is in *plain smell*. Dogs have made drug-sniffing a new field of search-and-seizure law, and the courts are now wrangling over what exactly "plain smell" is.

Animal instinct, whether canine, feline, or equine, has always been treated with utmost respect. Courts seem to believe that since animals can't lie, their testimony may be the most reliable of all. Even though they can't speak, their habits and actions speak for them and are often admissible in court.

Tracking fugitives with bloodhounds was customary in early U.S. history, and is still practiced today. Most courts recognized that the sensitive, trained canine nose—eight times more reliable than our own—led to valuable evidence, and so the baying of hounds at the cringing criminal's door was usually admissible.[14] (My bloodhound, Professor Moriarty, came from a Georgia prison camp where he was their finest tracker of criminals. He sniffs many of my clients with homesickness.)

Today, the baying bloodhound in the bayou has been replaced by the sharp-nosed shepherd in the baggage room. Although the courts haven't lost esteem for canine prowess in smelling, they are concerned about whether a sniff is the same as a search.

In a California case, the court called "Bourbon's Nose Knows, or the Case of Bourbon's Bust," a random sniff was held unlawful. Bourbon, the canine cop involved, was 92 percent accurate in detecting marijuana. That fact no one denied. Deputies took Bourbon to an airline baggage area and turned him loose on a "sniffing expedition." Sure enough, Bourbon came to an alert and chewed and scratched at a bag that contained marijuana.

Despite Bourbon's impeccable credentials, the evidence was not admissible at trial. The sniff *was* a search, and the officers had no probable cause whatsoever to think there would be contraband in that baggage room. Without any probable cause, this was a general, exploratory search, and no better than the use of writs of assistance and general warrants, which the Fourth Amendment was created to prevent.[15]

The same court looked more favorably on the dog involved in a case it called "Link's Link with Destiny, A Short Tale." The now-notorious Link was deadly accurate. In his whole marijuana-sniffing career he had only made two mistakes and those were by *missing* marijuana, never by reacting to objects that *didn't* contain it. On a tip, Link was taken to an airline baggage area where he ran directly to the suspected bag. The tip—and Link—were correct.

The court said "admissible," lauding Link's high-level performance and great accuracy as an investigator. But this wasn't a general "sniffing expedition." Link was brought in to look for specific evidence based on a reliable informant's tip—probable cause. So Link was allowed to provide the missing link in this case.[16]

THE "OFTEN COMPETITIVE enterprise of ferreting out crime" leads our men and women in blue into the most ludicrous attempts to trap the unwary offender. A good deal of these attempts go on in the public restroom, supposedly a personal sanctuary. The vice squad apparently spends considerable of its time peering under toilet stall doors.

In their diligent efforts to find out who is offending in restrooms, our noble peace officers spy from ceiling vents and holes drilled in walls, install observation devices, and spend days on end watching and photographing any "crimes against nature" that may occur therein.

The Fourth Amendment applies *anywhere* we reasonably expect privacy, it protects people's expectations, not places, and we don't lose its protection at the restroom door. But one may lose his Fourth Amendment rights depending on *where* he chooses to violate a taboo.

If you choose a toilet stall with a door, the courts realize that you probably decided to do your biological or recreational thing in private. You have a right to be free from random, clandestine observations going on while you don't even know your private parts and bodily functioning are being exposed to the gaze of the law.

In one case, police drilled holes in a bathroom wall and for several days had a concealed photographer taking pictures of what went on inside. The court said this was proper and *not* a search because the defendants were brazen enough to commit their offenses in open, public areas, not behind locked doors.[17]

In other cases, in which the cops ran an observation pipe through a ceiling and saw an offense committed "by means of a hole in the partition,"[18] and in which an officer crawled into the space between the bathroom ceiling and the floor above and used a movie camera and radio transmitter to record the dramatic events, the courts have drawn the line: "Man's constitutionally protected right of personal privacy not only abides with him while he is the householder within his own castle but cloaks him when as a member of the public he is temporarily occupying a room— including a toilet stall—to the extent that it is offered to the public for private, however transient, individual use."[19] (A rented hotel room is obviously private.)

Even where the parties involved managed dexterously to commit "the act" while kneeling on the floor through a twelve-inch space between stall partitions, the court said they had a right to privacy. It was an impermissible search—even though some part of "the act" might have been visible to the public.

It appears that Big Brother is finally growing tired of restrooms, however. Many states have laws permitting homosexual intercourse between consenting adults[20] and laws insuring our restroom privacy by outlawing two-way mirrors in bathrooms, showers, and hotel rooms.[21] We've either realized that "the act" has always been popular and we're not likely to stop it, or else the vice squad has realized it would rather spend its afternoons elsewhere.

R EMEMBER THAT the Fourth Amendment protects people's "right to be secure in their *persons*, houses, papers, and effects against unreasonable searches and seizures." The courts have taken this commandment literally; an invasion of the privacy of our own bodies is a search, and the Fourth Amendment can apply to blood tests, stomach pumps, and any other attempt to enter a body to search for evidence. Looking at some of the following search tactics, it's a good thing our founding fathers remembered to add "persons."

Antonio Rochin swallowed some pills while the police were coming for him. Three officers jumped him and tried to get the capsules out of his mouth. When that didn't work, they handcuffed him and took him to a hospital where he was force-fed an emetic through a tube in his nostrils until he vomited and the police retrieved their evidence.[22]

Kenneth Cameron was trying to cross the U.S.-Mexican border. Customs officials thought he looked suspicious. A strip search was fruitless, so Cameron was taken to a hospital where he was forcibly subjected to two rectal examinations, two enemas, and a liquid laxative. Eventually, a heroin balloon was retrieved.

To these body searches, the courts said: "This conduct shocks the conscience of the court!"[23] The Fourth Amendment won't permit such improper, humiliating, and abusive invasions; they are "too close to the rack and the screw," and cannot even be used for legitimate police purposes.

But (and there's always a "but") in *some* circumstances, even invading the body without a warrant can be reasonable.

When Armando Schmerber was arrested for drunk driving, the police had doctors take a sample of his blood, which had an alcoholic content high enough to pickle Schmerber. On appeal, he claimed this was an unreasonable search, because the police never had a warrant for his blood.

The court was unsympathetic. Since the percentage level of blood alcohol drops quickly after drinking stops, it was imperative that the evidence be extracted immediately, or it would have been forever lost. (Schmerber also tried to claim the blood sample compelled him to be a witness against himself in violation of the Fifth Amendment, but the court was out for Schmerber's blood, too, and said the blood, although intimately part of him, wasn't speaking for him. The chemical analysis was what incriminated him.)[24]

Law enforcement doesn't stop at emetics, laxatives, and needles. If those tactics don't work, police may try to go right *in* after the evidence.

Recently, in Arkansas, one John Bowden showed up at a hospital with a bullet wound. An x-ray revealed a .38 caliber bullet resting near his spine. Police had evidence that Bowden had been involved in a crime involving a .38 pistol, so they asked the court for a search warrant. The area of the search was "the lower part of petitioner's spinal canal." It was clear that this would involve risky and painful major surgery. The court said "unreasonable" and no warrant was issued. The evidence will go with John Bowden to his grave.[25]

In Washington, D.C., however, when James Crowder was arrested for the murder of a dentist and x-rays showed a bullet in his arm, the court said "reasonable" to the requested surgery. After all, the doctors had said this was "minor surgery," requiring only local anesthesia, and wouldn't involve a greater risk than "crossing the street."[26] So in they went, out it came, and Crowder was convicted, all because he had the misfortune to have suffered a *less* serious wound than John Bowden.

It's been held that fingerprinting *is* a search,[27] but voice exemplars aren't. A grand jury subpoenaed twenty persons and asked them for voice samples to compare with recorded conversations in a gambling investigation. One of the witnesses refused, claiming that compelling him to speak would force him to incriminate himself and would be an unreasonable "seizure" of his voice. But the court said there's no expectation of privacy in one's own voice:

> The physical characteristics of a person's voice, its tone and manner, as opposed to the content of a specific conversation, are constantly exposed to the public. Like a man's facial characteristics, or handwriting, his voice is repeatedly produced for others to hear. No person can have a reasonable expectation that others will not know the sound of his voice, any more than he can reasonably expect that his face will be a mystery to the world.

Since nothing was being requested that had not previously been exposed to the public, the witness was compelled to speak. (The court also said that there was no self-incrimination, since the voice samples were to be studied solely for their physical properties and not for the communicative content.)[28]

B LACKSTONE REPORTED that eavesdroppers, the world's first buggers, were a nuisance and actionable at common law: "Eaves-droppers, or such as listen under walls or windows or the eaves of a house to hearken after discourse, and thereupon to frame slanderous and mischievous tales, are a common nuisance and presentable at court-leet or are indictable at the sessions, and punishable by fine."[29]

As the art of surreptitious spying advanced from the naked ear to the electronic bug, the danger of the uninvited ear became more serious, and so did the consequences.

Charlie Katz was convicted of gambling. At his trial, the government had introduced Charlie's end of telephone conversations that FBI agents overheard by attaching an electronic device to the outside of the phone booth.

The FBI defended its eavesdropping, and said it wasn't a search. After all, a phone booth is made of glass, so how could Katz have reasonably expected his phone conversation to be private? The court disagreed and said Katz's rights had been violated. Even though he might be seen from outside, he still expected to be safe from the intruding ear, if not the intruding eye: "One who occupies [a phone booth], shuts the doors behind him, and pays the toll that permits him to place a call is surely entitled to assume that the words he utters into the mouthpiece will not be broadcast to the world."[30]

You can trust the privacy of your phone booth more than you can trust your friends. On Lee was suspected of dealing in opium, but the cops couldn't prove it. So they paid Chin Poy, an old friend of Lee (of "defective character" and "low morals" himself) to elicit incriminating statements from him. Chin Poy talked to On Lee in his laundry with a small microphone in his coat pocket and an antenna running along his arm. A narcotics agent with a receiver sat outside and listened while On Lee talked to his "friend."

The Supreme Court said this wasn't an unreasonable search. Since Chin Poy consented to the transmission, it was the same as if Chin Poy listened and testified himself. Lee talked indiscriminately to a friend he trusted, but the law won't protect misplaced confidences. The use of false friends may be dirty business, but it is constitutional, so long as one party consents.[31]

In 1962 Jimmy Hoffa was on trial in federal court in Nashville for violating the Taft-Hartley Act (labor relations). The feds got wind of his attempts to bribe jurors and decided to investigate. They hired Ed Partin, a Louisiana Teamster official, to spy on Hoffa in exchange for clemency on Partin's outstanding embezzlement charges. Partin testified that Hoffa tried to buy off two jurors and Hoffa claimed Fourth Amendment protection. But the court said secret informants are *not* searches, they're misplaced confidences. All too true was the court's conclusion that: "The risk of being ... betrayed by an informer or deceived as to the identity of one with whom one deals is probably inherent in the conditions of human society. It is the kind of risk we necessarily assume whenever we speak."[32]

If you ever have the misfortune to spend a night (or more) in one of our fine penal institutions, you will discover that there is very little expectation of privacy in jail. Your mail can be read and censored and your phone conversations tapped, all in the name of prison security. Surveillance and search can go on unimpeded by the Fourth Amendment, *except* for communication with your attorney. The attorney-client relationship is given at least the same respect as prison security in this case.

Recorded and very indiscreet conversations between Patty Hearst and her friends in the San Mateo County Jail were among the most damaging bits of evidence in her entire bank robbery trial. She should have been advised that in jail anything you say can and *will* be held against you.

We're not always free to expect that our *movements* will go undetected, either. In one case, agents suspected a man of manufacturing amphetamines. When he drove his pickup to get a drum of caffeine, the agents installed an electronic tracking device (a beeper) on the drum and traced and searched his house. At trial the court said the beeper wasn't an unreasonable search since the driver had exposed his movements to the public anyway (and theoretically could have been followed with or without electronic assistance), and, because the drum was owned by the chemical company, he couldn't reasonably expect it to be private.[33]

In another James Bond special, a beeper was used quite effectively. Police got a tip that Stuart Smith was about to fly a rented plane to Mexico to pick up a huge marijuana shipment. Police brought the plane's true owner and an airplane mechanic to the airport at 1 A.M. and they clandestinely installed a transponder, a tracking device that would appear as an unusual blip on any radar screen. The plane was both tracked on the ground and in the air by two customs aircraft.

Smith and the contraband were nabbed upon his return to the States, but at trial the court found this scientific sleuthing illegal. Smith may not have expected his route to be private, since any pilot knows his flight path can always be checked by sophisticated air traffic monitoring equipment. But Smith *could* reasonably expect that police would not invade the plane itself and install a hidden tracking device to gather incriminating evidence. The detectives were effectively told, "You should have had a warrant."[34]

IT IS OBVIOUS that eavesdropping has come a long way from Blackstone's literal listening at the eaves. Elaborate devices have made bugging (and debugging) a science-fiction art involving microwaves, satellites, and lasers. Things have gotten so out of hand that most states have criminal statutes outlawing intentional interception of communication; just suppressing the evidence apparently isn't enough to discourage Big Brother.

The federal and state laws vary. California's Invasion of Privacy Act[35] was written by a legislature that considered new eavesdropping techniques "a serious threat to the free exercise of personal liberties and cannot be tolerated in a free and civilized society." So, except for law enforcement officers with a warrant, any intentional eavesdropping without the consent of *all* parties to the conversation is a crime.

The federal Omnibus Crime Control and Safe Streets Act of 1968[36] was enacted after years of war protests and ghetto clashes, and its purpose was to *allow* wiretapping, so long as a proper warrant procedure was followed. Congress wanted to sit on the fence on this one. They were worried enough about domestic security (a 1984 doublethink catch-all) to see the need for infiltrating radical groups, but they *also* apparently distrusted the FBI and the Justice Department, and feared giving them total control over communications. So federal law only requires that *one* party to the conversation consent to the eavesdropping. Without consent, a fairly protective warrant procedure has to be followed. (Warrants cannot normally exceed thirty days, for example, and police have to show why other investigative tactics would not be effective.)

This hodgepodge of privacy law leads to seemingly ridiculous results, especially since some state laws (Maryland's, for example) are stricter than the federal law. Maryland forbids interception without the consent of *all* parties. Federal law requires the consent of *one* participant. This led Richard Nixon into the following legal labyrinth, revealed during Watergate.

Nixon made an unfortunate habit, as we now know, of taping all his phone conversations, as well as what went on in the Oval Office. During a phone call to former FBI Chief Patrick Gray, Nixon handed the phone to John Ehrlichman. When Nixon was speaking to Gray, the taping was perfectly legal, since Nixon was one party and he certainly consented—*he* was doing the recording. But when he handed the phone to Ehrlichman, neither participant knew of the taping and the recording instantly became illegal.

To make things seemingly even more absurd, when Nixon taped phone calls at Camp David, Maryland, it was totally illegal, since Maryland, unlike Washington, D.C., requires the consent of *all* parties. Had Nixon ever stood trial for his Watergate offenses, these eavesdropping shenanigans would undoubtedly have confounded everyone involved in the trial.

In 200 years we've progressed from writs of assistance to satellite surveillance. It is another tribute to the prudent authors of the Constitution, and to the sculptors of the law, that the Fourth Amendment remains a valuable weapon against invasions of our personal privacy.

Notes

1. Tudor, *Life of James Otis*, pp. 60–61 (1823).
2. II May's *Constitutional History of England* 246 (1864).
3. *Wilkes v. Wood*, 19 How. St. Tr. 1153 (1763).
4. *Entick v. Carrington*, 19 How. St. Tr. 1029 (1765).
5. California Penal Code §1533.
6. California Penal Code §1534.
7. *Buckley v. Beaulieu*, 104 Me. 56, 71 A. 70 (1908).
8. *Mapp v. Ohio*, 367 U. S. 643, 81 S. Ct. 1684 (1961).
9. *People v. Krivda*, 5 Cal. 3d 357, 486 P. 2d 1262, 96 C.R. 62 (1971).
10. *People v. Sirhan*, 7 Cal. 3d 710, 497 P. 2d 1121, 102 C.R. 385 (1972).
11. *People v. Cohen*, 59 C. A. 3d 241, 130 C. R. 656 (1976).
12. *People v. Sneed*, 32 C. A. 3d 535, 108 C. R. 146 (1973).
13. *U. S. v. Kim*, 415 F. Supp. 1252 (1976).
14. *Burks v. State*, 240 Ala. 587, 200 S. 418 (1941).
    Fisher v. State, 150 Miss. 206, 116 S. 746 (1928).
15. *People v. Williams*, 51 C. A. 3d 346, 124 C. R. 253 (1975).
16. *People v. Furman*, 30 C. A. 3d 454, 106 C. R. 366 (1973).
17. *People v. Roberts*, 256 C. A. 2d 488, 64 C. R. 70 (1967).
18. *Bielicki v. Superior Court*, 57 C. 2d 602, 371 P. 2d 288, 21 C. R. 552 (1962).
19. *Britt v. Superior Court*, 58 C. 2d 469, 374 P. 2d 817, 24 C. R. 849 (1962).
20. California Penal Code §288(a), for example, which permits "oral copulation" between consenting adults after July 1, 1977.

21. California Penal Code §653(n).

22. *Rochin* v. *California*, 342 U. S. 165, 72 S. Ct. 205 (1952).

23. *U. S.* v. *Cameron*, 538 F. 2d 254 (1976).

24. *Schmerber* v. *California*, 384 U. S. 757, 86 S. Ct. 1826 (1966).

25. *Bowden* v. *State*, 256 Ark. 820, 510 S. W. 2d 879 (1974).

26. *U. S.* v. *Crowder*, 543 F. 2d 312 (1976).

27. *Davis* v. *Mississippi*, 394 U. S. 721, 89 S. Ct. 1394 (1969).

28. *U. S.* v. *Dionisio*, 410 U. S. 1, 93 S. Ct. 764 (1973).

29. Blackstone, *Commentaries*, Ch. IV, §168 (1884).

30. *Katz* v. *U.S.*, 389 U. S. 347, 88 S. Ct. 507 (1967).

31. *On Lee* v. *U. S.*, 343 U. S. 747, 72 S. Ct. 967 (1952).

32. *Hoffa* v. *U. S.* , 385 U. S. 293, 87 S. Ct. 408 (1966).

33. *U. S.* v. *Hufford*, 539 F. 2d 32 (1976).

34. *People* v. *Smith*, 67 C. A. 3d 638, 136 C. R. 764 (1977).

35. California Penal Code § 630-637.

36. 18 U.S.C. 2510–2520.

12

The Right to Be Let Alone

WHEN I WAS IN COLLEGE, our beloved astronomer/
teacher Dean Leutchner told us a story of astral discovery
that is one of the truly romantic episodes in science.

What was thought to have been the last planet in the heavens,
Uranus, had been discovered. A student at Cambridge, however,
in reading astronomical reports relating to the orbits of the
planets, noticed that there was a strange and unaccountable
deviation of Uranus's orbit.

This young mathematician reasoned that only the gravitational
pull of some unknown body could cause Uranus to behave so
mysteriously. But search the heavens as they would with their
most powerful telescopes, astronomers were unable to find any
planet that could account for the weird perturbation of Uranus.

Although a planet could not be seen, this young Englishman
was convinced by his reasoning that one *must* be there. Repeatedly
he said, "There *ought* to be such a planet." So convinced was he, in
fact, that he set about calculations in abstract mathematics to
determine the precise position in the heavens that this phantom

planet had to occupy. When he completed his observations, he had arrived at a precise celestial latitude and longitude, and wrote to astronomers, saying, "Point your most powerful telescopes at the heavens to this latitude and longitude and you will see a new planet."

The astronomers did point their telescopes as the young man directed and faintly, ever so faintly, for the first time the light of the planet came into view.

For his faith, the boy got what an unrewarding world often gives its greatest: neither fame nor the credit of discovery. Although the planet was named Neptune and a Frenchman credited as its discoverer, this cannot detract from the faith of the boy who said, "There ought to be ... "

COULD A STORY OF SUCH ROMANCE and discovery be possible in staid old law, where every good and bad deed that could be done by modern man must have been done a thousand times before, his every whim, caprice, crime, and idiosyncrasy judged and rejudged and passed upon by a thousand tribunals since the world began?

There is such a story in the law. The year is 1890. It is the story of a young lawyer, then a student at Harvard Law School, a boy who was truly destined. He, too, had faith and said, "There ought to be ... "

The judges and lawyers at the turn of the century were perplexed as to whether there was any such legal right as the "right to be let alone." Could one go to court to enforce a right to be left alone if it had been infringed?

As an example, at the turn of the century, the picture of a beautiful and socially prominent young woman had been surreptitiously snapped, reproduced, and used without her consent as a trademark for a certain flower company under the slogan "The flower of the family." At a time when morals were as long as the bathing suit, young women were genuinely distressed to have their pictures appear commercially in public, and the young lady brought suit to enjoin the use of her picture and for damages.

The New York court denied her relief, and her picture continued to adorn the flower company packages, though she had given no consent, and though her anonymity and privacy were destroyed. The reason for her lack of remedy was that there had been no defamatory libel or slander. The trick picture was a true and flattering likeness. She was not held up to ridicule, nor was she maligned in any way; only her right to be let alone had been infringed.[1]

THE LAW PROVIDED a remedy for defamation, the injury of a reputation by either of the twin torts, libel or slander. Though the law of defamation has been accused of making little sense and containing "anomalies and absurdities for which no legal writer has ever had a kind word,"[2] it does preserve the right to live one's life free from false and detrimental tongue-wagging.

Libel was traditionally the tort of written defamation, and slander the tort of oral defamation, but modern media communication has made this distinction troublesome. A movie can be considered *libelous*, on the theory that a sound track physically accompanies the film.

If that seems fanciful, the debate over radio and television defamation reaches even greater heights of creative legal distinctions. Some courts say libel, some slander. Some say the decision turns on whether the material is read from a script. If the offending words are extemporaneous, they are slanderous; the words are libelous if the broadcaster is reading or reciting (which seems an absurd test since the audience frequently won't know whether or not the broadcaster is reading). Other courts say the case lies somewhere between the two and call this twentieth century tort "defamacast."[3]

Defamation is more than an insult; it is a publicized communication that holds an identifiable plaintiff up to "hatred, contempt or ridicule" in his community. It is not slander to call someone a police informer because, supposedly, only criminals would consider this an insult (although it's "true that informers are not always held in too high esteem"[4]) and it *was* slander to call someone a bootlegger during Prohibition, even though in *some* circles "where bibulousness is ever the dominant thought, and the proverbial hip pocket is seldom a vacuity, is he not recognized like Robespierre as the saviour of popular liberty?"[5]

Mere vulgarity and verbal abuse (i.e., swearing) won't do either, since they are products of personal dislike and no matter how rude, in most situations they won't injure a reputation. The law won't provide a remedy for the slings and arrows of daily life.

You may have to bear the brunt of daily insults, but not ridicule because ridicule tends to lower one's esteem in the eyes of the law.

It was defamation to use an imitation of Bert Lahr's voice as the voice of a duck in a Lestoil commercial—the "duck trespassed on plaintiff's reputation."[6] With certain kinds of defamation, however, the offended plaintiff doesn't even have to prove actual harm to his reputation. If the jury decides the communication was false and defamatory, the plaintiff wins.

The first special category of defamation that is actionable without proof of damages is falsely accusing the plaintiff of a crime. For example, it was libelous for a magazine article called "The Pill That Can Kill Sports" to accuse the Oklahoma University football team of using amphetamines during the 1956 season, since use of that drug is criminal.[7]

It is slander to call someone a queer in Texas because sodomy is a penal offense with criminal consequences more unbearable than this pun.[8]

Imputations of bestiality on the part of either sex are actionable without proven damages where such acts are criminal, even though the act charged may be a biological impossibility![9]

The particular person who has been vilified has to be the one to bring suit. A Texas court refused to allow Clyde Barrows's sister and brother to sue Warner Brothers for portraying Clyde as a homosexual and sodomist in the film *Bonnie and Clyde*.[10]

A second special category of defamation is imputation of a "loathsome disease," since in the good old days certain diseases would pretty well ensure your exclusion from most social circles. This category was usually restricted to venereal disease and leprosy, and is rarely used today. (A suggestion that someone had had venereal disease in the past never sufficed; old sins were apparently forgiven.)

The third category is defamation affecting a plaintiff's operation of his trade or profession. Thus, it is defamatory to accuse a kosher butcher of selling bacon.[11]

The last category is imputing unchastity to a woman, but the trend has been to include both sexes in this category. The rule was originally restricted to women because the courts felt a man's reputation would not suffer from such an accusation. In view of modern feelings, this defamation double standard is no doubt doomed.

IN ALL OF THESE defamation cases, the plaintiffs had been unjustly and falsely exposed to hatred or ridicule. But what could be done for the plaintiff whose solitude had been invaded and peace of mind disturbed, not from false or malicious motives but from mere curiosity or hunger for news?

It was such cases as these that caused the young law student to say "There ought to be a law." He and a fellow student prophetically wrote about this concept for an 1890 issue of *The Harvard Law Review:*

THE RIGHT TO PRIVACY

That the individual shall have full protection in person and in property is a principle as old as the common law; but it has been found necessary from time to time to define anew the exact nature and extent of such protection. Political, social, and economic changes entail the recognition of new rights, and the common law, in its eternal youth, grows to meet the demands of society.

Thus, in very early times, the law gave a remedy only for physical interference with life and property, for trespasses *vi et armis* [with force and arms]. Then the "right of life" served only to protect the subject from battery in its various forms; liberty meant freedom from actual restraint; and the right to property secured to the individual his lands and his cattle.

Later, there came a recognition of man's spiritual nature, of his feelings and his intellect. Gradually the scope of these legal rights broadened; and now the right to life has come to mean the right to enjoy life, the right to be let alone; the right to liberty secures the exercise of extensive civil privileges; and the term "property" has grown to comprise every form of possession, intangible as well as tangible.[12]

The student's name was Louis D. Brandeis, a man destined to become one of the great expounders of liberal justice on the United States Supreme Court. It was he who said more than ninety years ago "There ought to be a law."

WE JUMP FORTY YEARS to California in 1931. The student is now a justice of the United States Supreme Court. A case reaches the California Appellate Courts in which the plaintiff is the widow of Wallace Reid, the then-famous moving picture hero.

The story of Mrs. Reid's life was not one that could appear in any juvenile magazine, and the widow plaintiff freely admitted in her complaint that she had been a prostitute and had been tried for murder, but that the trial for murder had had its salutary effect, that she had given up her "life of shame," and had married Bernard Melvin (Wallace Reid).

She further alleged that after her marriage and reformation, a movie company produced a picture called *The Red Kimono*, which was an exposé of the plaintiff's life. Her maiden name was used, and her whole past revealed to her friends and to the public in general.

Mrs. Reid could not sue for libel or slander because the production was a true representation, and telling only the facts as they are is one defense to libel and slander. The plaintiff, however, complained that she had been held up to ridicule and scorn, and sought damages, not for libel or slander, but because her right to privacy, or the right to be let alone, had been infringed. The California Supreme Court upheld her complaint, saying:

> The right to pursue and obtain happiness is guaranteed to all by the fundamental law of our state. This right by its very nature includes the right to live free from the unwarranted attack of others upon one's liberty, property, and reputation. Any person living a

life of rectitude has that right to happiness, which includes a freedom from unnecessary attacks on his character, social standing, or reputation.

The use of appellant's true name in connection with the incidents of her former life in the plot and advertisements was unnecessary and indelicate and a willful and wanton disregard of that charity which should actuate us in our social intercourse and which should keep us from unnecessarily holding another up to the scorn and contempt of upright members of society.[13]

THE RIGHT TO PRIVACY is growing daily in our era of bugging, CIA and army surveillance of private citizens, microwave eavesdropping and computerized records kept by electronic Big Brothers on millions of Americans.

Congress tried to remedy these wholesale invasions of privacy by the Freedom of Information Act[14] and the Privacy Act,[15] which guarantee each citizen the right to know exactly what kind of information "the system" has about him. These acts have been extremely powerful weapons in the fight against unwarranted government intrusion into our private lives. The Freedom of Information Act provides for attorney's fees if an agency refuses to disclose the information it has on an individual.

Although the right of privacy has been recognized by Congress and the Supreme Court, snooping and prying by the media, the government, and the private intermeddler continues. (The Supreme Court recently refused to enjoin U. S. Army surveillance of private citizens because the plaintiffs couldn't show any actual harm to themselves.)[16]

OF COURSE ONE MAY LOSE the right to privacy in direct proportion to the fame and prominence he has achieved in this world. Certainly, politicians and public figures of prominence can't claim a violation to their right of privacy in most instances. For them, photographs, articles, and interviews are the tools of their trade.

I remember staying at the Georges Cinque Hotel in Paris with Errol Flynn. I wanted him to go to a tailor with me one morning. He said, "No, I can't. I'd be mauled by autograph hunters." I said, "Maybe I can stop them." He answered in feigned shock, "What, and spoil my livelihood?"

However, some people have sought to achieve "the man of mystery" attitude despite their prominence by refusing interviews, photographs, and the like (as did Howard Hughes). Prominence, however, is a privilege people have sought, and this may be the reason the world demands they accept the bad with the good and realize they may have lost their right to anonymity.

Thus, the widow of the very prominent Colonel Atkinson, upon his death, sued to prevent a cigar concern from selling cigars under the trade name of "Colonel Atkinson Cigars."

It was true, as she alleged in her complaint, that the cigar firm took the name "Colonel Atkinson" without her consent or the consent of the late Colonel, but the court held that there was no libel or slander, and there could be no right to this prominent person's privacy. Long after the Colonel's death his face and name appeared upon a brand of cigar labeled "His Favorite," a brand that he may never have smoked.

A CONVICTED GANGSTER once sought to prevent the portrayal of his life in a series of radio thrillers. The court denied him relief on somewhat the same theory, that he was a public character and the notorious accounts of his convictions were public record.

In these "public record" cases, the layman feels that if he has been erroneously arrested, his charge dismissed, and his "slate wiped clean," he is entitled to have his rogue's gallery portrait and fingerprints returned. However, this is not the case.

It has been held that an innocent person, arrested through mistake, has no *right* to have the record of his arrest made under statutory authority cancelled. However, this record states that the person in question was merely arrested and not convicted and this record is in no sense false. (Some states now have statutes that provide for expungement of criminal records under certain conditions of good behavior.)

As to persons who have been convicted of crime, their photographs and descriptions are properly circulated, and the courts will not necessarily order the destruction of such photographs and descriptions even after a pardon.

The relation to the public of one who has been convicted of crime is such as to forfeit his right of privacy, at least to the extent that the protection of society requires such forfeiture. But if the use of the photographs or description is wanton or malicious, it is actionable. Prior to a person's conviction, however, it has been held that that person's picture should not be placed in the rogue's gallery.

Upon like reasoning, i.e., the price of fame, underwear manufacturers, chocolate makers, and face powder purveyors have successfully used the names of prominent people and colleges without redress. However, another question may seriously intervene and this is one of property right, which the manufacturer may have to buy to feel secure.

SO THE RIGHT TO PRIVACY is a daily struggle. Each volume of the law reports brings new decisions of its enhanced use by harassed people.

Oddly enough, this legal right that grew out of a story of great romance finds a more common application in a most unromantic and practical business, the business of that villain, seemingly without soul, heart, or morals—the collection agent and his entourage of legal bloodhounds.

We have seen that while truth is a defense in libel and slander, the right to privacy may intervene. What about the collection of money? How far may the creditor go when money is actually owed?

A Washington court said, "The law does not countenance forceful and unlawful collection even of just debts."[17]

For the rules in the following cases the debtor may thank Justice Brandeis. In the Washington case just quoted, the creditor had threatened the debtor with assault, seduction, larceny, and other crimes. The creditor, instead of being the plaintiff, became the defendant and was convicted by the court of blackmail, the court saying, "One can commit this crime even though he is of the opinion that the money is actually due him."

But suppose a creditor takes a gun and holds up his debtor, robbing him only of the amount of money that he owes the creditor. Is this robbery?

A Texas court said no, and reversed just such a conviction for assault with intent to commit robbery where the testimony was that the robber had demanded payment at the point of a pistol only of the sum that he claimed and believed to be due, and threatened the debtor with bodily harm, if he did not pay.[18] (This procedure is not recommended.)

Dr. Morgan of Kentucky, on his way to the office one morning was startled to see the following sign in a store window:

> Notice. Dr. Morgan owes an account here of $49.67. If promises would pay an account, this account would have been settled long ago. This account will be advertised as long as it remains unpaid.

The sign was entirely on the property of the creditor, and there was no question that the good doctor owed the amount claimed. But the doctor felt that while the account might truly be owing and consequently that he could not sue for libel or slander, there ought to be some remedy for this embarrassment.

Dr. Morgan hired a lawyer (for more than the cost of the account) and took his case to court. The doctor stated that "My right of privacy has been infringed...decidedly." The court agreed with him, and awarded him judgment for a much larger amount than the bill, saying that the account was a *private* matter between the debtor and the creditor, in which the public had no interest. A creditor cannot usually *publicize* his debtor's delinquencies.[19]

Nonetheless, Mayor Kevin White of Boston conducted the most widely publicized collection campaign possible. On September 8, 1977, he appeared on local television flanked by large displays labelled "Professional Tax Delinquents." On each display was emblazoned the name and logo of a corporation owing city taxes, including Penn Central Railroad, Eastern Airlines, and even a state senator. The national media picked up the story and the debtor's names were publicized nationwide, including names of former debtors who had mended their ways by paying up.

Fortunately for the mayor, the traditional sovereign immunity of government officials may protect him from the lawsuits that are surely lurking around his corner.

Then there are the cases in which the collection agency, blocked by direct methods, and with more ingenuity than finesse, takes to the mails. The plan may backfire, however. A New York telephone operator had neglected a bill far beyond the first of the month and a credit clothing house wrote a letter to her employer that said "Frankly speaking, the only basis upon which we extended credit to your employee was the fact that she was a person in your employ, from each of whom you require a certain standard of honesty."

The telephone operator brought suit upon this letter and a jury awarded her not only $1,500 actual damages, but $500 punitive damages as well. (Big money in those days).

Another method that infringes on Mr. John Doe's right to be let alone is the "accompanying list" type of subtle collection. A secretary of a New York board of trade sent a letter to a debtor demanding that unless he paid his bill, notice of nonpayment would be sent to "Our Membership—See Accompanying List." There followed a long and imposing list of names of New York businessmen that read like a "Who's Who" in the commercial world.

New York has a statute that makes it a criminal offense to send letters with "intent thereby to cause annoyance." The secretary was convicted under that statute, the court holding that the threat to send the debtor's name to the accompanying list of people was made to annoy as well as to effectuate payment. (In other states, even without such a statute, a civil suit might lie under the cases cited above if mental suffering resulted.)

Sometimes the collection agency by subterfuge indicates that it has already draped the majesty of the court's robes about its shoulders. In the language of the legal community, this is known as "simulating legal process." Thus a Minnesota attorney was suspended for six months for sending out a form across the top of which was printed in large black type "Advance and File Notice Before Suit, Garnishment, Levy and Sale." The names of the creditor and debtor were written as in a title of a court case, and they were designated as plaintiff and defendant. The attorney's name was subscribed at the bottom of the paper and opposite this was a red seal of a size that would have done credit to any court clerk. Said the court: "Nothing resembling this practice will be tolerated. The use of a notice simulating legal process in the collection of debts is wrongful."[20]

Closely akin to this problem is that of corporations practicing law. It has been held that attorneys lending their names to collection agencies so that the collection agency can itself practice law, is not only a civil but a criminal offense. Furthermore, attorneys who prepare forms for collection agencies, leaving blanks for these agencies so that the clerks may fill them in, are themselves guilty of a serious breach of professional ethics.

IN CASES IN WHICH the creditor decides to carry the ball straight through the line relying upon force rather than deception, the law meets force with force. Such a case was that involving a dentist at Logan, Utah. This overzealous individual had repaired a dental plate for a female patient. She put the plate in her mouth and handed him less than the amount he claimed due, whereupon the dentist became abusive and excited, and finally locked the doors to his office, saying that the woman could not leave unless she left her money or her teeth. Finally, he shook his fist at her and telephoned the town marshal.

Upon the advice of the marshal, the patient left the teeth, went out and got the additional money, paid the dentist in full, and received her teeth back. However, from the excitement, she became nervous and sick, and as a result suffered a miscarriage a few days later. She brought suit against the dentist for false imprisonment and the court awarded her a judgment for both punitive and compensatory damages.[21]

Then there's the case of the kind-hearted dentist. In 1929 Dr. Kennedy of New York made dentures for the plaintiff's upper and lower jaws. As her jaws shrunk from age he made necessary alterations. At the end of two years he had the temerity to ask the plaintiff for the balance of her bill.

Such affrontry amazed her. Tears, curses, and letters to dental associations followed. Here's a sample: "Most of the presidents (of dental associations) only bathe themselves in the honor of the position, making every bid they can for popularity and use the office for their aggrandizement—consider our bar associations, their feeble efforts wind up in a fizzle but if those associations really exerted themselves, hundreds of lawyers would get their walking papers and the open challenges to the competence of judges would be less." That's just a sample.

This activity of the plaintiff culminated in 1934 when she not only refused to pay the balance but sued for the money she had already paid, claiming the dentures had never fit.

A sympathetic jury awarded her every cent.

What won the case was a kind-hearted offer from the dentist in 1931 to again fix her teeth free of charge if she would not bother him further. The New York Supreme Court construed that as a tacit admission of liability by the defendant that the teeth didn't fit.

Justice Bonynge's was the only dissent: "From Biblical times, or before, good men and true have paid money or sought acquittances in order to get rid of pestiferous women. The defendant had experienced one Niagara of tears and had no stomach for any more."

ANOTHER EFFECTIVE COLLECTION tactic was the gruesome action indulged in by a Washington undertaker to collect his bill. A Mrs. Gadbury had engaged the undertaker to conduct the funeral and bury the body of her son. For this he was paid in full. However, her son-in-law had died about fifteen months prior to this and this account was still owing.

Several weeks after the funeral of Mrs. Gadbury's son, the undertaker drove up to Mrs. Gadbury's home and told her that he was there to collect for the funeral of her son-in-law. On being told by Mrs. Gadbury that she did not consider herself responsible for this account, the undertaker said that he was still holding the uncremated body of her son and would hold it until the bill for her son-in-law was paid.

Of course Mrs. Gadbury had thought that her son's body had already been cremated and she had just begun to recover from the grief caused by his death. This news caused her to become severely ill and affected her health.

Finally, after friends had importuned the undertaker to cremate the body of the son, he did so. When Mrs. Gadbury brought suit against the undertaker, he pleaded a peculiar rule of law that was applicable years past, viz: That damages are not recoverable for mental suffering unaccompanied by actual physical contact. However, the Supreme Court of Washington announced a distinction, saying that "If such suffering is the direct result of a *willful* wrong as distinguished from one that is merely *negligent*, then there may be a recovery."[22]

The amorous railroad conductor who rained kisses upon the proper young school teacher cost his company $1,000 compensatory damages for her "terror and anguish, her outraged feeling and insulted virtue, her mental humiliation and suffering."[23] Two thousand dollars was the award in a case in which a hotel manager came to the plaintiff's room one night and accused her of being a "common prostitute," although in fact the gentleman who had come to visit her was her husband.[24] (Note that these were willful, not negligent, acts.)

Of course every father has heard the story that he would not be allowed to take junior home from the hospital until he had paid the stork's bill. However, if the hospital actually attempted this, the officers thereof might well be charged with false imprisonment or even kidnapping. Indeed, in an Alabama case, southern hospitality worked in reverse and damages of $1,500 were allowed to a patient who was about to leave the hospital and was detained eleven hours for nonpayment of his bill.[25]

In two contrasting cases, dissimilar in facts but identical as to the right infringed, the courts of Maine and Maryland reached opposite results. This is, however, not unusual in a country where decisions can be as various as the state boundaries and particularly in a growing field of law.

In the Maine case,[26] a newspaper negligently published the wrong photograph in connection with a true news item announcing the death of a person named therein. The mother of the person whose picture appeared suffered greatly from the shock but recovery was denied.

However, in the Maryland case,[27] the defendants had negligently permitted a dead rat to be wrapped up in a package of groceries and delivered to the plaintiff. Here damages *were* awarded for the resultant shock.

Wouldn't it seem reasonable that the shock of hearing of the death of one's son must be more severe than the learning of the demise of an unknown rat?

What about the cases of the practical joker who infringes upon what might be termed the "right to complacency"?

In an English case,[28] the defendant was held liable for a woman's mental suffering when he told her, as a practical joke, that her husband had been "smashed in an auto accident." In another case in which the practical joker had told someone other than the wife that the husband had "hanged himself" and this report later reached the wife through the tongues of gossipers, the practical joker was held liable.[29]

When gentle Miss Nickerson visited a Shreveport fortune teller and was advised she would soon find a pot of gold, twin fires of romance and finance were kindled in her spinster heart.

The mystic sold her a map (part of his trade), and she started digging. Fervently and eagerly though she dug, days passed without finding so much as a pirate's note.

Several practical jokers, seeing only the brave smiling face and not knowing how piteously low the fires burned within, provided a pot of gold for the fortune hunter: They filled an old copper kettle with rocks and wet dirt and buried it near where Miss Nickerson was digging. A note, wrapped in tin, was fastened to the pot and dated 1784. "Do not open for three days—notify all heirs," it said.

The pot was to have been found April first, but Miss Nickerson was so busily digging elsewhere that she did not get to it until April 14. What excitement when her shovel gave a metallic clang; what tears of joy came to her eyes as she tremblingly hauled to the surface the deceptively heavy old kettle.

Her eager eyes blazed when she read the note. True to pirate ethics she kept faith, took the "gold" to the bank for safekeeping, called the heirs.

Everyone in town knew of the joke save the poor old woman. All were present when the bank opened the kettle. Miss Nickerson seemed to age a thousand years in that minute. There lay all her dreams unwrapped and crumbled in dirt. Yet how they roared with laughter, the bankers, the doctors, the lawyers, and the others.

Her mind slowly began to crumble, then her body, like her gold. Two years later she died.

Before she died, Miss Nickerson's lawyer brought suit for her shock and humiliation, asking $15,000 damages. Once again the poor little lady missed her pot of gold for the Supreme Court of Louisiana, where the case finally went, said, had she been living, they would have allowed her the $15,000 damages. Since only her heirs lived, $500 was the damage allowed.[30]

Yet Miss Nickerson's case is a warning to all practical jokers: If their subject lives longer than poor Miss Nickerson, he or she may have the last laugh.

TODAY THE RIGHT TO PRIVACY has expanded into a broad protection against all sorts of emotional indignities visited upon all sorts of plaintiffs, famous, notorious, or John Does.

Concomitant physical injury is no longer always required, nor is any intent to harm the victim. Even a careless gesture or thoughtless word may be cause to sue for "negligent infliction of emotional distress." And the famous do not lose their rights altogether; even in the limelight there are limits to what one must pay for fame.

Jackie Onassis has some right to privacy. Ron Galella, a *paparazzo* free-lance photographer, made it his mission in life to photograph Jackie and her children. Wherever they went, no matter where they turned, Galella was there—following in speedboats, jumping in front of her children's bikes, bribing restaurant employees, romancing her servants.

Although Jackie couldn't claim that *use* of her picture was unwarranted, since she was so famous as to be within the public domain, she *could* claim that Galella's manner of photography was so obnoxious that it amounted to invasion even of her privacy.

The court agreed, and Galella was enjoined from coming within twenty-five feet of Jackie and from any further harassing or annoying picture-taking.[31]

WHAT ABOUT OUR cherished "freedom of the press"? Can we allow huge libel judgments against newspapers for merely slipping up on detail or two? After all, newspapers are the backbone of free speech and press, and they report thousands of items a day. Chances are pretty good that someone will overlook a copy error now and then. How can we protect the press and at the same time compensate someone wrongly presented?

The Supreme Court provided the answer to this question in a case involving the *New York Times*. In 1960 the civil rights struggle was raging in the South. A group of activists paid for a full-page ad in the *Times* that accused Montgomery, Alabama, police of teargassing students on the state capitol steps. L. B. Sullivan was the Montgomery commissioner in charge of the police and he sued for libel.

The United States Supreme Court decided that protection of a free press reporting on events of public interest involving public officials was more important that Sullivan's feelings.[32]

The rule, and it is law today, was that a newspaper must be responsible for actual malice and gross disregard of the facts before a public figure can recover.

Even though the ad was not totally correct, the error was unintentional on the part of the *Times* and Sullivan's judgment was reversed. Simple negligence, the old law, is no longer enough when a public figure seeks to sue for his claimed defamation.

Thus privacy and press struggle on, the right of a free press versus the right to be let alone. The recent contests over the Pentagon Papers and the Nixon tapes are living examples. In these and many other areas the right to be let alone is constantly being applied. Countless individuals have benefited from this right since it was presented by a farsighted law student who felt "There ought to be a law."

Notes

1. As a result of this case, New York passed and now has one of the most stringent "right to be let alone" laws in the United States.

2. Prosser, *Law of Torts*, §111 (4th ed. 1971).

3. Ibid. §112; 50 Am. Jur.2d, Libel and Slander §5; *American Broadcasting-Paramount Theatres, Inc. v. Simpson*, 106 Ga. App. 230, 126 S. E. 2d 873 (1962).

4. *Connelly v. McKay*, 28 N. Y. S. 2d 327, 176 Misc. 685 (1941).

5. *In re Kirk*, 101 N. J. L. 450, 130 A. 569 (1925).
Curtis Publishing Co. v. Birdsong, 360 F. 2d 344 (1966).

6. *Lahr v. Adell Chemical Co.*, 300 F. 2d 256 (1962).
Tidmore v. Mills, 33 Ala. App. 243, 32 S. 2d 769 (1947).

7. *Fawcett Publications Inc. v. Morris*, 377 P. 2d 42 (Okla. 1962).

8. *Buck v. Savage*, 323 S. W. 2d 363 (Tex. Civ. App. 1959).

9. 50 Am. Jur. 2d, *Libel and Slander*, §70 at 575.

10. *Keys v. Interstate Circuit Inc.*, 468 S. W. 2d 485 (Tex. Civ. App. 1971).

11. *Braun v. Armour & Co.*, 254 N.Y. 514, 173 N. E. 845 (1930).

12. S. Warren & L. Brandeis, *The Right to Privacy*, 4 Harv. L. Rev. 193 (1890).

13. *Melvin v. Reid*, 112 C. A. 291, 297 P. 91 (1931).

14. 5 U. S. C. 552.

15. 5 U. S. C. 552(a).

16. *Laird v. Tatum*, 408 U. S. 1, 92 S. Ct. 2318 (1972).

17. *State v. Richards*, 97 Wash. 581, 167 P. 47 (1917).

18. *Barton v. State*, 88 Tex. Cr. Rep. 368 (1921).

19. *Brents v. Morgan*, 221 Ky. 765, 299 S. W. 967 (1927).

20. *In re Dows*, 163 Minn. 6, 209 N. W. 627 (1926).

21. *Salisbury v. Paulson*, 51 Utah 552, 172 P. 315 (1918).

22. *Gadbury v. Bleitz*, 133 Wash. 134, 233 P. 299 (1925).

23. *Croker v. Chicago & N. W. R. R.*, 36 Wisc. 657 (1875).

24. *Emmke v. De Silva*, 293 F. 17 (1923).

25. *Gasden Gen. Hosp. v. Hamilton*, 212 Ala. 531, 103 So. 553 (1925).

26. *Herrick v. Evening Express Publishing Co.*, 120 Me. 138, 113 A. 16 (1921).

27. *Great Atl. & Pac. Tea Co. v. Rock*, 160 Md. 189, 153 A. 22 (1936).

28. 2 O.B. 57, 123 Engl. Rep. 45 (1968).

29. *Bielitski v. Obadiak*, 65 D. L. R. 627 (1922).

30. *Nickerson v. Hodges*, 146 La. 735, 84 S. 37 (1920).

31. *Galella v. Onassis*, 487 F. 2d 986 (1973).

32. *New York Times Co. v. Sullivan*, 376 U. S. 254,84 S. Ct. 710 (1964).

13
Animals and Objects in Court

ALTHOUGH IT WOULD BE a preposterous sight to see Uncle Sam in court actually suing a barrel of whiskey, nevertheless many cases have been entered in the law books with such titles as *United States* v. *One Barrel of Whiskey*.[1] Not without history and logic, the whiskey is considered the wrongdoer, and, while it cannot be sentenced to jail, this is one instance in which spirits may be subdued and confiscated.

One ship collides with another; the owners do not sue, the ships do. The suit appears as *The Spray* v. *The Mary Jones*. The ship is considered the actor, the wrongdoer, regardless of the fault of the captain or owner.[2]

More legal black magic? Not at all. Let us trace the origins of the whiskey barrel's and the ships' suits.

To early man, all the world was vividly animate. In ancient Greece, lightning was the anger of a god, and morning and love were goddesses. Mountains too were gods, and trees and marble pillars were minor gods. Everything was thought to possess a mind and a soul and was consequently responsible for its acts.

Thus, when a marble pillar fell upon an ancient Greek, the pillar was brought to trial for its misdeed.[3] Since it could not speak, a public defender was assigned to defend it. An elaborate jury trial was held,[4] and if the pillar (or rock or tree) was found guilty, it suffered the punishment of being cast into the sea or banished forevermore to a foreign land. Counsel for the pillar no doubt remained unpaid.

THIS CHILDISH DISPOSITION to punish inanimate objects and irrational creatures, which is common to the infancy of individuals and of races, has left a distinct trace of itself in a peculiar institution of English law known as *deodand* and derived partly from Jewish and partly from old German usages and traditions: "If a horse," says Blackstone, "or any other animal, of its own motion, kill as well an infant as an adult or if a cart run over him, they shall in either case be forfeited as deodand."

In the archives of Maryland, mention is made of an inquest held as late as January 31, 1637, upon the body of a planter, who "by the fall of a tree had his bloud bulke broken. . . . And furthermore the jurors aforesaid upon their oath aforesaid say that the said tree moved to the death of the said John Bryand; and therefore find the said tree forfeited to the Lord Proprietor."

Until Queen Victoria's time, the common law required the thing that caused injury to be forfeited to the crown, and, if of value, to be distributed by the chief almoner among the poor.

This led to the rule that the worth of a deadly weapon must be set forth in the indictment for if it be not forfeited, then its value must. From this, there remains the present law that the weapon must be described with particularity.

It is true, as Blackstone asserts, that the church claimed deodands as its due and put the price of them into its own coffers; but this fact does not explain their origin. They were an expression of the same feeling that led the public authorities to fill in a well in which a person had been drowned, not as a precautionary measure, but as a solemn act of expiation; or that condemned and confiscated a ship, which, by lurching, had thrown a man overboard and caused his death.

When I was in Lasha, Tibet, recently, my guides told me the Tibetans were against capital punishment but they also told me that the birth of twins was evil. One was drowned. It was the *water* that was the executioner, not the people.

A NIMALS WERE LIKEWISE tried in ancient and comparatively modern courts upon the same theory as inanimate objects that they, the actual wrongdoers, were responsible for their own wrongdoing. We may smile as we read the following cases and consider the subtleties and quiddities of medieval theologians, but the importance attached to these trivialities was not so much the peculiarity of a single profession as the mental habit of the age, the result of scholastic training and scholastic methods of investigation, which tainted law no less than they did theology and medicine.[5] Then, too, we should not be intolerant of man's gropings in the past, for today's best legal procedures may be as heartily laughed at in the year 2000.[6]

For the lawyer, there are many roads to fame, but none as ingenious as that of the great French advocate, Bartholomew Chassenee, who, in 1522 in his first case, successfully defended all the rats of the French village of Autun.

Since the rats had committed the crime of destroying the crops, they were duly summoned into court to explain their actions. Chassenee was appointed to defend them.

He objected to the summons on the ground that since the case involved the reputation of all the rats nearby, the summons were of too local a character. This point was argued with all the seriousness a case commands before the United States Supreme Court today. The court ruled in favor of the rats on this first point. Delay was granted.

The summons were changed and deputies were dispatched to all the districts to read in a loud voice, so all the rats might hear, that "each and every, all and singular rats" were ordered to appear in court under penalty of death for disobedience to the court summons. Still no rats came.

The great defender then pleaded for an extension of time and again gained it on the grounds that since great preparations were needed by so many rats to put their homes in order, and to make arrangements to have their many children taken care of before leaving for what no doubt would be a long and protracted trial, they should be granted more time. Still no rats.

Then counsel for the defense delivered his final and unanswerable plea. He cited authority for the proposition that witnesses, while under summons, were protected while coming to and from the court. A great many cats were about, he argued, and his clients were afraid of summary execution before trial, and stood upon their "constitutional rights."

Chassenee then demanded of the plaintiffs, many of whom kept cats, that they post a bond to assure that their cats would do no harm to the rats. This the plaintiffs were unwilling to do, for they feared that perhaps their cats would not respect the sanctity of judicial process.

The judges were as perplexed, though not from the same cause, as present readers of this court record must be; but they could do no more and adjourned *sine die* (without assigning another date for the case), Chassenee having won the case to his everlasting fame.

Chassenee became one of the most famous lawyers of the Middle Ages.[7] His specialty? The trial of animals. He even wrote a learned treatise with all the intricate legal procedure for trying animals. This book was used as a handbook until comparatively modern times and was as revered as is *Wigmore on Evidence* today.

F ROM BASLE, SWITZERLAND (1474), comes the strange case of the rooster that laid an egg.

Now a rooster's egg was of inestimable value to sorcerers as containing magic of all sorts and potency. It was the principal ingredient of witch ointment and, when hatched by a serpent or toad or by the heat of the sun, it brought forth a basilisk that would hide in the roof of the house and, with its baneful breath and "death-darting" eyes, destroy all the inmates. Therefore, the devil surely must have employed the cock to lay the egg, and the cock was really in for trouble.

On behalf of the no doubt already bewildered rooster, who must have been sufficiently astonished and punished by the herculean feat of egg-laying alone (if indeed he did), counsel claimed that there was neither intent nor premeditation proved, and further-more, that no one was injured.

However, the state's attorney held that the cock had entered a compact with the devil.

Not to be outdone, the cock's lawyer demanded that the contract be put in evidence. The attorney, naturally, could not produce the document.

The court was packed against the poor rooster, however, and it was held that the devil had entered the rooster even though the defendant fowl did not so desire.[8] The poor cock was thereupon found guilty and burned at the stake, the punishment for heresy, with all judicial solemnity, accompanied by his egg.[9] (Is it any wonder that so many humans were burned at the stake and capitally punished when such feelings of vengeance and retribu-tion were evidenced even against animals and inanimate things?)

But the incident did not end there. The executioner alleged that upon cutting open the poor cock he found three more eggs inside "him."

THROUGH ALL THESE CASES ran the reasoning that the animals, even as the Greek pillar, were cognitive beings, somehow responsible for their actions. Villagers troubled by pests sought their relief in the ecclesiastical courts, for the obvious reason that the church could mete out punishment in the absence of the defendants—the punishment of excommunication and heresy.

The inhabitants of the infested town drew up their formal petitions and presented them to the court. The petitions were examined with great care and if the reasons were sufficient, an advocate was designated by the court to defend the accused. Summons were issued by the duly appointed officer of the court and were served by reading the same to the animals if they could be found, and if not, then read in the open fields.

After the summons were read three times, judgment went against the animals by default if they failed to appear. It was recorded as unusual that many judgments were by default. After judgment, a writ was issued warning the animals to leave upon pain of excommunication or death.

It is recorded that cases were "continued over" many times, the court not being desirous to force the issue of appearance because of the disrespect engendered by a judgment unenforced.

In the sixteenth century at the village of Saint Julien in France, a speedy conviction resulted against insects overrunning the vineyards. Judgment went unexecuted for more than a year and the villagers, complaining of the law's delays, were told to pay more tithes to the church and pray.

The insects disappeared but returned in forty-one years. This time the trial was so long it covered twenty-nine books, which are still to be seen in the village archives. Sentence was never executed; a compromise was reached granting an exclusive plot of land to the pests by judicial decree.

In 1394 a pig was found guilty of "having killed and murdered a child in the parish of Roumaygne, in the county of Mortaing, for which deed the said pig was condemned to be halved and hanged by Jehan Petit, lieutenant of the bailiff." The work was really done by the hangman, Jehan Micton, who received for his services the sum of "fifty sous tournois."

In 1499 a bear that had ravaged Schwarzwald villages came up for trial defended by a lawyer as able as Chassenee. The lawyer insisted upon a trial by a jury of the bear's peers. A delay of more than a week was occasioned because of this technicality.

In 1609 a cow had the distinction of being convicted by no less a body than the Parliament of Paris. Even Mrs. O'Leary's cow did not attain such distinction.[10]

As late as 1713, a swarm of ants in Brazil were charged with undermining cellars and carrying off flour from storerooms.

Counsel was appointed to represent them and the case was heard before a church court sitting in the monastery of Saint Anthony. The verdict was pronounced in open court by one of the friars; it was against the ants.

And fifty-five years later at Nismes, in Languedoc, a donkey was tried for the crime of sacrilege. The animal had drunk holy water from a basin in the church. Counsel pleaded in vain for the donkey but the defendant was hanged on the gibbet. The costs were borne by its owner, a gardener.

To carry the fiction of criminal responsibility in condemned animals still further, the animals were tried and executed only after they had been dressed in the wearing apparel of the times according to the sex.[11] On March 15, 1403, the bailiff of Nantes and Meullant presented a bill that contained the following items of expense incurred for the incarceration and execution of an infanticidal sow:

> Cost of keeping her in jail, six sols parisis.
>
> Item, To the master of high works, who came from Paris to Meullant to perform the said execution by command and authority of the said bailiff, our master, and of the procurator of the king, fifty-four sols parisis.
>
> Item, for a carriage to take her to justice, six sols parisis.
>
> Item, for cords to bind and hale her, two sols eight deniers parisis.
>
> Item, for gloves, two deniers parisis.[12]

Brutes and human criminals were confined in the same prison and subjected to the same treatment. One of the old records of account shows that the jailer charged "two deniers tournois a day," for boarding a pig accused of murdering a child, the same as for boarding a man, thus placing the porker, even in respect to its maintenance, on a footing of perfect equality with the human prisoners. He also puts into the account "ten deniers tournois for a rope, found and furnished for the purpose of tying the said pig that it might not escape!" In regard to imprisonment humankind has not much improved. When I was in Vietnam trying military cases, I visited many of the Viet native jails. The animals and men were locked up closely together, sometimes sleeping with heads on each other.

A NIMALS WERE ALSO competent witnesses in court. The barking of a dog, the crowing of a rooster, or the braying of an ass, when an accused was brought into its presence, was accepted as valid testimony from a reasoning being.[13] Today, dogs are competent witnesses, having sniffed out drugs in defendants' baggage.

Only the crow of a rooster could adjourn the original "night court" of Essex, England. This court heard petty collection cases and for more than 300 years met annually at midnight of the Wednesday following Michaelmas Day. The court session could not legally end until a rooster's shrill chanticleer was heard at daybreak.

Such bestial barristry was not unknown in the United States. Smoking was prohibited by Indiana law. To the wealth of himself and the amusement of the crowd, an organ grinder once allowed his monkey to smoke cigarettes. When the case came to court it was explained in defense that the poor monkey did not know the law. The judge correctly ruled that "ignorance of the law is no excuse" and found the monkey guilty.

An attending lawyer was said to have commented that he had heard of men being tried by men and animals being tried by men but this was the first time he had ever heard of a monkey being convicted by an ass.

The ass or the pig being executed in its dumb bewilderment may now be pitied by us. But aren't we just as cruel and stupid today, when we suggest, as did Ed Meese, one of Mr. Reagan's assistants, recently, that the insane should be capitally punished? They too, truly bewildered, know no more than the ancient condemned ass and pig.

THE RIGHTS OF ANIMALS, and the people to whom they belong, have been controversial in more modern times as well. As long as Bill Smith kept his five cats, no one bothered him, but when Bill, unwilling to await the natural increase of his feline friends, bought three more, trouble descended. Trouble in this case assumed the form of Chief of Police Steineuf and Bill landed in jail.

He had violated an ordinance of the sovereign state of Kansas that made it a crime for anyone to keep more than five cats. In fact, by having eight, he had violated the ordinance three times.

Now Bill loved cats, and having read that in 1865 a French judge had started a notable line of decisions by calling cats property, Bill came into the Supreme Court of Kansas with a writ of habeas corpus saying that he had been deprived of his property without due process of law.

First, the Supreme Court of Kansas examined the purported reasons for the passage of the ordinance and determined they were two-fold, olfactory and auditory.

As to reason one, said the court, "Not so long ago everyone kept driving horses in stables next to their homes and, especially in certain kinds of weather, characteristic odors would be quite pervading." If horses, why not cats?

As to reason two, said the court:

> What makes a cat a nuisance? The city resorts to the analogy of the dog—noise, stench, and lack of privacy of conduct in the mating season.
>
> In framing the ordinance, the city applied the principle of classification by numbers; five cats, no nuisance; six cats, nuisance. Surely none but the most sensitive ear and nose could tell the difference and the difference may not be determined on the basis of what may offend the fastidious.

So the problem of nuisance or no nuisance was solved as if according to the following mathematical formula: X equals maximum amount of nuisance ordinary folks must endure. To find the value of X, multiply the quantity of discomfort one cat produces by five. This computation gives the cat the benefit of the doubt, because the increment produced by associate relation is disagreeable.[14]

Since the court determined the ordinance was unreasonable in its classification limiting ownership to five cats, the petitioner's writ of habeas corpus was granted.

AMONG THE ANCIENT BRITONS (as among the Egyptians) the cat had an honorable and valued rank. He was the guardian of the king's granary. Any person guilty of killing a cat forfeited to the king an amount of wheat equal to the size of the cat.

The law provided the method of measurement: "Let the cat be hung by the tip of its tail with its head touching the floor and let the grains of wheat be poured upon it until the extremity of its tail be covered."

But in later law, when the theft of anything of value was punishable with death, the cat lost its rank and consequent protection. The test of value for animals became a gastronomic one. Was the cat edible? No. So out of the frying pan into the fire went the cat: not edible, no value, no protection. It was no crime therefore to kill or steal a cat.

Though the modern rule is that cats are valuable property, and protected by the law as such, a cat owner may not intercede in a fight between a cat and a dog if his cat is the aggressor. After noting that "there is a natural antipathy between the cat and the dog, the very presence of a cat in the wake of a dog is a challenge, an insult, a bait, and an enticement," a Tennessee court said:

This is an action in which the plaintiff seeks to recover for the unlawful killing of a hound dog who honorably bore the name of Speed.... The specific defense urged is that at the time Speed met his untimely fate, he was unlawfully and feloniously assaulting a member of the defendant's household, to wit, a Thomas Cat.

We are bound to take notice of the instincts as well as the outstinks of all animals.... Mr. Thomas Cat had no business being away from home. He should, like men, have kept his toes around the domestic hearth. He was evidently out for a fight. It seems plain that he had left his home for a "felineous" purpose of raising a row or creating a disturbance.

The court is satisfied that on the particular night in question, when Thomas Cat approached the path down which Speed was traveling, he bowed his back and growled and spit in the dog's face. That was necessarily a "felineous" assault on the part of the cat.

No power under heaven could have restrained Speed from pursuing Thomas Cat after this indignity—judgment against Mr. Thomas Cat's owner.

WHEN SOMEONE CRIED "RAT," Paulina Del Rosso did what any normal woman is supposed to do—she jumped on a table. But in jumping she fell and received severe injuries, about which she complained in the Massachusetts Supreme Court.[15]

Miss Del Rosso testified that she was, up until the time someone cried "rat," enjoying the food at defendant Woolworth's lunch counter. Out from the kitchen charged the offending rodent and scampered under the lunch counter.

Whether he had himself decided to eat at the counter instead of in the kitchen we are not told. However, such an answer is not even necessary for Mr. Rat ultimately decided not to eat at all and scampered from the store.

The law is made for humans and not for rats, otherwise Mr. Rat may well have been the plaintiff himself, suing to recover from his shock at Miss Del Rosso suddenly precipitating herself "with great force and violence" directly into his path. However, he must suffer in silence (*damnum absque injuria*, or loss without redressable injury, as the lawyers say), and at that he fared as well as did the plaintiff.

Said Chief Justice Rugg (adding insult and libel to poor Mr. Rat's injuries): "The rat is commonly recognized as an enemy of mankind. It is offensive from almost every point of view. There is nothing in this record to indicate effective and practicable means to keep occupied premises clear of this vermin."

In other words, the defendant had done everything possible to make the premises unattractive for rats. Beyond this he was not legally bound to go. In purveying his foods and delicacies for humans, he unconsciously invited the rats also.

IN THE SIXTIES AND SEVENTIES, the ancient Greek anthropomorphism of animals—and their subsequent day in court—came full circle. The environmental consciousness of the sixties gave rise to legislation protecting wildlife from extinction and abuse (laws like the Endangered Species Preservation Act, the Wild Horse and Burro Act, and the National Wildlife Refuge Act). The most creative environmental lawyers are beginning to argue —the late great Justice Douglas among them—that animals should be given standing to sue in court, assisted by human counsel, for wrongs done to them.

A thousand-year-old idea has re-emerged in the late twentieth century and is considered avant-garde.

Notes

1. In the case of *United States* v. *350 Cartons of Canned Sardines* (7595 Dis. Ct. W. Penn.), the jury returned the following verdict: ·"The jury finds a verdict in favor of the United States and recommends the mercy of the court."

2. However, the owner may be deprived of the ship for its misdeeds.

3. In 1900 at Fouchow, China, a wooden idol fell on a man, killing him. As a result, several similar wooden idols were tried, convicted of this murder, and sentenced to the punishment of beheading.

4. As many as 500 jurors could serve on the jury of ancient Greece.

5. Consider the crudity of the medical art at comparable times: Harvey did not discover the circulation of the blood until 1628; anesthetic was not used until 1846; appendicitis was invariably fatal in 1875.

6. I remember trying a case in which it took an hour to put a hypothetical question to an expert. After I finished stating the entire question, there was an objection to his answering it. This objection was argued for the balance of the day with the judge finally ruling in favor of the expert being allowed to answer. The expert's answer was "I don't know."

7. At a later period of his life, when Chassenee had risen to fame and was presiding as the head of a judicial assembly, there was discussion of exterminating all the people of a certain village, without trial, for heresy. Counsel reminded President Chassenee that he had once pleaded, as a rule of law, that even animals should not be adjudged and sentenced without trial. Chassenee, reminded of his earlier idealism, requested a decree from the king granting a trial.

8. It was cited in support that even though the swine possessed by devils (as related in the New Testament) were involuntary agents, they, nevertheless, were punished by being caused to run down a steep incline into the sea of Galilee, where they were drowned.

9. In citing this actual case to a somewhat skeptical audience, the question was asked the author if this was also the origin of the hard-boiled egg.

10. Evans, in his *Criminal Prosecution and Capital Punishment of Animals*, sets forth a remarkable compilation of animal trials showing the animal, the place of trial, and the date. The animals run all the way from caterpillars, horseflies, serpents, weevils, dolphins, eels, snails, and vermin to wolves and bears. His earliest date given is 824, his last, 1906. In the latter, a man named Marger was killed and robbed by Scherrer and his son in Switzerland with the fierce cooperation of their dog. The three murderers were tried and the two men sentenced to life-long imprisonment. But the dog, the chief culprit, without whose complicity the crime could not have been committed, was condemned to death.

11. The appropriate garments for the rooster must have perplexed the court attachés.

12. This account, which amounted in all to sixty-nine sols, eight deniers parisis, was examined and approved by the auditor of the court, De Baudemont, who affixed to it his own seal with signature and paraph and "in further confirmation and approbation thereof caused it to be sealed with the seal of the Chatellany of Meullant, on the 15th day of March in the year 1403."

13. In some islands of the South Seas, to this day, the suspects of a crime stand in a circle, a rooster is thrown into the center and him against whose leg the rooster first runs is guilty.

14. *Smith v. Steineauf*, 140 Kan. 407, 36 P. 2d 995 (1934).

15. *Del Rosso v. F. W. Woolworth*, 293 Mass. 424, 200 N. E. 277 (1936).

14

Torts and Other Tribulations

THE PERSONAL INJURY LAWYER used to be called the "ambulance chaser." But back about thirty-five years ago, NACCA, the National Association of Claimants Compensation Attorneys, was founded in Portland, Oregon. The guiding spirit was Sam Horovitz of Boston, a workmen's compensation lawyer who could have passed for Ichabod Crane. He was gentle but forceful. Above everything else, he was compassionate. That quality became the badge of the personal injury lawyer, whose image we set out to change—and did.

I joined the association a few years after it started and became one of its first presidents. It is now called ATLA, the Association of Trial Lawyers of America, and there are 50,000 of us worldwide, principally in the United States and Canada.

For the most part we try personal injury cases or torts, but we also try cases on workmen's compensation, crime, domestic relations, wills, and all sorts of other actions since, succumbing to my entreaties, the organization agreed that a well-rounded lawyer must try a variety of legal issues.

More than 50 percent of the cases tried in American courts today are personal injury or tort cases. They are glutting our courts, cases involving colliding autos (with or without alcohol or drugs); fall after fall on slippery or allegedly slippery sidewalks; injury in buses, airplanes, lurching trains, bobbing boats and any other type of personal injury or wrongful death. In all of these cases the defendant was *negligent*, for negligence is the *gravamen* of the action, or the name of the game.

In the personal injury mainstream of law, one particularly sees outmoded laws superseded. But lately one also sees the lobbying and legislative fights between two great suitors, the trial lawyer organizations for the people and the many and well-heeled insurance companies for their own special interests.

In the earliest legal cases there was no distinction between criminal and civil cases. There was the blood feud and then there was the fine assessed by the crown for damages to its peace or dignity or subjects.

We've seen the growth of civil law and the jury in chapter 2. While criminal law and civil law separated ages ago, civil law today still has, remarkably, some of the old intendments of the law of 1200 and even before.

I've never been able to understand how a lawyer could be such without knowing from whence his modern law came any more than a doctor could be less than curious in not inquiring about leeches and powdered unicorn horns and bleeding and the "standard practices" of bygone ages. A lawyer can better propose legislative changes knowing the law of 1200, from whence the present rules come.

AFTER MY INVESTITURE by *Life* magazine as the "King of Torts," I reported on personal injury or tort law in *Ready for the Plaintiff* (which is now being revised), so I will only touch lightly on this most active specialty of the law here.

Perhaps the best place to start is a decision by Judge William H. Teompkins of Rochester, New York. Every now and then one gets a literate and humorous jurist who views the modern tort action with perspicuity.

Said Judge Teompkins in his opinion of the classic automobile collision:

> The episode culminating in this engagement was an unannounced encounter between two evenly matched lightweights—a Ford and a Chevrolet. The squared circle was the intersection of Court and Chestnut streets, supposedly safeguarded by signal lights, one at each corner of the improvised ring. The hour was 1 A.M. on a gloomy drizzly morning. Each contender for the championship rushed toward his opponent, foregoing the usual preliminaries of dodging or ducking. The result was an unexpected and disastrous meeting in the center of the arena. Each took the count. There was no second round.
>
> No referee being then present, this engagement results. The challenger (plaintiff) had fortified himself with two beers. Defendants were boys homeward bound from a fraternity function via some downtown restaurant where they hoped to find sufficient appetizing vitamins to quiet the demands of growing youth till breakfast time.

Each reached the intersection at the same time and as the signal lights were changing. Defendant was going twenty-five miles an hour, too fast at that intersection on a wet street. He was negligent, said the judge.

But what did plaintiff recover? Not a cent. *He* should have *looked* for approaching cars. He didn't, and therefore he was *also* negligent. His negligence in law is called *contributory* negligence, for, no matter how slight it is, if it contributes or helps cause the accident or injury of which he complains, the plaintiff cannot recover at all.

In this, law philosophizes, but for *your* negligence, no matter how negligent your opponent was, the accident would not have happened.

In the spirit of "it takes two to tango," *comparative* negligence jurisdictions reduce your recovery in proportion to the percentage you were negligent. Where that reaches 50 percent, and you and the defendant stand equally blamed, you may recover nothing. In some jurisdictions, you may always recover to the extent of the other person's fault, even if you were more at fault. In these so-called "pure" comparative negligence states, a person who was 99 percent negligent may recover from the other for the latter's 1 percent negligence. But in contributory negligence jurisdictions, *any* negligence on your part may bar recovery. Comparative negligence is modern law, ever more tolerant of human errancy.

I tried a federal tort claim case recently in Minot, North Dakota. This type of case is a suit by someone against the federal government, which has waived its sovereignty; a federal judge hears the case and a jury is not allowed.

My young plaintiff, the son of an army sergeant, had been paralyzed on a trampoline on an army base.

The federal judge awarded $2,500,000 but cut the award to $1,500,000 because of the boy's comparative negligence. Had the tolerant judge cut the award by another 5 percent to 50 percent comparative negligence for both the plaintiff and the defendant, my plaintiff would have gotten nothing under North Dakota law, which the federal court followed.

B UT WHAT IS NEGLIGENCE? When one fails to come up to the standard of care or conduct that a "reasonable and prudent person"[1] would ordinarily have exercised under similar circumstances, he is negligent. How may one tell what this chameleonic legal myth, the "reasonable and prudent person," would have done?

The judge or the jury hears all the facts of how the defendant acted, and must then answer this question to the best of their judgment and experience (and sometimes, unfortunately, prejudice). That's the personal injury suit. If the defendant hasn't come up to the judge's or the jury's standard of the reasonable person, the verdict is for the plaintiff.

After thousands upon thousands of juries have considered as many different questions of man's capricious conduct, by precedent we now may know beforehand if certain conduct is "reasonable and prudent" and not negligent.

Of course, the standard of care the plaintiff or the defendant must exercise varies with the circumstances and the person. Thus the reasonable and prudent person may be a reasonable and prudent blind person, old person, cripple, or child. The jury decides if the litigant before them acted as a reasonable and prudent person of that class under the given circumstances.

There is no particular age at which a child is deemed wholly without capacity or fully accountable. This is generally a question for the jury. Some states have legal *presumptions* that a child below a certain age is incapable of negligence (it used to be fourteen at common law and is now five or under in California), but even these presumptions can be rebutted in some cases.

For example, a boy of fifteen purchased gunpowder from the defendant and constructed a toy cannon. The cannon exploded and the boy was injured. In a suit against the store that sold the gunpowder, the Supreme Court of California held that the boy was old enough to appreciate the danger of explosives and was responsible (not *guilty* since that's a criminal term) of contributory negligence as a matter of law. He could not recover for the negligent sale.[2] Now with comparative negligence, California would just reduce the verdict for the plaintiff boy the amount of his negligence.

In another California case, an eight-and-a-half-year-old girl suddenly ran from the curb out into the street to retrieve an article. She was struck by a speeding automobile. No recovery. The court held that she was old enough to be responsible for contributory negligence as a matter of law.

Other California cases have held that children of four and three-and-a-half cannot be negligent as a matter of law. That is presumably because, as we all know, there is no such child as the "reasonable three-year-old."

WHEN YOU COME to a railroad crossing, if the view is obstructed, do you stop, look, and listen?[3] If you can't get a good view of the track both ways, do you get out of the car and look? If you don't, you're responsible in some states in contributory negligence as a *matter of law*. You can't recover if the train hits your car; so said, at one time, the United States Supreme Court. (But then do you have to get out *again* to look once you have gotten back in?)

An auto driver may be speeding and negligent, but if you've walked from the sidewalk to the street without looking to the right or left you may be contributorily negligent and cannot successfully sue for your injury.

Then again, a streetcar may have been negligently operated, but if you alighted from another car and failed to look for this car coming in the opposite direction, you might have avoided the resulting accident. You may be barred from recovery—if the jury finds both you *and* the streetcar negligent in a contributory (not comparative) negligence state.

Common carriers must accord their passengers the *utmost*, not just ordinary (the usual yardstick), care. Streetcars, escalators, airplanes, etc., are all common carriers. Not only must they exercise the utmost care while in the actual process of transporting you from place to place, they must exercise the utmost care while a passenger is entering or departing the car. Thus, if the car jerks forward while a person's trying to board, or a passenger leaving a car at night falls in an unseen pothole, the common carrier is liable.

MERE DRUNKENNESS of a pedestrian who is struck by a negligent auto driver is not contributory negligence as a matter of law, but presents a question for the jury to decide. Did the drunkenness help cause the accident, contribute to it? If so, no recovery or, under comparative negligence, diminished recovery. If the accident would have happened despite the plaintiff's drunkenness, he may recover.

The drunk has many things to thank Old Lady Law for. When he becomes incompetent, she gives him a guardian; in some cases she reduces the consequences of his crimes because of his lack of sobriety. When he falls into a hole in the street she gives him damages.

In one case, the defendant had dug, and left unguarded, a hole in the sidewalk in front of his San Francisco premises back in 1855. Came the plaintiff, having difficulty holding to the sidewalk with his feet. Abruptly he filled the hole—with himself.

In the bottom of many an unguarded hole lies a waiting lawsuit. The plaintiff landed on his, and went to court for damages.

The jury was instructed that "if at the time of the accident plaintiff was intoxicated from the use of ardent spirits," he could not recover. They found for the defendant.

But old Justice Heydenfeldt of the California Supreme Court held the instruction in error. Tersely but accurately he said: "If the defendants were at fault in leaving an uncovered hole in the sidewalk of a public street, the intoxication of the plaintiff cannot excuse such gross negligence. *A drunken man is as much entitled to a safe street as a sober one, and much more in need of it.*" [4]

The wisdom of the California court was later matched by the Supreme Court of Oregon.

A bridge upon which the plaintiff was crossing broke and dropped him into the water. In his condition of alcoholic absorption, the shock of touching actual water was too much. He sought a lawyer and sued for damages, alleging the bridge was unsafe. The bridge company defended, declaring the plaintiff had had too much whiskey and too few chasers.

Said the Oregon court:

> The traveling public are not required to be bridge inspectors. Their attempting to cross such a structure could not be negligence, whatever might be their condition of intoxication or sobriety.
>
> Possibly his judgment as to its strength [the bridge's] might have been better while sober than while drunk, but defendant cannot claim anything on that ground.
>
> Whether plaintiff was drunk or sober, he had the right to suppose that a bridge open to the use of the public and under the control of the company officials would bear up his load [sic!] in crossing it.

One Zeb Frugia had a large family. One day Zeb rode his "hoss" down the railroad tracks. Next immediately following (as the lawyers used to say), Zeb's family no longer had him and he no longer had his hoss.

Suit against the railroad for wrongful death—the jury finds Zeb worth his weight in gold, judgment for his family, the railroad appeals.

Claimed the railroad: Zeb had been drinking when the Angel of Death appeared in front of him in the shape of one of our engines. His drinking made him negligent; his negligence made him ride his horse on our railroad track and meet his doom.

The Supreme Court of Texas found that the deceased was "'considerably organized,'" but not so drunk as to establish negligence as a matter of law: "Intoxication affects different men in different ways. In some it quickens the intellectual faculties and sharpens the physical senses; and in some the first are, for the time, destroyed and the latter blunted. It largely depends upon the kind of man and liquor."

In affirming the judgment for Zeb's family, the Supreme Court announced:

> Men have been getting drunk ever since Noah celebrated the subsidence of the flood. The ancient Germans, from whom the Anglo-Saxon race sprung, used to propose their laws in their Legislature while drunk and consider their passage while sober. And it is suspected by some that their descendants propose laws in Legislatures of the present day while in the same condition, though their enactment may not be considered while sober, as by their ancestors."[5]

When you voluntarily accept a ride with a drunken driver, knowing him to be drunk, you've assumed the risk of an evident danger and may be contributorily negligent in the resulting accident. You may not successfully be able to sue either your host or a negligent third person.[6]

Accepting a ride with *any* driver used to prevent an injured passenger from suing the negligent driver. "Guest statutes" provided that a guest in a vehicle, one who was there voluntarily and without paying for the privilege, had no right to sue his driver for any injuries inflicted during his ride (unless the accident was intentional or the driver was reckless). The rationale was to prevent fraudulent, collusive suits between friends in order to claim and split insurance proceeds. The other rationale was to reward and protect the "hospitality" of the driver. (Passengers who paid some consideration for the ride could sue.)

But courts have realized that it's a bit unfair to bar a whole class of plaintiffs from suing just because of a few bad faith lawsuits, and "guest statutes" have been declared unconstitutional in most states.[7]

CONSUMERS' SUITS HAVE BECOME the order of the day and plaintiffs' lawyers have patrolled the manufactured product, whether it be a drug, tire, cosmetic, automobile, or airplane, with larger and larger awards until insurance companies have cried "ouch" and manufacturers have said, "We'll have to be more careful." This is the tort of the day.

For a particular bit of judicial understatement, we turn to a consumer case that requires not so much a strong mind as a strong stomach. If you've ever found in your food an article perceptibly extraneous to the established cuisine of our better hostelries, you may sympathize with one Bryson Pillars of Mississippi.

Pillars had just replenished his supply of chewing tobacco. As the Mississippi Supreme Court said of him in 1918:

> [He] consumed one plug of his purchase, which measured up to representations, that it was tobacco unmixed with human flesh, but when [he] tackled the second plug it made him sick, but, not suspecting the tobacco, he tried another chew, and still another, until he bit into some foreign substance, which crumbled like dry bread, and caused him to foam at the mouth, while he was getting "sicker and sicker." Finally, his teeth struck something hard; he could not bite through it. After an examination he discovered a *human toe, with flesh and nail intact.*

Pillars consulted a physician, who testified that he exhibited all the characteristic symptoms of ptomaine poisoning.

The physician identified the human toe as in a state of putrefaction and said, in effect, that the plaintiff's condition was caused by the poison generated by the rotten toe.

In giving judgment to Pillars the court succinctly said that certainly a manufacturer would be liable for intentionally placing a toe in his tobacco, therefore he should be held for negligently allowing the toe to come there.

Tersely the court concluded: "We can imagine no reason why, with ordinary care, human toes could not be left out of chewing tobacco, and if toes are found in chewing tobacco," summarized the court with great wisdom and perspicuity, "it seems to us that *somebody has been very careless*." [8]

Despite the court's adminition, in 1924 someone was again "very careless" with the same tobacco, for a Mr. Loftin, in biting into his purchase, found, not a human toe, but the body of a small, partly decomposed snake!

A jury of his gastronomic peers, prospectively suffering, undoubtedly, a loss of appetite for months to come, gave Mr. Loftin judgment for $1,500. But the Supreme Court of a southern state was composed, as aged appellate justices sometimes are, of men more hardy and mellowed with the years and certainly of vigorous digestion. They reduced the judgment to $500 and allowed as how this was sufficient money damage for anyone who saw snakes in his tobacco. [9]

A word should be said about *judicial discretion*, the *cormotio celebri* that allows an appellate justice to substitute his *discretion* for that of the trier of facts below (the jury at the trial court level): You toss your coin and take your chances that the appointing power has picked an appellate justice with a social and economic philosophy matching your own.

O F ALL THE PERSONAL INJURY SUITS ever filed, the most notable effort has to be Gerald Mayo's suit against Satan, alleging that "Satan has on numerous occasions caused plaintiff misery . . . , placed deliberate obstacles in his path and has caused plaintiff's downfall." Unfortunately, the Devil had his day, for the court admitted it couldn't grant relief:

We question whether plaintiff may obtain personal jurisdiction over the defendant in this judicial district. The complaint contains no allegation of residence in this district. While the official reports disclose no case where this defendant has appeared as defendant, there is an unofficial account of a trial in New Hampshire ["The Devil and Daniel Webster"] where this defendant filed an action of mortgage foreclosure as plaintiff. The defendant in that action was represented by the preeminent advocate of that day, and raised the defense that the plaintiff was a foreign Prince with no standing to sue in an American Court. This defense was overcome by overwhelming evidence to the contrary.[10]

I T HAS BEEN SAID "Where there's a wrong, there's a remedy," and the following cases illustrate that there is no indignity too petty for our justice to place a value upon.

The Court of Appeals of Georgia awarded a plaintiff $500 for the wrong it described as follows:

> [T]he plaintiff was an unmarried white lady, and . . . while in attendance as a guest of the defendant at a circus performance being given by the defendant, . . . a horse, which was going through a dancing performance immediately in front of where plaintiff was sitting, was . . . caused to back towards the plaintiff, and while in this situation the horse evacuated his bowels into her lap . . . [A]s a result thereof plaintiff was caused much embarrassment, mortification, and mental pain and suffering, to her damage.[11]

This case is a delight to law students. But I hasten to advise that the law treats of *all* man's actions and inactions, and inadequate is the trial lawyer who trifles or makes fun of the litigant because the tort is bizarre.

The Supreme Court of Wisconsin affirmed a judgment of seventy-five dollars for this grandiloquently described insult to plaintiff's cow. On September 14, 1907, the plaintiff was the owner of a thoroughbred Holstein-Friesian heifer, which was born on January 8, 1906, and had been thereafter duly christened Martha

Pietertje Pauline. The name is neither euphonious nor musical, but there isn't much in a name anyway. (See Shakespeare's *Romeo and Juliet*, Act II, scene 2.) Notwithstanding any handicap she may have had in the way of a cognomen, Martha Pietertje Pauline was a genuine highbrow, having a pedigree as long and at least as well authenticated as that of the ordinary scion of effete European nobility who breaks into this land of democracy and equality and offers his title to the highest bidder at the matrimonial bargain counter.

> The defendant was the owner of a bull about one year old, lowly born and nameless as far as the record discloses. The plebeian, having aspirations beyond his humble station in life, wandered beyond the confines of his own pastures and sought the society of the adolescent and unsophisticated Martha, contrary to the provisions of sec. 1482, Stats. (1898), as amended by ch. 14, Laws of 1903. As a result of this somewhat morganic *mesalliance*, a calf was born July 5, 1908.[12]

In the law of negligence, "The Jackass Case" is a cause célèbre.

It is the irony of our world that of the most deserving, praises are often unsung. Man works ceaselessly in a garret to die unknown, his invention sold to a receptive public by one who toiled not. The famous NRA case of President Franklin D. Roosevelt's time interested a nation, but the crate of chickens that caused it—does anyone know or care if they were white or black or gray, or even roosters for that matter? The Dred Scott case provoked the Civil War, but who remembers, who has written, of Dred Scott himself? The tears, the laughs, the rights, the wrongs of the suitors after lending their names to cases, are bound and wrapped in buckram in the anonymity of "plaintiff" and "defendant."

So it was with a donkey. Back in 1842 Mr. Davies fettered his donkey in the middle of a public road. Mr. Mann, driving down an incline in his wagon at a "smartish pace" (as was later said), came upon the poor little donkey, and, unable to stop, ran over and killed him.

When Mr. Davies sued Mr. Mann in the English court of the exchequer for the value of the donkey, Mr. Mann countered by saying that the wrong was that of Davies in illegally tying the donkey in the center of the road, even while admitting that he, Mann, drove his team negligently.

The court, in giving judgment of forty shillings to Mr. Davies, enunciated a rule of jurisprudence that was to remain in our law until today. Although the plaintiff was negligent originally, the defendant, acting as a prudent person, could and should have seen the negligence and incidentally the donkey, and had he himself not been negligent, he could easily have prevented the accident. Thus the doctrine of "last clear chance" was first announced.

So, regardless of how egregious your negligence, if the operator of the streetcar or train bearing down upon you is likewise negligent, and in exercising his faculties could have prevented the accident, you may recover damages—thanks to the poor little donkey, worth but forty shillings.

While he remains nameless, to his anonymous and undying glory *Davies* v. *Mann* is cited as "The Jackass Case," and since November 4, 1842, when the case was decided, it is said the piteous moans of the dying jackass have been heard in the jurisprudence of courts the world round.

A MAN SEES a child drowning. He could save its life by stretching out a helping hand with no danger to himself. If he stands idly by and watches the child drown, he has broken no earthly law. Yet, once he even begins to rescue the child, he becomes liable for any harm he might cause in so doing—to the child or to others—if he fails to exercise the care of a "reasonable person."

But if ever you can't decide whether or not to be charitable and rescue your brethren in peril, the following legal doctrine may help you make up your mind.

The "rescue doctrine" of the common law protects a rescuer from harm befalling him during his heroic efforts. "Danger invites rescue," says the law. If you place a person in danger by your negligence, you must not only compensate the victim, but his rescuers as well, for rescue is foreseeable where there is danger, and rescue is merely another incident in the chain of causation you started by your negligence in the first place.[13]

For example, in 1893, New York State owned a bridge over a canal and bridge authorities failed to notice an opening in the bridge railing. A small child fell through this opening, and his father immediately plunged into the canal to save him. Both child and father drowned, and the court held New York liable for *both* deaths.

The rescue attempt by the father was deemed "natural and instinctive," and as much a result of the broken railing as the child's death.[14]

The rescue doctrine was at issue again in New York in 1921.[15] Arthur Wagner and his cousin Herbert had gone for a ride on the New York Central and Erie Railroad to Niagara Falls. Herbert was standing near an open door—there was a sudden, violent lurch—and "Man overboard!"

The train was stopped on a bridge, and a rescue party was formed. Night and darkness fell, but Arthur still walked along the bridge searching for Herbert. Other rescuers went beneath the trestle, and had just come upon poor Herbert's body when *another* body crashed to the ground beside them. Arthur had found his cousin's hat on the bridge beam, and, reaching for it, had slipped in the darkness and joined Herbert below.

Arthur lived, sued for his injuries, and won because of the "rescue doctrine," which the court eloquently explained: "Danger invites rescue. The cry of distress is the summons to relief . . . the wrong that imperils life is a wrong to the imperiled victim; it is a wrong also to his rescuer. . . . The risk of rescue, if only it be not wanton, is born of the occasion. The emergency begets the man. The wrongdoer may not have foreseen the coming of a deliverer. He is accountable as if he had."

That is the law in all its benign sovereignty. It imposes no duty upon us to rescue, but protects us if we do.

Notes

1. The common law refers to the "reasonable and prudent man" as its standard, and more than one court declared that was due to the lack of any "reasonable" women. Today, the term "person" is agreed upon.

2. California was formerly a contributory negligence state, but has recently followed the progressive trend toward comparative negligence since the latter does not operate so harshly upon the slightly blameworthy plaintiff.

3. A Kansas law provides, "When two trains approach each other at a crossing, they shall both come to a full stop, and neither shall start up until the other has gone."

4. *Robinson v. Pioche, Bayerque & Co.*, 5 C. 460, 461 (1855).

5. *Frugia v. Texarkana & Ft. S. Ry. Co.*, 43 Tex. Civ. App. 48, 95 S. W. 563, 565 (1906).

6. The owner of a building negligently left open an elevator shaft. Plaintiff came into the building at night and knowing that the elevator might not be at the ground floor, failed to make an inspection and fell into the shaft. His *contributory* negligence prevented a recovery.

7. *Brown v. Merlo*, 8 Cal. 3d 855, 506, P. 2d 212, 106 Cal. Rptr. 338 (1973).

8. *Pillars v. R. J. Reynolds Tobacco Co.*, 117 Miss, 490, 78 S. 365, 366 (1918). Emphasis added.

9. *Reynolds Tobacco Co. v. Loftin*, 99 S. 13 (1924).

10. *U. S. ex. rel. Gerald Mayo v. Satan and His Staff*, 54 F. R. D. 282, 283 (W.D. Pa. 1971).

11. *Christy Bros. Circus v. Turnage*, 38 Ga. App. 581, 144 S. E. 680 (1928).

12. *Koplin v. Quade*, 145 Wis. 454 (1911).

13. Some states give comfort to the heroic rescuer (or his family) who rushes in where angels fear to tread: They provide government compensation to reward such meritorious actions, which may otherwise go unrewarded. (See Calif. Gov. Code §13970.)

14. *Gibney* v. *State*, 33 N.E. 142, 137 N. Y. 1 (1893).

15. *Wagner* v. *International Ry. Co.*, 232 N. Y. 176, 133 N. E. 437 (1921).

15

May It Please Your Honor

ORD AVORY, presiding over a criminal court in old England, had a prisoner arraigned before his bar.

The lord looked at the defendant and inquired, "You have been convicted before, have you not? I seem to remember your face."

"That I have, your lordship, but it was due to the incapacity of my lawyer. It was through no guilt of mine," answered the prisoner.

"That is always said," exclaimed Lord Avery with a grim smile, "and you have my sincere sympathy."

"Thank you, my lord," answered the prisoner. "I deserve it, seeing you were my counsel on that occasion."

Members of the bench, except some justices of the peace,[1] were all once members of the bar, although there is no law that requires U. S. Supreme Court justices to be lawyers. Federal judges and justices are appointed by the president for life; state judges are elected except when they are appointed to fill an untimely vacancy.

It is notorious that an incumbent judge is difficult to defeat at the polls. First, he uses the word *judge* before his name to the disadvantage of the opposing candidate; second, few members of the bar have the courage to refuse a judge their support against an aspiring brother lawyer not yet so elevated; third, every other incumbent judge lends support, fearing that the defeat of one judge will make vulnerable any judicial tenure.

A LAYMAN ONCE had good reason to be disgusted with the law; but rather it was due to the vagaries of two different judges. He was sued by his wife for divorce on the ground of impotency and at the same time was made defendant by his stenographer in an action for seduction. He lost both cases.

In another case, Mr. Musselman's wife had been awarded a divorce in the lower court and Mr. Musselman appealed to the Supreme Court of Indiana on two grounds: The judge both smoked and slept during the trial.

As to the first contention, the court said even if the judge and all the attorneys did smoke during the trial, the defendant, not indulging in tobacco, should have had a clearer head and profited instead of suffered.

As to the sleeping, the defendant alleged: "The court erred in sleeping, or sitting with his eyes closed in open court during the reading of the written evidence upon the part of the plaintiff at the trial of said cause, by which the plaintiff was prevented from having a fair trial."

To this the Supreme Court of Indiana made the following answer:

> The above reason for a new trial is very vague and indefinite. If the appellant who was personally present in the court was unable to determine whether the Judge was really asleep or only had his eyes closed how are we to determine?
>
> It is said to have occurred while appellant was reading his written evidence. If he had a reason to suppose the Judge was indulging in a gentle doze after dinner, he should have suspended his reading or awakened the Judge [the court does not indicate the polite or

effective manner of doing the latter]. Nor does it appear what portion of the written evidence was being read. There was much of it wholly immaterial and irrelevant.

We might reasonably conclude that the Judge but imitated the example of many of the profoundest thinkers and most distinguished Judges and closed his eyes that he might hear the more accurately and more fully comprehend what he heard (even the immaterial and irrelevant).[2]

In an early California case the defendant fared better. The judge had stepped from the courtroom for a few moments to heed nature's call[3] while counsel was arguing his case. The California Supreme Court gave the defendant a new trial observing with great wisdom, "There can be no court without a judge."

Quite appropriate to the antics above is the allegedly true (the word *allegedly* is a lawyer's sword and shield) story of the lawyer-father who took his quite young son to the supreme court of a certain state that its awesome majesty might permanently inoculate the boy against the dangers of ever practicing any lesser profession. An impassioned argument was being heard as father and son arrived. The judges sat motionless. Not a judicial muscle quivered under the several black robes.

This went on for a good half hour. Then a fly, hovering over the well polished landing field that was the dome of the chief justice, made a four-point landing. The chief slowly and deliberately raised his hand to brush off the fly.

Young Blackstone turned excitedly to his father and whispered in amazement, "Dad! Why, they're alive!"

ON THE SUBJECT of appeal and reversal, courts have dryly made the following observations.

Said the Kansas Supreme Court: It is grounds for reversal that the trial court erroneously decided a question "as transparent as the soup of which Oliver Twist implored an additional supply."[4]

Said the Idaho Supreme Court, "On appeal it is not sufficient that God knows a thing, but the record must show it."[5]

The Georgia Supreme Court: "On appeal, a point which appears in its virgin state, wearing all its maiden blushes, is out of place."[6] And the Georgia Supreme Court gave hope to litigants with: "The appellate court will not allow a judgment to be ambushed."[7]

The reason for occasional dejection may appear from this Georgia Supreme Court opinion: "In every forensic season the courts have a considerable flock of cases which are tomtits furnished with garbs of feathers ample enough for turkeys, which are to be stripped and dissected for the cabinets of jurisprudence."[8]

The judicial tongue can be sharp to other members of the bench as well as to lawyers and laymen, as the following case illustrates.

Born in 1891, in the placid little trickle that was Idaho's Gooseberry Creek, was a torrent of judicial language that we would say, were it not for the mixed metaphor, administered a most thorough judicial spanking by a supreme court to a lower court.

The waters of the creek ran 100 inches and plaintiff had appropriated all that water. Every witness so testified.

Years later, the defendant, settling beside the creek and above the plaintiff, took the entire supply of the stream. Who was entitled to the water? That was the contest.

Not only did the trial court give judgment to the defendant when he should have found for the plaintiff, but he gave judgment for 800 inches when there were only 100.

On appeal he was reversed by the Idaho Supreme Court and the following judicial spanking was administered:

> To the ordinary mind this question might present a somewhat difficult problem for judicial solution, unaided by the statutes; but the learned Judge [always "learned" when about to be reversed] found no difficulty whatever in reaching a conclusion as unique as it was unprecedented.
>
> Heroically setting aside the statutes and the decisions in the cases, he assumed the role of Jupiter Pluvius and distributed the waters of Gooseberry Creek with a beneficient recklessness, which makes the most successful efforts of all rain wizards shrink into insignificance and which would make the hearts of the ranchers of Gooseberry Creek dance with joy if only the judicial decree could be supplanted with a little more moisture.

The individual who causes two blades of grass to grow where but one grew before is held in highest exaltation as a benefactor of his race. How then shall we rank him, who, by judicial fiat alone, can cause 800 inches of water to flow where nature only put 100. We veil our faces, we bow our heads before this assumption of judicial power and authority.

Evidently the court assumed that Gooseberry Creek was as inexhaustable as the widow's cruise, or else that its decree possessed the potency of Moses' rod.

A question is settled when it has been decided in one way, twice by the Supreme Court of the United States, seventeen times by the Supreme Court of California, five times by the Supreme Court of Colorado, six times by the Supreme Court of Nevada, twice by the Supreme Court of Montana, once by the Supreme Court of New Mexico, twice by the Supreme Court of Utah, once by the Supreme Court of Oregon and repeatedly by the Supreme Court of Idaho.[9]

Despite the old saying "as sober as a judge," the judicial eye twinkles as much as any other. Judges can be human and humorous beings. While sitting at the Newcastle assizes in England, Justice Grantham was staying at a country house. Late one evening he had finished writing some letters and, putting on an overcoat and cap for a stroll to the letter box to post his mail, he passed an English bobby, who had been assigned the disagreeable duty of guarding the house through the cold night.

Not recognizing the justice in his hasty attire, and thinking he was perhaps a servant of the house, the bobby inquired, "Has the old s.o.b. gone to bed yet?"

"Not yet," truthfully answered the justice.

After posting the letters, the justice returned to the house, retired to his bedroom, turned out the lights, and went to the window and called down to the bobby, "Say, officer, the old s.o.b. is just going to bed now."

Said an old English court, showing the venerable roots of judicial humor: "The very definition of a good award is that it gives dissatisfaction to both parties."[10]

Within the confining limits of age, the bench, or even the folds of a black gown, there are many other twinkles in the judicial eye. Recently, Justice Bonynge of the Supreme Court of New York, upholding option betting in dog racing, had this to say of judicial naiveté:

> For a generation or more betting at horse races was unlawful. After this prolonged burst of morality the Legislature suddenly discovered the need of "improving the breed of horses."
> In a backhanded way this legislation restored racetrack betting by removing the criminal penalties. But let no one suspect that our best citizens repair to Belmont Park and other nearby tracks for the purpose of gambling.
> Perish the thought, for their minds rest on higher things. Improving the breed of horses is their aim, and their conversation, aside from formal greetings, deals solely with sires and dams, foals and fillies, blood lines, consanguinity, and inherited characteristics. These things a judge must believe, even at the risk of being chided as naive, because they are contemporary America.

Justice Dent in a West Virginia case said that "A boy may satisfy his mother that his wet hair is the result of sweat, and not of his going swimming contrary to his commands, but he will hardly convince her that his back and arms were sunburned, and his shirt turned wrong side out in crawling through a rail fence backward."

THEN WE HAVE the nasal digit drama. No word spoken, no life lived, no gesture made, that Old Lady Law at some time has not probed with her insatiable curiosity. There's a perplexing gesture, for example, originating so long ago that the "memory of man runneth not to the contrary"—but let Justice Roy of the Supreme Court of New York tell of the gesture and the case:

> Is it disorderly conduct for one individual to publicly greet another by placing the end of his thumb against the tip of his nose, at the same time extending and wiggling the fingers of his hand?
> That momentous question is involved in this appeal. What meaning is intended to be conveyed by the above described pantomime?
> Is it a friendly or an unfriendly action; a compliment or an insult?

Is it a direct invitation to a fight, or is it likely to provoke a fight?

In the Knickerbocker History of New York we read that when William the Testy sent an expedition to treat with the belligerent powers of Rensselaerstein, the ambassador who accompanied the expedition demanded the surrender of the fortress.

In reply, the wachtmeester applied the thumb of his right hand to the edge of his nose, and the thumb of his left hand to the little finger of the right, and spreading each hand like a fan, made an aerial flourish with his fingers.

No breach of the peace ensued, but this was apparently owing to the fact that the ambassador was ignorant of the significance of the wachtmeester's salutation. It is, however, recorded that the practice became widespread, and that up to the author's day the thumb to the nose and fingers in the air is apt to be a reply made by tenants to their landlords when called upon for any long arrears of rent.

In the case at bar the circumstances attending the enactment of the nasal and digit drama aforesaid tend to show a design to engender strife.

My answer to the question stated at the beginning of this opinion is: It depends on the circumstances.

So, under some circumstances, the "nasal digit drama" may be legally as well as emotionally justified.[11]

THE SCOPE OF judicial eloquence and knowledge sometimes seems unlimited: Witness "Tuba v. Crickets."

Under the common law, eviction by the landlord meant a forcible ouster. Now there is a new doctrine. When premises become uninhabitable, the tenant may take a *constructive* eviction, for which the landlord must pay damages and during which the tenant need not pay rent.

This example of a constructive eviction is from New York; a tuba-playing tenant felt he couldn't live with the landlord's crickets.

The tenant claimed they were black, green, and silver and at least as big as hummingbirds. The landlord claimed he found only three—all dead and no larger than ants.

Said the landlord, "The Chinese put crickets into cages and pay to hear them sing. The tenant heard the crickets gratis."

Said the New York Supreme Court:

> While a cricket is technically a "bug," it would appear from a study of his life, that instead of being obnoxious, he is an intellectual little fellow, with certain attainments of refinement and an indefatigable musician par excellence.
>
> It is singular that a musician should complain about another musician. The tenant with his tuba, which is similar to the ancient bombardon, is able, in an artificial band, to dispense all the music within its compass, nearly four octaves. The cricket, with his musical armature, is capable of emitting his intermittent notes, though mainly for selfish purposes in love-making.
>
> That there was in this case what may be termed a unilateral affinity between the crickets and the tuba player, is demonstrated by the fact that not only were they attracted by the tuba's deep notes, but they wished to be his personal companions, each a concomitant adjunct in the production of orchestral melody.
>
> The tuba player's nonreciprocating attitude toward the crickets must have caused dismay among them, and if the hosts would leave the premises it would mean misery for them. A loss of habitation in these days is a disastrous event, and three of the crickets must have become so melancholy that to use a bit of criminal phraseology, they suffered pains of which they languished, and languishing, did live until of said pains they did die.

The landlord won his case against the tuba-playing tenant.

THE TASK OF JUDGING is truly a most difficult job. Yet all the rules are written. To the judge, as well as the lawyer, one may well say, "Seek and ye shall find." There is no such thing as the unwritten law, though juries have often followed it.

One judge, in answer to the plea of unwritten law by a woman romantically wronged said, "Madam, the law for you is clear. It is summarized in one word that you should have employed—*no*."

Sancho Panza, the famous servant of the even more famous Don Quixote, in one instance at least was a good judge and gave a decision which is still law. In the crime of rape the advances of the unsought suitor must be fought off (unless his verbal or physical threats make resistance useless) by the complaining witness; otherwise, it is not rape.

A complaining witness against a herdsman defendant had successfully resisted the attempt to take her purse but alleged she was not as successful in warding off defendant's other advances.

In acquitting defendant, Sancho said, "Sister of mine, had you shown the same, or but half as much courage and resolution in defending your chastity as you have shown in defending your money, the strength of Hercules could not have violated you."

Here are some other judicial bons mots.

Solemnly announced the high court of Missouri: "It is an inalienable right of the citizen to get drunk."[12]

An English court came up with this one: "Adultery is the highest invasion of property."[13]

From New York, the wry observation: "A man intending seduction may blunder into bigamy."[14]

A Nevada judge commented on the morals of the parties before him by saying, "One may not litigate all day in this court and fornicate all night even in Nevada."

And this decision from the Supreme Court of Georgia: "In order for an assault with intent to rape to be committed, is it necessary that the persons of the two should be in such proximity as that the organs of the male shall be within what may be termed 'striking distance' of the organs of the female? Or, is the virile member to be treated as a gun which is harmless until brought within 'carrying distance' of the target? We think not."[15]

In Florida, an elderly gentleman was convicted of "the abominable and detestable crime against nature." On appeal, the court phrased the issue in such graphic terms that the case has since earned an X rating among bored law students looking for lively reading:

> Does the one specific crime definitely defined and limited by Section 7567 . . . comprehend or include the action of a 76 year old, aged Indian War Veteran, feeble physically and mentally ill, after having met the two girls of 11 and 13 years of age who solicited him, went to his residence and there they both got on the bed, pulled up

their dresses, and dropped down their panties, when he in turn on his back in the same bed allowed them to diddle with his rag-like penis, unerectable, lifeless and useless except to connect the bladder with the outside world for more than six years since the death of his wife, utterly incapable of either penetration or emission, and wad it like a rag into their mouths, and then, in his feeble and aged condition impelled by the irresistible impulse, in turn he would kiss and put his tongue in their little though potentially influential and powerful vaginas?

Unfortunately for this spry individual, the court decided the issue against him.[16]

I HAVE BEEN READING judicial opinions for fifty years, and, within the often somber limits of jurisprudence, they range, like all literature does, from the most vapid to the most profound, from the banal to the sublime.

The Public Local Laws of Maryland (Vol. 2, p. 315) contain the Police Act of the City of Baltimore, passed in 1860. This provides that "No Black Republican" shall be appointed to any office under the board of police. The unconstitutionality of the act was brought to the attention of the appellate Maryland court, presumably by a Republican. It took the Maryland court over 100 pages to state that they didn't exactly know what a "Black Republican" was.[17]

Some cases have come before the courts that judges have frankly admitted their inability to solve.[18] A clever and justiciable solution to one perplexing case was the following: Courts of equity in the old days could not issue injunctions ordering a party to do an affirmative act because of the difficulty of supervision. Their jurisdiction was confined to the *restraining* or enjoining litigants from doing an act.

Came a case in which a ditch owner allowed his ditch to break and flood a neighbor's land. The court could not tell him affirmatively to repair the ditch, but the court effectively used the rule of the negative by ordering the owner to "cease keeping his ditch in a state of disrepair."[19]

In another case, the plaintiff, a very obese woman, was alighting from the defendant's train when the latter started up before the plaintiff had safely reached the ground.

The Illinois Appellate Court, in affirming judgment for the plaintiff considerately held: "A fleshy woman has a right to ride on a train and to have a valise and parcels, and she is entitled to more time for alighting than might be required for a foot-racer or a greyhound."[20]

ONE OF THE MOST beautiful decisions of the Supreme Court of the State of Georgia is a poem entitled "In the Matter of Rest."

When Justice Bleckley resigned from the Supreme Court of Georgia in 1879 after a full judicial life, he read an exquisite little poem and it was ordered spread upon the minutes of the court as an official decision and given a place in the law books at Volume 64, Georgia Reports, page 452:

Rest for hand and brow and breast,
  For fingers, heart and brain!
Rest and peace! A long release
  From labor and from pain;
Pain of doubt, fatigue, despair
Pain of darkness everywhere,
  And seeking light in vain!
Peace and rest! Are they the best
  For mortals here below?
Is soft repose from work and woes
  A bliss for men to know?
Bliss of time is bliss of toil:
No bliss but this, from sun and soil,
  Does God permit to grow.

COMPASSION CAN BE another judicial attribute. Chief Justice Hale was strongly opposed to the severity of that old English law that made most penalties capital ones. From the bench he put this conviction into practice.

Once a half-starved lad came before him on a charge of burglary. The defendant had been shipwrecked upon the Cornish coast and, being refused food or clothing, suffered the pangs of extreme hunger.

He had the choice of starving or committing a capital offense, burglary. He chose the latter, broke a baker's window, and stole a loaf of bread.

Justice Hale heard the lad's story and directed the jury to acquit. But, less merciful than the judge, the gentlemen of the jury returned a verdict of guilty.

Hale, however, seized upon another severity of the old law: Jurors could not eat until they had rendered a verdict. The judge refused to discharge the jury until they had changed their verdict. Finally, experiencing the pangs of hunger the defendant had suffered, they thought the better of their bitter verdict and set the prisoner free.[21]

Several years passed and Justice Hale, while riding circuit in the north counties, was caught in a sudden rainstorm.

Cold, shivering, and hungry, he was amazed to see a sheriff in a carriage beckoning to him with dry clothes and food.

Taken to the sheriff's house, the justice finally exclaimed at the lavish hospitality of the sheriff. The sheriff answered with emotion: "I am only showing my gratitude to the judge who once saved my life. Had it not been for you, I should have been hanged in Cornwall for stealing a loaf of bread instead of living to be the richest landowner here."

We can never tell what the future holds for us. The sixteenth century Judge Popham, who started his career as a highwayman, ended up as Queen Elizabeth's Lord Chief Justice.

JUSTICE JAMES MINTURN of the New Jersey Supreme Court wrote an opinion in 1925 that, for me, is the apotheosis of judicial eloquence.

The defendant had appealed his conviction of disorderly conduct for publicly informing a member of the town council that he was a "souphead." Said the court:

> The mystical term *souphead* ... awakens delectable memories of the early well-kept home, fast disappearing, like many other cherished American institutions, before the tinsel invasion of that birdlike roost, appropriately termed a flat. This euphonious appellation seems to have had a local application peculiar to days when that attractive dish was made and consumed with relish and avidity, by the habitués of that ancient comfort station known as a barroom.
>
> The libraries and lexicons of neighboring municipalities furnish no clue to its origin, doubtless due to the fact that, in those less-favored localities, the canned variety fulfilled the local needs. Nor are we in any wise assisted in this research by the erudite researches of learned counsel, possessed as they are with a large and varied experience in the sociological conditions of the past.
>
> The difficulty of classification and etymology is therefore quite manifest, and as in all such researches, when modern learning fails, recourse must be had to the ancient founts of inspiration. The antique genus "souphead" was doubtless the proud possessor of a mentality surcharged, among other things, with the diluted essence of succulent garden products, not radically distinguishable from the modern vegetarian, whose dietary code has its genesis in soup as a fundamental substratum.
>
> In the light of these circumstances it will be quite universally conceded that the head which invented this popular gastronomic edible, like the genius who discovered the attraction of gravitation, or the rotundity of the earth, is entitled to the applause and gratitude, rather than the condemnation, of mankind. Obviously, therefore, the term cannot be deemed either undignified or offensive, and the defendant, whether conscious of his complimentary ebullition or not, cannot be adjudged guilty of disorderly conduct.[22]

Judicial wit can sparkle where we least expect it and add color to what might otherwise be prosaic cases.

Notes

1. "A justice of the peace is generally a man of consequence in his neighborhood; he writes the wills, draws the deeds, and pulls the teeth of the people; also, he performs divers surgical operations on the animals of his neighbors." *Bendheim Brothers v. Baldwin*, 73 Ga. 594 (1884).

2. *Musselman v. Musselman*, 44 Ind. 106 (1873).

3. It would "perhaps be considered indecent now for a judge, as was once the custom, to retire to a corner of the court for a necessary purpose in the presence of ladies." *Reg.* v. *Webb*, 61 E. C. L. 933 (1848).

4. *Searle* v. *Adams*, 3 Kan. 513 (1866).

5. *Pence* v. *Lemp*, 4 Id. 526, 43 P. 75 (1895).

6. *Cleveland* v. *Chambliss*, 64 Ga. 353 (1879).

7. *Swindle* v. *Poore*, 59 Ga. 336 (1877).

8. *Lukens* v. *Ford*, 87 Ga. 541, 13 S. E. 949 (1891).

9. Justice Bleckley, in ruling that if the trial judge had fortunately reached the correct result, even though his reasoning was wrong, the case should be affirmed, said:

   > The pupil of impulse, it forc'd him along,
   > His conduct still right, with his argument wrong;
   > Still aiming at honor, yet fearing to roam,
   > The coachman was tipsy, the chariot drove home.

   Lee v. *Porter*, 63 Ga. 345 (1879).
   "One of the greatest difficulties of the trial judge is to keep his mouth shut." *Kaye* v. *Kinnare*, 69 Ill. 81 (1896).
   A fit occasion to deliberate on a question of practice which has not been satisfactorily settled is "when the court

is full." *Postmaster General* v. *Trigg*, 36 U.S. (11 Pet.) 173 (1837).

10. *Goodman* v. *Sayers*, 2 Jacob & Walker 249, 37 Eng. Rep. 622 (1820).

11. I can remember a very learned San Francisco trial judge, recently deceased, who, before California law for a short time provided that a judge could comment on the credibility of a witness's testimony, made gestures for the benefit of the jury and concerning the witness far worse than those in the "nasal digit drama." The appellate courts of course took no note of them for a judge's "manner and accent cannot be made a part of the record." *State* v. *Kerns*, 47 W. Va. 266, 34 S. E. 734 (1899). (Really they can be if counsel at the time of the judge's gestures is courageous enough to describe them for the reporter to record.)

12. *St. Joseph* v. *Harris*, 59 Mo. App. 122 (1894).

13. *Reg.* v. *Mawgridge*, J. Kel. 119, 84 Eng. Rep. 1107 (1708).

14. *Hayes* v. *People*, 25 N. Y. 390, 82 Am. Dec. 364 (1862).

15. *Jackson* v. *State*, 91 Ga. 322, 18 S. E. 132 (1892). Voltaire wrote, "In order to obtain an equitable verdict in an action of adultery, the jury should be composed of twelve men and twelve women, with an hermaphrodite to give the casting vote in the event of necessity."

16. *Lason* v. *State*, 12 S. 2d 305, 152 Fla. 440 (1943).

17. *Baltimore* v. *State*, 15 Md. 376 (1859).

18. See for example *Hoag* v. *Sayre*, 33 N. Y. Eq. 552 (1881).

19. It is pointed out that the court does not actually order the performance of an act or acts but prohibits the doing of an act, the violation of which prohibition can be immediately reported to the court by the plaintiff without necessity of continued supervision on the part of the court. *Associated Oil Co.* v. *Myers*, 217 C. 297, 18 P. 2d 668 (1933).

20. *Pierce* v. *Gray*, 63 Ill. App. 158 (1895).

21. It is said that a judge, learning that the jury stood deadlocked six to six, called them back into court and asked: "I suppose

the complexity of the case has confused you, eh?" Answered the foreman, "Not at all Your Honor, it's just that six of us want to decide the case on the basis of the law involved and the other six want to decide it on the basis of your charge to the jury."

22. *In re Kirk*, 101 N. J. L. 450, 130 A. 569 (1925).

16

Killing Elves Prohibited

I N THE LEGISLATIVE ACTS, local and national, we find history written. The act bespeaks the age. At the time of Henry III, it was thought that fairies and elves actually roamed the streets, lived in the woods and danced in the meadows. To them were attributed deeds in fact. Consequently a law was passed visiting the death penalty upon anyone "Kyllynge, woundynge or [even] mamynge" a fairy or an elf. (This law is still on the English statute books. No one has thought it necessary to repeal it.)

We build for permanence with mansions of brick, stone, and steel. Yet nothing in this world is permanent except change.

The mighty eternal Maginot Line became as outmoded as the plug hats and morning pants the French politicians wore in dedicating "this eternal work of man."

So it is with the law. Be not too positive with your "shall not" and "be it enacted." Tomorrow others may laugh just as heartily at your ponderous efforts, Mr. or Ms. Legislator, as we do today at the following records of York County, Maine, written in 1666:

> Wee present the wife of Christopher Collins for knitting on ye Lord's day.... This woman fined for her offence 10S–13S 4d to ye witnesses & 5S ye officirs fees.
>
> Wee present Michaell Tomson and his wife for not frequenting of the publique meeting on ye Lords day to heare the word of God preached about halfe a yeare. For Miles Tomson his absenting his selft from the publique meeting & his wife is fined Tenn shillings & the officirs fees of five shillings.
>
> Wee present Joane Ford the wife of Stephen Forde for calling the Constable horne headed Roge & slowheaded Roge—Joane Foard punished for this offence by nine stripes given her at ye post at a Court Houlden at Yorke 28 December 1665. [Note the different spelling of the name "Ford" in the same record.]

Poor Goody Mendum must have been an habitual criminal for three times in the same year are noted her derelictions:

> Wee present Goody Mendum for sailing to Hugh Gullison & John David—Ye devills. Fined 2s 6d for swearing. We present Goody Mendum for cursing & sailing at the devill take Mr. Gullison and his wife. Fined five pounds. Wee present Goody Mendum for abusing Mrs. Gullison in words.

These were common, everyday derelictions and goings-on giving a picture of man's social customs of those times.

In 1770 an act was introduced in the English Parliament for the necessary purpose of protecting the bachelor. It provided:

> That all women of whatever age, rank, profession, or degree, whether virgins, maids, or widows, that shall, from and after such Act, impose upon, seduce, and betray into matrimony, any of His Majesty's subjects by the scents, paints, cosmetic washes, artificial teeth, false hair, Spanish wool, iron stays, hoops, high-heeled shoes, or bolstered hips, shall incur the penalty of the law in force against witchcraft and like misdeameanours and that the marriage, upon conviction, shall stand null and void.

NOT SO LONG AGO in a great majority of states the destination of all Sunday travelers was jail and Sunday drives were criminal conspiracies.

The idea of a Sabbath is of ancient origin. The keeping of one day holy whereupon no work or play shall be done is found in the Commandments. Even before the Jews, the Babylonians recognized a Sabbath. However, the first legal recognition of a day of rest was by Constantine the Great in the year 321 A.D., and thereby a service done for all judges throughout history.

Whether from religious motives alone or because of the quality of his court's decisions, Constantine decreed that upon one day of the week the judges should rest their weary minds. He ordered, in fact, all judges and inhabitants of cities to rest on the venerable day of the sun.

In 517 an Asiatic church council declared Sunday a "nonjudicial day" and prohibited any court proceedings during that time.

Most American law is traced to English common law origins and Sunday statutes are no exception. By the statutes of Charles the Second, Sunday observance was officially ordered. Copying this law, the Virginia colony, three years before the landing of the Pilgrims, passed a law ordering Sunday a day of strict rest. This was the earliest "Blue Law" in America.

For Jews the Sabbath is Saturday. Consequently, New York State, out of deference to its large Jewish population, enacted a law that no court proceeding could be brought against a Jew on Saturday,[1] and, since the courts were not open on Sunday, a Jewish litigant had only five court days.

In fact, some Jewish lawyers claimed that their Sabbath was not from midnight Friday to midnight Saturday, but from starlight Friday to starlight Saturday. The courts refused to so extend their legal holiday.

In an early Florida case,[2] authority is cited for the proposition that Sunday extends from dawn on Sunday to sunset the same day; therefore, jury deliberations held between midnight Saturday and sunrise Sunday are not illegal for it is still "legally" Saturday.

While journeying through Connecticut, George Washington noted in his diary under the date November 8, 1789:

> It being contrary to the law and disagreeable to the people of this state to travel on the Sabbath day, and my horses, after passing through such intolerable roads, wanting rest, I stayed at Perkin's Tavern (which by the way is not a very good one) all day; and a meeting house being within a few rods of the door, I attended the

morning and evening services and heard a very lame discourse from a Mr. Bond.

It was remarked in a "Sunday case" of 1892 that "Connecticut has improved her inns and the intellectual character of her preaching and has mended her ways, but has not altered particularly the laws spoken of; at least Sunday traveling and work are still prohibited, except in cases of necessity and mercy."

In Massachusetts, it was not only unlawful to travel on Sunday, (except from necessity or charity), but a fine of ten dollars was inflicted for every violation. There was certainly no amusement in that, but there is in some of the decisions on the subject.

Proof was offered in one Massachusetts case that the Sunday traveler was his master's only servant and that at that season fresh meat was only fit for use on Monday when slaughtered and dressed on Sunday, but the judge said the law was too clear to admit of discussion. This wicked servant had to bear his smarts unrecompensed. The judge undoubtedly was not one of the persons who suffered from the "temporary inconvenience caused by the failure to supply provisions on Monday." As it was, the court held that "the servant received a meet punishment for his transgression, and thus the sound morality taught at the famous Theological Seminary at Andover was recognized by the Massachusetts statutes and saved that town from a bill of damages."

This is not the only case showing the prudence with which Massachusetts reconciled a due observance of Sunday with the inviolability of the public purse. It is deemed a work of necessity for the public to repair the highway on Sunday in order to prevent accidents on Monday. It was so held in an action for damages occurring on Monday through a defect in the highway, the defendant setting up as a defense that it would have been unlawful to repair the road on Sunday. The court wisely held that no day was better than Sunday for a community to mend its ways!

In Pennsylvania, to visit one's father on Sunday was a work of necessity, but in Massachusetts it was left undecided whether a young man who received injuries arising from a defect in the highway on a Sunday visit to his betrothed was a lawful traveler.

A New York statute (perhaps with a view to restricting inordinate and excessive church-going), wisely provided that no one should ride more than twenty miles to church on Sunday.

Massachusetts was impartial in the administration of its laws and in 1792 the chief justice of the state and his associate justices were indicted for traveling on Sunday. They were compelled to petition the legislature to authorize a dismissal of their case so they could be on hand Monday to decide the cases of others who had violated the law by traveling on Sunday.

Sunday is not the only special day in the eyes of the law. It is against the law to celebrate Christmas in Scotland. This law has been in effect since 1645 when a Parliamentary Act forbade celebration on the ground that it was a heathen festival and an occasion of needless expense. (This law has never been repealed.) England likewise prohibited the celebration of Christmas for twenty-eight years and the colonists in America would not allow it to be celebrated because it reflected of "popery." Furthermore, all the incidents of Christmas were frowned upon. Thus, some of the colonies would not permit the use of turkey or pig on festive days for even that might remind some of the diners of the custom.

OLD LAWS MAY NOW cause as much wonderment as the contents of strange bottles on the apothecary's shelf of yesterday, and they were undoubtedly just as bitter to take. Yet, some still have a sweet nostalgic aroma.

An old Tennessee statute provides that a motor vehicle may not be driven along any highway without a herald preceding it, and a Tacoma, Washington, ordinance provides that the chief of police must be informed by an advancing motorist by telephone before he enters the city.

It took an act of the United States Congress to provide: "Hereafter women shall not be allowed to accompany troops as laundresses."[3]

A Virginia law made it illegal to keep a bathtub in the house; it must be kept in the backyard.

In Ohio it is a felony for a roller-skating instructor to seduce a female pupil!

In Kentucky anyone operating a still must blow a whistle.[4]

It is a misdemeanor, punishable by a year's imprisonment or a fine of $250, or both, for anyone to appear naked anywhere in

New York State in the presence of two or more naked persons of the opposite sex.

It is against the law for a barber to threaten to cut off a youngster's ears in Shreveport, Louisiana, and a thoughtful Waterloo, Nebraska, ordinance of 1910 provides: "It shall be illegal for any barber in this town to eat onions between 7 A.M. and 7 P.M.."

In Wisconsin all bills of fare must be printed in English, and a Pennsylvania law demands that all restaurants must be equipped with stretchers and wheelchairs.

When a person's house burns down in Cuba, the owner goes to jail for three days, which at least insures he has a place to stay.

Do you live in Los Angeles? Then you are subject to more than 77,000 regulations passed by the various councils since Los Angeles grew from pueblo to city.

For example, if you are planning Sunday dinner with more than twenty-five relatives, you must apply for a permit to hold a picnic, otherwise you are breaking the law. However, with the courage to have twenty-five relatives under the same roof at the same time, one should certainly be able to get a picnic permit.

Don't shake your carpets out of the window; that's illegal. Furthermore, don't keep a flowerpot on your window sill; that's also a crime. If you bury a dead cat, place more than two "for sale" signs on a vacant lot at the same time, feed the pigeons in Pershing Square, keep a goat within twenty feet of your doorway, or promise to get husbands for old maids you may find yourself in the Los Angeles city jail.

Don't make mince pie in Kansas—it's against the law. (King James the First forbade the eating of pie to anyone below the rank of baron.) In San Francisco don't carry bread or pastry in an uncovered basket; that's illegal. In Arizona, if you own more than twenty-four chickens at any one time you are breaking an old law.

San Francisco prohibited the spraying of clothes in laundries by means of water emitted from the mouth.[5] Ordinance 888 also prohibits the carrying along the sidewalks of bags or baskets suspended from poles, and San Francisco has further provided that bootblacks must furnish leg straps to keep down the dresses of female patrons.

In Charleston, South Carolina, prisoners are compelled by law to pay one dollar for each ride to jail in the "black maria," and in Oregon it is against the law for a college fraternity man to "hang" his pin on anyone not a member of his fraternity.

It is against the law to tickle a girl under the chin with a feather duster in Portland, Maine, and in New York if a man tells a girl he cannot live with her, this is a proposal of marriage.[6] Furthermore, in Wisconsin, if you tell a girl you are "crazy about her" you are practically engaged; if you repeat the phrase in the presence of witnesses, you are.

In Chicago, Illinois, it is a crime for people to kiss in public parks. (In 1935 a husband was fined fifteen dollars for kissing his wife.) In Rhode Island a proposal of marriage was only valid when the man was on his knees. Six visits to the home of a girl in Maryland was tantamount to a marriage proposal.

THEN THERE ARE the odd laws that come from the advancement of selfish interests. One of the oddest legislative nightmares comes from New Zealand where "A Chinaman is a girl under 18." It happened this way:

In 1910, it was found that the Chinese had monopolized the laundries of that country. White laundry workers, unable to compete with the lower Chinese prices, were thrown out of work.

One legislator found the solution. Laundries were "factories" within the meaning of the Factory Act. The Factory Act prohibited girls under the age of eighteen from working in factories. So the legislature introduced a bill that was passed, which provided: "for the purpose of the Factory Act, a Chinaman shall be deemed to be a girl under 18."[7]

Then there were the odd laws that were passed late at night when most of the legislators were presumably not quite wide awake:[8]

Virginia provided[9] "To prohibit corrupt practices or bribery by any person other than candidates ... "

An Ohio law provides, "A person assaulted and lynched by a mob may recover, from the county in which such assault is made, a sum not to exceed five hundred dollars."[10]

IN 1937 REPRESENTATIVE THOMAS WEIDEMANN introduced a bill with the title "To Cure All Lawyers' Mistakes": "All mistakes by lawyers are hereby erased, but everyone shall be required to abide by the letter and spirit of the laws. This statute shall work prospectively and retroactively forever."[11] Unfortunately, it wasn't passed.

Notes

1. *Martin v. Goldstein*, 39 N. Y. Supp. 254 (1896).
2. *Hodge v. State*, 29 Fla. 500, 10 So. 556 (1892).
3. U. S. Rev. St., Vol. 18, Title XIV, §1240 (1878).
4. "Where a pack of dogs are on a railroad track, it is not necessary to blow the whistle for each particular dog." *Fink v. Evans*, 95 Tenn. 413 (1895).
5. San Francisco Health Ordinance 3065 (March 15, 1897).
6. *Button v. McCauley*, 1 Abb. Dec. 282, 4 Tr. App. 447 (1867).
7. *The New York Appellate Division, Onondaga Nation v. Thacher*, 53 N. Y. App. Div. 561 (1900) held that "the University of the State of New York is not an Indian and has no statutory right or power to be constituted an Indian."

   However, no less a body than the United States Supreme Court, *Silver v. Ladd*, 74 U. S. (7 Wall.) 219 (1868), held that the term "a single man" includes an unmarried woman!
8. It has been said that "The King, being God's lieutenant, can do no wrong," 77 Eng. Rep. 1235, 11 Coke Rep. 72(a). As a corollary, it is thought likewise that "Parliament can do no wrong, though it may do several things that look pretty odd." And said the New York Supreme Court: "No man's life, liberty, or property are safe while the legislature is in session."
9. Va. Code Sec. 242 (1930).
10. Ohio Gen. Code Tit. 2, Ch. 20, P. 1590, Sec. 6281.

    This is now §3761.04 of the Revised Ohio Code, Tit. 37, Ch. 3761. The amount recoverable by the representative of the victim is $5,000. A limit of $500 to the attorney assisting in the recovery is set.

11. A bill was introduced into the Minnesota legislature which at one time provided that lawmakers should be assessed ten dollars for each bill introduced without any hope of passage. The "cinch bill" is a familiar one to lobbyists and legislators and is one of the greatest evils in democratic legislative bodies. It is a bill introduced by the legislator that he intends to kill himself for a price from the people at whom the bill is aimed.

Epilogue

"That is no excuse," replied Mr. Brownlaw. "You were present on the occasion of the destruction of these trinkets, and indeed are the more guilty of the two, in the eyes of the law; for the law supposes that your wife acts under your direction."

"If the law supposes that," said Mr. Bumble, squeezing his hat emphatically in between his hands, "the law is a ass—a idiot. If that's the eye of the law, the law is a bachelor; and the worst I wish the law is that his eye may be opened by experience—by experience."

—Charles Dickens
Oliver Twist

AND OPENED I HOPE it has been. We've seen the omnipresent eye of the law survey the ever-changing antics of our curious species century after century. The eye has reflected and recorded our evolution from use of the ducking stool to the study of criminology as a sociological discipline, from the subjugation of women under the marriage yoke to the acceptance of common-law and equal marriage, from writs of assistance to strictly circumscribed search procedures. As the eye continues observing, it will also continue to change as we do, though, in its wisdom, always more slowly and prudently, maybe unfortunately even belatedly.

These legal tales must have convinced the reader that "the law is a ass" unless he forgetteth "not the reason thereof," to paraphrase Lord Coke.

A burglar in Stockton, California, was recently surprised in the act by the local police. He was caught red-handed, but he remained undaunted.

At his trial, he claimed his Fourth Amendment rights had been violated by the unannounced police entry without a warrant while he was burglarizing.

The court was incredulous at this defense, creative though it was. For a burglar to assert that an unannounced entry violated the sanctity of his *victim's* house—the very sanctity the burglar was industriously invading—was called "doublethink beyond the capacity of the ordinary mortal."

To make *quite* sure that the burglar understood what the court felt about his preposterous defense, it judicially noted "The law is neither an ass nor an idiot!"[1]

Generally, it's still some of *us* who would bend it to our own advantage who are.

Notes

1. *People* v. *Cook*, 69 C. A. 3d 686, 138 C. R. 263 (1977).

Index